R. D. Laing: The Philosophy and Politics of Psychotherapy

R. D. Laing: The Philosophy and Politics of Psychotherapy

ANDREW COLLIER

Lecturer in Philosophy,
University College of N. Wales, Bangor

The Harvester Press

First published in 1977 by
THE HARVESTER PRESS LIMITED
Publisher: John Spiers
2 Stanford Terrace,
Hassocks, Sussex,
England

British Library Cataloguing in Publication Data

Collier, Andrew
  R. D. Laing: the philosophy and politics of psychotherapy.
  Bibl.–Index.
  ISBN 0–901759–68–6 (cloth) 0–901759–58–9 (paper)
  1. Title
  616.8'914'0924 RC454
  Laing, Ronald David
  Psychology, Pathological

Printed in Great Britain by
Latimer Trend & Company Ltd Plymouth

Contents

Acknowledgements

I would like to thank Dr. Margaret Boden for suggesting that I should write this book; John Mepham for his criticisms of the book in draft; and all my friends from London, Leamington, Brighton and Bangor for the stimulation provided by discussions with them of some of the issues raised here.

I am grateful to the following publishers for kind permission to quote from nine of the works by R. D. Laing and his coworkers, of which complete bibliographical details are given on pages 204/205: Pantheon Books, New York; Penguin Books, Harmondsworth; Tavistock, London; and Basic Books, New York.

The book is dedicated to my wife, Heather, with thanks for her encouragement and her ideas.

Andrew Collier,
August 1976.

Preface

The aim of this preface is to justify the subtitle of the book. Why write a *philosophical* book on psychotherapy, and what has this to do with politics? In answering these questions I will also be putting my cards on the table with respect to my philosophical and political positions.

There are those who think that a philosopher is entitled to pontificate about anything, and there are those who think that every issue is political. I disagree with both of these views, so these questions are serious ones for me.

Traditionally there have been two conceptions of the role of philosophy—as the queen of the sciences, or as their under-labourer. Philosophy of the first type does not only try to legislate for the sciences, it represses them. Its exponents have taken up their positions between the sciences and various ideologies —whether ecclesiastical, moralistic, or commonsensical—and have said to the sciences, 'Thus far shalt thou come, and no further!' (Thus, Kant relegated the moral will to the world of things-in-themselves, and restricted scientific knowledge to the world of appearances; 'ordinary language' for many linguistic philosophers, and 'lived experience' for many phenomenologists, are sanctuaries within which any irrationality is immune from scientific criticism.) The sciences have advanced in spite of these philosophers, and like King Canute they have got their feet wet. Their successors have not learnt humility, but only changed their ground. Nobody now disputes the exclusive right of science to investigate the origin of the world and man. Some still dispute its competence in the areas of human history and the human mind. Almost no one admits the right of science to legislate in moral questions.

If as I believe, philosophers must accept the role of under-labourers to science, 'removing some of the rubbish that lies in the way of knowledge' as Locke says, such philosophers also must move on to ground where their services are needed, i.e. where there is still ideological rubbish obstructing the progress of knowledge. The appearance of the sciences of historical and mental processes, associated with the names of Marx and Freud, defines the task of philosophy in our time as I see it.* Misconceptions which stand in the way of the extension of knowledge on the basis of these sciences, must be cleared away. This involves clarification of the method and structure of these theories, and the refutation of claims by the Canutes that they are unscientific or inappropriate to their specific objects. And this is precisely what most philosophers do claim.

Now Freud had little to say about questions of method in the sciences, or more particularly in psycho-analytical theory. For the most part, he was prepared to take over the methodology of his natural-scientific training, adapting it as necessary to the new object of his researches—the unconscious, and mental processes generally.

R. D. Laing on the other hand has been almost obsessed with methodological questions, and belongs to an established philo-sophical tradition with regard to them—namely, existential phenomenology. In the light of what I have said about the relation of philosophy to the sciences, it is by no means the case

---

* To avoid misunderstanding: I do not think there can be a Marxist or Freudian philosophy as such—no single science can claim exclusive rights over philosophy, and neither can any non-theoretical practice, such as politics or psychotherapy.

that the philosophical *naïveté* of a Freud or the philosophical erudition of a Laing should predispose us to favour Laing where there are differences of methodology between the two. Rather, it means that a philosophical reflection on Laing cannot limit itself to elucidating the method and structure of his theory and its relation to its object; it must also address itself critically to Laing's philosophical premises.

There will therefore be more than one theory under discussion in this book. The foremost philosophical influence on Laing is that of Sartre, and many of Laing's methodological formulations seem *on first sight* to be lifted straight out of Sartre. On the other hand, Laing's therapeutic viewpoint is nothing if not psychoanalytical, and therefore he does not follow Sartre in rejecting the notion of the unconscious. If one leaves aside Laing's methodological proclamations and follows what he is actually doing in most of his writings, one can see far more continuity from Freud than is usually admitted, either by Laing's followers or by his opponents. But of course it would be much too simplistic to say that Laing is a Sartrean in theory and a Freudian in practice. It is necessary to distinguish between the method Laing talks about and the one he uses, but they exert a reciprocal influence, and he is never an uncritical disciple of anyone. Anyway, his theories cannot be understood as a mere convergence of influences—they are also a result of his researches into matters not studied by either Sartre or Freud.

There are two other theoretical traditions which I do not discuss in this book, though they are always present in the background. First of all there are other contemporary investigators of social inter-action in the family, family contexts of madness, and so on. Laing's work does not stand alone in this area, but is part of a set of ongoing and reciprocally influencing programmes of research. But it is no part of my intention to map out this area, or to establish credentials of originality, or corroboration. Laing refers often enough to the writers in question, and anyway the concepts used by Laing must be understood according to their place in Laing's system, not their place of origin. I therefore deliberately avoid discussion of other writers in this field, with the exception of those with whom Laing has collaborated in his literary production—David Cooper and Aaron Esterson.

The other theoretical tradition I refer to is Marxism. The relevance of Marxism here is primarily that Laing believes that the micro-social contexts in terms of which he seeks to understand individuals can themselves only be understood in terms of their own macro-social context. I take it that a Marxist analysis is required in order to understand this context.

This brings us to the question of 'politics'. Laing's work is political in that to understand the micro-social structures which he is studying is also implicitly to criticise them—in Marxist terms, it is to expose contradictions in them. So much, of course, is also true of Freud; but in Laing's case, the critical conclusions are also made explicit in various places. The politics involved however is 'micro-politics'—the transformation of small groups. How this relates to politics in the larger sense —whether they are independent practices, or complementary, or perhaps even alternatives—is another question which must be answered in this connection. I take it for granted that the relevant 'macro-politics' will be socialist in content, and based on a Marxist account of how capitalist society works. This book is not of course the place to justify this assumption, so to readers who do not share it I can say only that it appears to be shared by Laing and his collaborators themselves.

Chapter 1

The Self and its Vicissitudes

I was once at a lecture given by R. D. Laing, at which he was asked what the differences of method were between the various schools of analytical psychotherapy—Freudian, Kleinian, etc. He replied, as I remember, that there were no differences of method, only of terminology; for instance, in the course of an analysis by a Kleinian, the word 'breast' might be used a hundred times more than in an orthodox Freudian analysis, while the orthodox Freudian would use the word 'penis' and 'vagina' a hundred times more. Laing was then asked what words he would use more than other analysts, and he said he would be inclined to use the same words as the other person (who was being analysed).

I think this is symptomatic of a striking feature of all Laing's psychiatric writings—the capacity, one might almost say the compulsion, to see others as they see themselves. This ability is one of Laing's strengths, but it also has its dangers. Both these facts will emerge from an examination of his first major work, *The Divided Self*.

I propose to examine first the descriptive parts of this book, which are aimed at understanding what it is like to experience the world in certain ways characteristic of a 'schizoid'[1] condition,

1

and then return to the two theoretical chapters with which the book opens to ask what is the relation of that theory—existential phenomenology—to the subject matter which it has been used to clarify. I shall for the time being try to ignore as far as possible the claims which Laing makes that go beyond pure description of the way an individual of a particular kind experiences his relation to the world and to himself—claims which no longer belong to the order of appearances (phenomenology) but make assertions about how things are in reality.

The key concept in Laing's understanding of schizoid experience is 'ontological insecurity'. In the chapter of *The Divided Self* devoted to this concept, Laing is describing the fundamental difference between two ways of experiencing oneself and the world—those of the ontologically secure and of the ontologically insecure person. Only on the basis of an understanding of ontological insecurity can the neurotic and psychotic modes of experience and behaviour described in parts two and three of *The Divided Self* be understood.

By using the term 'ontological' insecurity, Laing means to indicate that it is about one's 'being' that one is insecure. This should not be taken primarily as meaning anxiety about one's continued presence in the world as a living being—i.e. it is not fear of death. Death would be one way of losing one's being, but it is other ways which are prominent here. One's 'being' includes not merely 'that one is' (one's existence) but 'what one is' (essence) and 'who one is' (identity). There is a fear that what is most essential to oneself as an individual might be lost.

This prospect is not of course necessarily undesirable. One may wish to change from being one kind of person to being a totally different kind. But there are also states of mind in which the loss of certain qualities is feared and constantly guarded against. It is quite possible that most ontologically insecure people would not accept this description of their fears, which are experienced more as fears of loss of one's soul, in the sense of some real 'inner' entity, which is the essence of an individual, but which he can lose while remaining biologically alive. But Laing, while rejecting more radical redescriptions of these fears (e.g. as castration fears) should not be thought to endorse this description in terms of a spiritual substance, at any rate in his earlier writings.

It is perhaps best at this point to quote at some length Laing's characterization of the world of the ontologically insecure person:

The individual in the ordinary circumstances of living may feel more unreal than real; in a literal sense, more dead than alive; precariously differentiated from the rest of the world, so that his identity and autonomy are always in question. He may lack the experience of his own temporal continuity. He may not possess an over-riding sense of personal consistency or cohesiveness. He may feel more insubstantial than substantial, and unable to assume that the stuff he is made of is genuine, good, valuable. And he may feel his self as partially divorced from his body. It is, of course, inevitable that an individual whose experience of himself is of this order can no more live in a 'secure' world than he can be secure 'in himself'. The whole 'physiognomy' of his world will be correspondingly different from that of the individual whose sense of self is securely established in its health and validity. Relatedness to other persons will be seen to have a radically different significance and function. To anticipate, we can say that in the individual whose own being is secure in this primary experiential sense, relatedness with others is potentially gratifying; whereas the ontologically insecure person is preoccupied with preserving rather than gratifying himself: the ordinary circumstances of living threaten his *low threshold of security*. (*The Divided Self*, p. 42)

Two aspects of the ontologically insecure individual's experience may be noted here: his sense of the unreality and foreignness of the world including his own body, and the experience of other people as objects of anxiety rather than of pleasure.

Specific to this mode of experience are three fears, in terms of which many of its phenomena can be understood. Essentially they are all fears that relations with others will lead to loss of the self. Laing calls these fears (1) Engulfment, (2) Implosion, (3) Petrification and depersonalization. As Laing expresses it, the ontologically insecure person becomes 'absorbed in contriving ways of trying to be real, of keeping himself or others alive, of preserving his identity, in efforts, as he will often put it, to prevent himself losing his self'. (*The Divided Self*, pp. 42–43)

The self is seen as something which is endangered and which it is up to one to guard, and which relations with other people put at risk. In fear of engulfment,

the individual dreads relatedness as such, with anyone or anything, or indeed, even with himself, because his uncertainty about the stability of his autonomy lays him open to the dread lest in any relationship he will lose his autonomy and identity. (*The Divided Self*, p. 44)

In particular, to be loved and to be known are feared.

To be understood correctly is to be engulfed, to be enclosed, swallowed up, drowned, eaten up, smothered, stifled in or by another person's supposed all-embracing comprehension. It is lonely and painful to be always misunderstood, but there is at least from this point of view a measure of safety in isolation.

The other's love is therefore feared more than his hatred, or rather all love is sensed as a version of hatred. (*The Divided Self*, p. 45)

This isolated self then, in the poverty of its experience, feels empty, and while in one way wishing for relatedness to the world to fill it, fears this relatedness as being a filling with something alien, a threat to the integrity of the self. This is what constitutes implosion-anxiety.

A curious feature of these fears is that, though in one sense they are intuitively very 'understandable' (to me at least), when one asks what they are fears *of*, it seems impossible to give an answer except by piling up metaphors—implosion, stifling, drowning etc. In this respect they resemble fear of ghosts, in which there is rarely any conception of what a ghost would do; its mere presence is horrific enough. An even closer analogy is the numinous horror which many people feel at the thought of another living organism inhabiting their body—a tapeworm, for instance; or again, at the presence of mice in their house; or the way some people are completely shaken to discover their house has been burgled, even though no serious harm has been done and they can prevent its recurrence. These are all fears of the uninvited intrusion of a living being into some projection of the self. Whether the horror of rape is simply one case of this class of fears, or the unconscious basis of all of them, I shall not discuss.

The third fear is perhaps even more 'normal', in the statistical sense, yet just as difficult to elucidate in terms of its rationale. Laing lists three aspects of the fear of petrification:

(1) A particular form of terror, whereby one is petrified, i.e. turned to stone.

(2) The dread of this happening: the dread, that is, of the possibility of turning or being turned, from a live person into a dead thing, into a stone, into a robot, an automaton, without personal autonomy of action, an *it* without subjectivity.

(3) The 'magical' act whereby one may attempt to turn someone else into stone, by 'petrifying' him; and, by extension, the act whereby one negates the other person's autonomy, ignores his feelings, regards him as a thing, kills the life in him. In this sense one may perhaps better say that one depersonalizes him, or reifies him. One treats him not as a person, as a free agent, but as an it. (*The Divided Self*, p. 46)[2]

Here the dichotomies of person/thing and subject/object make their appearance. One may ask (1) how does one treat a person as a thing? In most of the contexts in which this expression is used, it is strictly inaccurate. For instance, to take the extreme case, sadism involves a sharp recognition of the humanity and feelings of the victim; one cannot treat a thing sadistically. Genuine 'reification' of another person would mean total indifference to him, the absence of the possibility of any relationship. Laing however distinguishes reification and indifference. (2) If on the other hand the subject/object dichotomy is used to describe the fear and project of depersonalization—as it is by Sartre in *Being and Nothingness*, which Laing mentions here as a brilliant discussion of this phenomenon—the reverse conclusion follows: any attempt to relate to another person is an attempt to depersonalize him, for it involves treating him as an 'object', i.e. the object of love or hate, sexual desire or aggression, perception or knowledge. The only way to treat someone as a subject would be to be intellectually aware of his existence as a subject, but to avoid any relationship with him. It will be necessary to discuss this later in the chapter. Nevertheless it is worth noting that Laing, despite his indebtedness to Sartre, does not share this conception of man and the consequent belief that 'Conflict is the original meaning of being-for-others.' (Sartre, *Being and Nothingness*, p. 364) His conception of the matter is clear enough: the other-as-threat is not seen by Laing as a necessary feature of any experience of the other, as it is for Sartre. It is seen in the first place as a feature of bad relationships, in the second as the general experience of some unfortunate people:

The issue is in principle straightforward. One may find oneself enlivened and the sense of one's own being enhanced by the other, or one may experience the other as deadening and impoverishing. A person may have come to anticipate that any possible relationship with another will have the latter consequences. Any other is then a threat to his 'self' (his capacity to act autonomously) not by reason of anything he or she may do or not do specifically, but by reason of his or her very existence. (*The Divided Self*, p. 47)

If we are to compare this way of seeing the world with that of the ontologically secure person, it is first of all evident that it is an unpleasant fate to be ontologically insecure. Whereas anyone may be unhappy through the frustration of his desires, or unsatisfactory relationships with other people, the ontologically insecure person is cut off by his fears from the possibility of satisfying relationships. Given then that it is possible for a person who is at one time ontologically insecure to become ontologically secure, this would seem desirable, and perhaps the aim of analytical psychotherapy for him. This supposes in addition that the way that the ontologically secure person sees the world is truer, for all analytical schools aim at increasing the self-awareness and understanding of the analysand, not at peddling comforting illusions. I am assuming here that these different ways of seeing the world involve different *claims* about how the world is, and that these differences are not purely subjective in the sense that one view would not contradict the other.

In discussing one of the manifestations of ontological insecurity, the feeling that the self is unembodied, Laing says:

We would almost have, if the embodiment or unembodiment were ever complete in either direction, two different ways of being human. Most people may regard the former as normal and healthy and the latter as abnormal and pathological. Throughout this study such an evaluation is quite irrelevant. From certain points of view, one may regard embodiment as desirable. It is possible to suggest from another point of view that the individual should try to disentangle himself from his body and thereby achieve a desired state of discarnate spirituality. (*The Divided Self*, p. 66)

These two extreme possibilities require to be examined in terms of the way in which an individual whose position approximated to one or other of these possibilities would experience his relatedness to other persons and the world. (*The Divided Self*, p. 67)

In these passages, Laing is apparently making the claim that the two ways of relating to the world are equally valid. In the same section he argues that there are even some advantages in feeling unembodied—relative immunity to bodily dangers and frustrations, etc. Thus he seems to be putting the two modes of experience on an equal footing as to truth, and a more or less equal footing as to value. Finally, he is arguing that each mode must be understood in its own terms, i.e. the understanding which the psychotherapist has of the patient's world must not contradict the appearance of that world to the patient. The psychotherapeutic theory of ontological insecurity must therefore be couched in the terms in which it is understood by an ontologically insecure person. Hence the therapeutic task in relation to an ontologically insecure person would not be to 'cure' the ontological insecurity, but to resolve the specific problems arising from this condition, i.e. help him for instance to avoid the occurrence of those states which he fears (engulfment, etc.), to help him to attain the sort of security which the ontologically insecure person pursues by means of the various stratogems Laing discusses, not to help him to achieve '*primary* ontological security', which would necessitate getting him to revise his whole self-understanding.

It is interesting to note also that in his desire to clarify the way that the world appears to the ontologically insecure person, he actually misdescribes its appearance to the ontologically secure person. His description is in terms of the ontologically secure person's world having various characteristics that the ontologically insecure person's one conspicuously lacks. It seems to me that it is not correct to describe the ontologically secure person's self-conception as 'a firm sense of one's own autonomous identity', or to say that relations with other people are not threatening to him *because* they are based on individual autonomy. Rather questions of autonomy or identity are simply not an issue for him.

However, the second and third sections of *The Divided Self* deal with the various ways in which an ontologically insecure person may become neurotic or psychotic in an attempt to cope with his specific problems as he sees them, i.e. essentially, to preserve his self; Laing's descriptions of these leave no doubt as to the desirability of 'cure'; they do leave doubt as to its possibility *within* the schizoid world view. It is these sections which I will now consider.

On the first page of part II of *The Divided Self*, Laing tells us that 'In the absence of (ontological) security, life must, nevertheless, go on.' The vicissitudes of the self as described in this section—the splitting of the self, etc.—are seen as ways of coping with the problems confronting the person with the fears specific to ontological insecurity. Insofar as these vicissitudes are neurotic, they appear as, not so much intrinsic to the state of ontological insecurity, but neuroses to which ontological insecurity predisposes the individual, but which need some immediate cause to set them off.

However the situations which are found threatening to the ontologically insecure person are so intrinsic to human life that one cannot conceive of someone being ontologically insecure without having recourse to these neurotic defences; if he did not have recourse to them, it seems to me that he would cease to be ontologically insecure. If ontological insecurity 'explains' the splitting of the self, in that the latter is a defence against fears specific to ontological insecurity, it is also true that the splitting of the self 'explains' ontological insecurity, in that it appears to be presupposed in an account of those fears. It is just this circularity, among other things, which makes one feel that the real problem is elsewhere, that one cannot take ontological insecurity at its face value and explain other phenomena in terms of it— rather it is itself in need of explanation.

The splitting of the self into 'embodied' and 'disembodied' selves is seen by Laing as in the first place a normal reaction to abnormal stress. In a particularly threatening situation, anyone may react by treating his body as external to him, and hence conceiving the real self (i.e. that to which the body is perceived as external) as invulnerable. The ontologically insecure person, finding as he does all social life threatening, comes to have this split into 'real' self and body as his normal mode of experience. Both poles of this split are then considerably elaborated. The embodied 'false' self, which is observable by others and hence vulnerable to their threats, is perhaps developed compliantly with the demands of others (i.e. of those particular others whose influence is most inescapable—parents, bosses, sexual partners etc.) while the 'inner self' keeps its attitudes and aspirations scrupulously secret.

Laing gives a number of brief case histories in which it is clear enough that the people he is describing experience themselves as split in this way, perhaps take the split for granted as a basic fact. In describing and documenting this kind of experience, Laing does the service (among others) of showing up the hollowness and misleading nature of many recent philosophical treatments of the problem of 'other minds'. One of the few substantive doctrines of the linguistic analysis school of philosophy is a sort of logical behaviourism (whether or not it admits to the title) which, in its rather embattled attempt to prove that other people are real, rules out of court any talk about inner states, mental phenomena which cannot be observed except by their possessor. Insofar as this doctrine is merely a rejection of the Cartesian tradition of philosophy of mind, which tends to make mental states private in principle and by definition, it is no doubt correct; but by concentrating on this unreal philosophical problem, it plays down the real problems about interpersonal perception. In so doing it actually tends to give credence to the Cartesian tradition which it attacks (and which incidentally includes Sartre, but no other existentialist thinker), as being less unrealistic. It should be noted that Laing does not hold either Cartesian or logical behaviourist views, and I would claim, shows in practice the untenability of either view. Note in this connection his account of 'sudden' outbreaks of schizophrenic psychosis in previously 'normal' people:

It is only when one is able to gather from the individual himself the history of his *self*, and *not what a psychiatric history in these circumstances usually is, the history of the false-self system*, that his psychosis becomes explicable. (*The Divided Self*, p. 148)

It is important to recognise that, although the schizoid worldview may be pathological in the sense of presenting insoluble problems and perceiving reality in a systematically mistaken way (points which Laing seems to sometimes stress and sometimes ignore) it is neither uncommon nor limited to people who have found their way into a psychiatrist's clinic. It is one of the many conflicting views of life which are widespread enough and taken sufficiently for granted by their adherents to be described as 'commonsense'. There is a very large proportion of people who, when they are talking seriously about their lives, will use terms like 'the real me', make the distinction between someone's 'true self' and 'facades', worry about whether other people recognize their true self, and if they do, worry about having given themselves away, and so on. This 'schizoid commonsense' is reflected in popular culture—e.g. in the lyrics of many popular songs.[3]

The Outer Self of the schizoid person, as compliant with social requirements, may appear (statistically) normal, unremarkable, lacking in outstanding qualities or particular wickedness— though of course it need not be so: it may be an elaborately concocted role, as in the case of 'David', who Laing says resembled 'an adolescent Kierkegaard played by Danny Kaye'. The Inner Self is likely to contain both a strong ideal of self-awareness and independence of others, and also certain violently antisocial desires, which are perhaps the objects of great feelings of guilt and self-contempt. It at once despises the Outer Self for its compliance (by contrast to its own claim to independence and infinite possibilities) and despises other people for not seeing through the Outer Self to the unpleasantness of the Inner Self; if they did, they would hate it—so it is all the more important that they should not. At the same time the schizoid person may demand precisely that other people recognize his 'true self'.

The schizoid person according to Laing's account is trapped in a set of insoluble contradictions. His inner ideal is of his autonomy and independence of others, yet it is precisely in order to adapt to the unlivable demands of others that he has had to take refuge in a wholly inward freedom—i.e. to renounce self-fulfilment in reality. The Inner Self needs experience to feed on, yet it avoids such experience as dangerous to its integrity, and comes to be more and more 'empty' in itself. This increases the fear of 'implosion'—there is nothing within to set against the dreaded inundations of reality.

A great deal of Laing's description of schizoid existence is devoted to showing the self-defeating nature of schizoid defences. The schizoid person separates his 'real' self from his body and his relations with the world in order to preserve his autonomy, to defend himself against being known by others. Yet this leads to loss of autonomy on the part of the 'false' self, impoverishment of the 'inner' self, increased vulnerability to the consciousness of others.

For instance, Laing describes the state of 'self-consciousness' in which a person is acutely and unpleasantly aware of the possible consciousness which others have of him. The splitting of the self, with its results that one takes a quasi-external view of one's 'public' self, desires reassurance about one's own reality, senses others as a threat, etc. causes such a self-consciousness to be normal in schizoid people. But the effect of self-consciousness is that one feels

more the object of other people's interest than, in fact, (one) is. Such a person walking along the street approaches a cinema queue. He will have to 'steel himself' to walk past it: preferably, he will cross to the other side of the street. It is an ordeal to go into a restaurant and sit down at a table by himself. At a dance he will wait until two or three couples are already dancing before he can face taking the floor himself, and so on. (*The Divided Self*, p. 107)

The schizoid person becomes both less able to relate to others and increasingly subject to feelings of his own unreality, and vulnerability to others.

Describing the role of the 'false self' of the schizoid person, Laing says it

exists as the complement of an 'inner' self which is occupied in maintaining its identity and freedom by being transcendent, unembodied, and thus never to be grasped, pinpointed, trapped, possessed. Its aim is to be a pure subject, without any objective existence. Thus except in certain possible safe moments the individual seeks to regard the whole of his objective existence as the expression of a false self. Of course . . . if a man is not two-dimensional, having a two dimensional identity established by a conjunction of identity-for-others, and identity-for-oneself, if he does not exist objectively as well as subjectively, but has only a subjective identity, an identity-for-himself, he cannot be *real*. (pp. 94–95)

The self-defeating nature of the schizoid project is again stressed. Two points can be noted about this: (1) the fears which constitute ontological insecurity in terms of which Laing explains schizoid experience can also be seen as the *result* of the schizoid splitting; this does not mean that Laing is wrong in describing this circular relation of fears and defences; but this real circularity does preclude cure within the schizoid terms of reference. The ontologically insecure or schizoid mode of experience is not just one mode among others—it is a pathological one. (2) This circularity tends to deepen into a spiral and thus leads of itself to the possibility of psychosis; the third part of *The Divided Self* is devoted to the description of such developments. Laing claims that a psychotic development—schizophrenia—is a comprehensible outcome of an unrelieved schizoid experience which was originally within the bounds of sanity. 'The Case of Peter' (pp. 120–33) illustrates this transition. Peter had been brought up sleeping in the same room as his parents and was treated by them as though he was not there. He had developed all the classic schizoid symptoms as described by Laing—self-consciousness, the conception of himself as split into inner and outer selves, contempt for his body, hatred of other people—and while not actually psychotic, his taste for life was severely impaired and he had certain delusions (he originally came for treatment because of his false belief that he was emitting a strong smell).

One aspect of this case history which bears noting is the role of sexual matters in it, despite the 'ontological' language used. The effects of sharing the parents' bedroom for instance need not have been purely ontological. Masturbation seems to have played an important part in determining his perception of others and of his body. His inability to combine physically sexual and affectionate feelings for a woman is after all an instance of what Freud called 'the most prevalent form of degradation in the erotic life'. His 'deliberate' practice of 'disconnecting' the world from himself and 'uncoupling' his true self from his body can be seen as a defence against sexuality, just as St. Clement of Alexandria described the ascetic life as a 'rational death', i.e. a deliberate uncoupling of body and soul as an escape from the world, the flesh and the devil.

At the outset of the subsequent chapter of *The Divided Self* Laing describes this case as coming 'perilously near to frank psychosis'. There is clearly a continuity between neurosis and psychosis for Laing, and we can already see in what this continuity consists: the schizoid (such as Peter) *tries* to say, 'All of me that can be an object-for-the-other is not me.' (p. 131). The schizophrenic has succeeded in effecting this split to such an extent that the inner self loses its sense of reality and identity because it is no longer an object for others, ('since *the sense of identity requires the existence of another by whom one is known*' p. 139), and the outer self disintegrates more and more into patterns of behaviour independent of the individual's conscious control.

There seem to be two aspects to this transition from neurosis to psychosis: first of all the descending spiral already noted; fear that relationships with others will destroy the self, leading to isolation from the outside world, leading to increased impoverishment and insecurity of the inner self, leading to still greater fear of the world at large, and so on. Then there is the collapse of the false self system at the end of this process, which constitutes the psychotic breakdown itself. The self, in cutting itself off from relations with others ' . . . has endeavoured to become its own object: to become in fact, related directly only to itself.' (p. 137) This is very close to the Freudian notion that a withdrawal of cathexis from the world to the self takes place in psychosis (i.e. that the psychoses are essentially narcissistic).

The concepts with which Laing seeks to understand schizophrenia in *The Divided Self* are the same as those he uses in describing sane forms of schizoid experiences—true and false selves, the fears associated with ontological insecurity, and so on. These are not of course Freudian concepts, but when it comes to the understanding of psychosis the gap between Freud and Laing is considerably narrowed. Freud only analysed sane, neurotic patients and his remarks on psychosis are somewhat in the nature of speculations. Nevertheless he did give a clue that has been taken up by some of his followers, namely that psychosis is a regression to the pre-oedipal phase, in which the child is part of a diadic relationship with its mother, rather than the oedipal triad mother-father-self. In this phase, self-preservation is the dominant drive (rather than sexuality, which is as yet 'anaclitic' i.e. 'leaning on' self-preservation). So it is not surprising if the anxieties of the psychotic are ontological, i.e. concern loss of being rather than castration.

For Freud, the oedipus complex is essential to the understanding of neurosis, but of course the oedipus complex is grafted on to the pre-oedipal experience of the child; and when an adult regresses to this phase, it is presumably the inner conflicts resulting from the oedipus complex that motivate this regression.

But despite this element of continuity between neurosis and psychosis, the discontinuity is stressed far more in Freudian theory than by Laing, for whom the transition seems at times like a natural outcome. However we must now look at the second aspect of Laing's theory about the pre-history of psychotic developments. This is a point which Laing makes very forcibly in the final chapter entitled 'The ghost of the weed garden: a study of a chronic schizophrenic'. It is that in the view of a schizophrenic's family, he or she has very often been through three stages, described as 'good—bad—mad'. 'Good' here is used in the negative sense of 'not troublesome', 'compliant with the parents' wishes'. The goodness turns out to be a false self, which does not express the individual's own wishes, but those of the parents. The 'bad' stage, which generally occurs in teenage, can be seen as the attempt of the repressed desires to find expression, or as Laing would perhaps prefer to say, the attempt of the individual to become autonomous, or of the true self to realize itself. It is the failure to become 'bad' i.e. to live according to one's own desires rather than those of one's parents, that leads to the third stage; here the repressed wishes and the concomitant aggression against the parents finds symbolic expression. For instance, Julie, in the chapter referred to, stopped accusing her mother of preventing her from living her own life, and started saying that she (Julie's mother) had murdered a child. Sudden outbreaks of schizophrenia in individuals previously considered as perfectly 'normal' are explained by Laing as cases in which the compliant, 'good' outer self has remained intact until the last minute, while the secret history of the inner self, which only the individual concerned can know about, has been one of increasing alienation from the outer self and its world, with the spiralling effect mentioned above.

It would seem then that for Laing an important factor in inducing schizophrenia is the continued non-conduciveness of the real world to the satisfaction of the desires of the inner self.

There are two things which it would be interesting to know in connection with Laing's discussions of the role of the family in inducing schizophrenia: one is the extent to which several of the schizoid patients he refers to, who seemed to be loners, were really so. For in the case of the loner the problem can hardly be

resolved by reference to current real pressures from the family—
the typical efficient cause of breakdown in Laing's later case-
histories; if the family is invoked as an explanatory element it
must be the internalized family, and the real infantile experiences
of the family which left this internalized family as their deposit.
Whatever other pathogenic processes can be attributed to the
family in such cases, it certainly cannot be blamed for 'labelling'
the patient as mad, for in these cases it is presumably his or her
own decision to seek psychiatric help. The second is a question
which Laing himself could probably not answer, as it concerns
events occurring before the treatment started, which the psychiatrist can only infer: it is the question whether the undoubted
delusions which some of the patients suffered from started occurring before or after that individual came to be seen as 'mad' by
his or her own family. An answer to this question would give us
some idea of just how seriously we should take talk of 'labelling'
people as mad, with the implication that such labelling has no
objective basis at the time it is initiated.

I now wish to turn to a consideration of the relation of the
foregoing account of Laing's description of schizoid experience,
to an assessment of the use he makes of existentialist concepts.
Laing describes his method as existential phenomenology, yet I
have indicated points of difference between his theories and
those of the existentialists. Therefore a disgression on the mean-
of these often rather loosely used labels seems necessary.

The aspects of existentialist thought which I regard as most
relevant will emerge from the following discussion of Laing's
divergence from them. By way of narrowing down the *list* of
existentialist thinkers, which is often so elongated as to defy anyone to find even a 'family resemblance', the best procedure is to
stipulate an 'inner canon' of existentialist writings, consisting of
Kierkegaard's *The Sickness unto Death* and *The Concept of
Dread*, Heidegger's *Being and Time*, and Sartre's *Being and
Nothingness*. These are probably the existentialist writings which
have most influenced Laing, along with those of the theologian
Paul Tillich, from whom the concept of ontological insecurity is
derived. Nietzsche can on no account be regarded as an existen-

tialist, as he denies every main tenet of existentialist thought. The works listed above share the doctrines: (a) that man is free, in the sense of being compelled to choose between infinite possibilities; (b) that he experiences his freedom in anguish (the Danish word '*angest*', the German '*Angst*' and the French '*angoisse*' in the above works are translated respectively as 'dread', 'anxiety' and 'anguish'. The meaning in these three writers is more or less identical); (c) that the unpleasantness of this state motivates man to hide the fact of his freedom from himself by absorption in the conventional practices of everyday life ('inauthenticity').

Phenomenology is a method developed originally by Brentano and Husserl purporting to acquire pre-scientific knowledge in a rigorous way. Roughly speaking, its essential features are: (a) 'pure' (presuppositionless) description of conscious phenomena as we experience them, not as we believe they must be in the light of commonsense or scientific knowledge; (b) analysis of these phenomena in terms of 'intentionality', i.e. directedness towards 'objects', which is said to be a feature of all mental phenomena. Thus a belief is a belief *that* . . ., a desire is a desire *to* . . . a sensation is a sensation *of* . . . The 'object' is that which fills the gaps in each case. It need not be real; e.g. ghosts are the object of fear of ghosts. When I use the word 'object' in this book, I will, unless otherwise stated, mean it in this sense, or the related sense of an object of a science, i.e. what it is the science of; I carefully avoid using 'object' in any of the other common English senses, i.e. aim, material thing, or lifeless material thing.

The term 'existential phenomenology' I take to mean, not the use of the phenomenological method to arrive at existentialist conclusions, but a phenomenology which, rather than simply describing and classifying 'intentional phenomena', seeks to understand these as forming, in the case of each individual, a structured whole—his way of 'being-in-the-world'. This is how Laing uses the term. He tells us that existential phenomenology 'is not so much an attempt to describe particular objects of (a person's) experience as to set all particular experiences within the context of his whole being-in-his world.' (p. 7)

Hence although Heidegger and Sartre were existential phenomenologists and also existentialists, Merleau-Ponty was an existential phenomenologist without really being an existentialist, and it is arguable that the same is true of Laing in *The Divided Self*.

Nevertheless Laing has undoubtedly been profoundly influenced by existentialist thought. In what way has this thought been relevant to his investigations in *The Divided Self*? The answer seems to be that the ontologically insecure and schizoid individual experiences the world in many ways just as the existentialist philosopher says that the world really is. The following points of contact may be noted:

(1) The ontologically insecure person feels 'not at home' in the world, he finds it uncanny, he experiences dread in the face of his possibilities. This is exactly how man be's[4] in the world according to Heidegger. Admittedly man does not 'in the first place and for the most part' experience this uncanniness ('*Unheimlichkeit*') consciously, according to Heidegger, but that is only a mark of the inauthenticity, the 'lostness in the world', of everyday existence. The ordinary experience of the schizoid individual is made into something of a norm here.

(2) According to Heidegger also, the characteristic of man (*Dasein*) is that *his being is an issue for him*. He holds in his hands the responsibility for how he be's—whether in an owned way (authenticity = '*Eigentlichkeit*', ownedness), or whether he does not really be at all, but rather allows himself to be beed by other people.

The fear of the ontologically insecure person is 'over his being'. He is afraid that it might not really be his.

(3) The fear of 'petrification and depersonalization', and the defence against this by seeking to 'petrify and depersonalize' others, is characteristic of the schizoid person according to Laing. But according to Sartre it is the necessary mode of all human relationships.

For Sartre, consciousness, which is what is specifically human about a person, cannot be an object for another person; hence the other person can only 'use' one's objective qualities, consciousness in principle escapes him. According to this conception it is objectionable to be 'used' and 'made an object' by the other, and one therefore seeks to avoid it by turning the tables on the other and 'using' him, 'making him an object'. It should be noted that 'object' is used here in the first place in the strictly phenomenological sense, so that to be 'made an object' or 'objectified' equals to be related to in any way by the other person. Hence the alleged unpleasantness of being objectified, as well as the possibility of using objectification of the other as a defence, need to be explained. The possibility of mutual use and objectification is ruled out because it is alleged that one cannot simultaneously be the 'subject' that objectifies the other, and oneself objectified by the other-as-subject. (Contrast Marx's statement that 'if I have a being as my object, that being has me as its object', which is not necessarily true, but at least, in spite of Sartre, it is—mercifully—possibly true.)

There is undoubtedly a conflation here by Sartre of 'object' in the phenomenological sense (object of knowledge, desire, perception etc.), and 'object' in the sense of a non-living or at least somehow subhuman thing. This is not just an accidental confusion however, but stems from the division of a person into a consciousness which cannot be an object (cf. the schizoid person's 'inner self') and an objective being ('facticity'), which includes all the actual qualities or characteristics of the person, but which he nevertheless constantly 'escapes' and therefore does not really be (cf. the 'false self' in schizoid conditions). Hence being an object for the other neutralizes one's consciousness and thus reduces one to an 'object' in the other sense (lifeless material thing). Objectifying the other in turn, by neutralising his consciousness, prevents him from objectifying oneself. The idea that objectification is a threat and a degradation, and that it can be forestalled by objectifying the other, are therefore common to Sartre and the schizoid person as described by Laing, and based on the same dualistic conception of man in both cases. It may be noted in passing that Heidegger's concept of man is less 'schizoid' in this respect.

(4) For Sartre, the 'psyche', the object of psychology and of

everyday knowledge of others, is not identical with consciousness, but is produced by consciousness at a distance. It is a conglomeration of the acts of consciousness. Hence, for Sartre, the 'character' or 'personality' has no real existence. (Sartre is supposed to have said of Heidegger, apropos of the latter's brief flirtation with Nazism in 1933, that he had no character. It is rather as if B. F. Skinner were to accuse an opponent of having no soul.) The psyche is constructed out of a person's acts and experiences, but the only reality behind them is the free spontaneity of consciousness (see Sartre's *The Transcendence of the Ego*). It is rather as if, in watching a film, one assumed that the images shown on the screen reflected a real drama going on behind the screen, instead of referring them back to the projector. This fictional drama would correspond to 'the psyche', the projector to consciousness, in Sartre's account. For Sartre the belief that the psyche has a life of its own independent of consciousness is at best a convenient fiction, at worst an enslaving illusion. For Sartre all the things a person actively be's—his psychological properties, social roles, etc.—he actually plays at being; 'consciousness is that which plays at being, and consciousness itself is "nothingness" and not being'. This corresponds exactly to the experience of Laing's patients who more or less consciously played a series of roles, retaining a distance from each of them, the 'inner self' becoming increasingly without qualities.

(5) The case of Kierkegaard.

Perhaps the most striking existentialist anticipation of and influence on Laing's account in the middle section of *The Divided Self* is Kierkegaard's *The Sickness unto Death*. Possibly the most schizoid individual in the history of philosophy, Kierkegaard had an unusual degree of insight into his condition. In *The Sickness unto Death* he puts forward the view that the self is a union of the infinite possibility of the spirit with the finitude of the body and everyday life. A self is sick to the extent that the two elements are in disrelation. Such a self lives on the one hand in fantasy (infinite possibility in detachment from reality) and/or on the other hand, in a mindless everyday existence. The cure (which for Kierkegaard is also salvation, and depends on the relation of the self to God) would be a unification of the two elements, in which the individual would be free to realise some of his possibilities instead of giving them indulgence for complete freedom in fantasy while remaining unfulfilled in reality.

Unfortunately these insights which we may (anachronistically) call phenomenological ones, did not enable Kierkegaard to cure himself of the sickness unto death, and in the last phase of his life he betrayed them and took sides wholly with the 'inner' self of pure possibility against anything tarred with the brush of finitude. His hostility to women was rationalized by the assertion that they stand in a dangerous rapport with finitude. His 'Attack on Christendom' (i.e. on the Lutheran Church) was an attack on any religion which failed to renounce life in this world.

Theoretically, he came to take his stand on a dualism according to which the spiritual self was edified to just that extent that the 'worldly' self was denied. This spirituality is the exact opposite of Blake's—there is no content to its infinitude but the negation of finitude, by denying the passions.[5]

We can learn from Kierkegaard's descriptive account of schizoid experience in *The Sickness unto Death* and his other psychological writings, but we can also learn from the fact that he could not sustain these insights, but had to take up a position more flattering to his own mode of existence.

It may occur to someone to say at this point that Laing is reading his existentialist ideas (if that is what they are) into the minds of his schizoid patients, and thus forcing the phenomena to fit his theory. This is not the case however. In the first place, it would hardly be a confirmation of existentialist theory that it was believed by schizoid people. But in addition to this, Laing quotes from his patients, he largely 'uses the words that the other person was using'. In one case ('Joan') he discusses the responses of a schizophrenic patient not treated by him or any other 'existential' analyst, and she does use similar language (distinguishing her 'animal body' from the 'part that was a person', the 'real self' etc.). As a description of schizoid and schizophrenic experience, Laing's account is clear and convincing; it evokes immediate recognition in people who have themselves experienced ontological insecurity. I am talking here, not about the explanatory force of Laing's account, but only its descriptive accuracy, and in this respect it leaves nothing to be desired. Finally, as I have already pointed out, Laing only claims that *some* people—those who are ontologically insecure, i.e. 'schizoid' people, experience the world in an 'existentialist' way, not that everybody must, or that those who do not are in 'bad faith'. So his relation with existentialist thought seems to be that he uses it to elucidate the self-experience of schizoid people, not that he accepts it as the correct theory about human existence, and explains schizoid experience in accordance with it.

At least in *The Divided Self* and Laing's other early works, though he uses a number of concepts derived from the existentialist tradition of philosophy and psychotherapy, he gives an empirical content to what were metaphysical doctrines in the writings of the existentialists proper—Kierkegaard and Sartre and to some extent Heidegger. The unhappy states of affairs which these thinkers portray as belonging inescapably to the human condition, are for Laing misfortunes which can befall people under particular circumstances.[6] Whereas the existentialists urge the recognition in anguish of these truths, but see them as inevitable Laing seeks to create understanding in the belief that it can lead to 'cure', at least if combined with a change in the circumstances which caused the trouble.

Thus Laing does not think—at least at this point in his career —that human beings are essentially isolated, that other people are our worst enemies, and so on. He repeats time and again that the schizoid defences, insofar as they lead to the withdrawal of the individual from interaction with other people, are self-defeating, leading to increasing feelings of 'emptiness' and anxiety. He merely recognises that these dogmas proclaimed by existentialist philosophers correspond to the self-experience of a large class of people, including his schizoid patients, and hence can be of assistance in 'understanding' these people, in the sense of being able to see things as they do (which is not the same thing as to endorse the view expressed by them).

Also one should not confuse Laing and his collaborators with other schools of existential psychiatry, despite a few points of contact. These schools in general (Frankl is a good example) are dominated by 'edifying' purposes, i.e. they seem to aim at securing adherence to moral ideals by flattering human vanity, not at lessening human misery by creating greater self understanding. One can certainly not imagine Laing dealing out this sort of 'ghostly comfort'.

However the 'existentialism' which Laing finds in his patients' self-experience does infect his own method of theorizing about psychological matters. In the first two chapters of *The Divided Self* he is concerned to show that existential phenomenology is the only appropriate method of understanding the schizoid person. The sort of understanding he means is primarily that involved in 'seeing the world through another person's eyes', rather than scientific explanation. If that were all that he was doing there could be no objection, but the danger is that it is easy to come to see description as an *alternative* to explanation, and to see a person's experience as *self-validating*. In that case it becomes impossible to acquire real scientific knowledge, which might show a person's self-experience to be radically mistaken. The phenomenological exercise of limiting oneself to pure description of the world-as-experienced is unobjectionable only if it can be and is consistently carried out—and this means not only that one refrains from making explanations, but also from ruling out specific explanations. Unfortunately it is not so easy to draw the distinction between descriptions and explanations. For instance a description of one's own experience will involve references to the motives of one's actions, which are seen as explaining those actions; but this is merely part of description. It would on the one hand be inaccurate to miss out of a phenomenological description of an action, the motives which were experienced by the agent as explaining it. On the other hand, to assume that they were the only and really effective motives would be to transgress the legitimate limits of phenomenology and place an unwarranted restriction on any scientific explanation of the action in question. Moreover an explanation may contradict the original description and make a redescription

B

necessary; phenomenology is not inviolate, even within its own limits. A process of description-explanation-redescription may take place in the course of a Freudian analysis: for instance a man may say 'I could have started an affair with that woman, but it just didn't seem worth it'. He is in all good faith describing his conscious motivation; he was indifferent to the possibility of this relationship. Later—perhaps in the course of an analytic session—he recognises that he had actually had a strong desire for such a relationship, which had showed itself in various symptoms, but had also felt strongly inhibited in relation to the woman, an inhibition which had also showed itself in various symptoms. The indifference which he felt, and which was all he could consciously introspect on the subject, was the product of two conflicting unconscious forces. Having come to see this to be the true explanation, he will no longer describe the experiences in the same way as before.

In Freudian psychoanalysis there is a 'phenomenological' element, firstly in the 'fundamental rule' that the analysand should say whatever comes into his head, should not rework his experience or subject it to the censorship of his moral or theoretical beliefs before describing it to the analyst; and secondly in that the process of making an unconscious belief or wish conscious is not simply that of convincing the analysand that he has just that belief or wish (which by itself would be therapeutically useless) but of bringing the unconscious material into consciousness out of the analysand's own unconcious. However between the original self-experience on which the analysis works and the self-awareness which is the product of the analysis, there is a process of explanation of conscious phenomena by unconscious processes, in accordance with the theoretical concepts of psychoanalysis, and this explanation contradicts the original experience.

A phenomenology which claimed to be an independent science, on whose territory other sciences, however valid in their own sphere, could not trespass, would prevent any such process as this. Yet it would seem that Laingian psychotherapy is at least psychoanalytical enough to allow such processes of explanation and redescription as I have just described. Why has Laing chosen to use a phenomenological method in his scientific project?

On the second page of the first chapter, he tells us:

The particular form of human tragedy we are faced with here has never been presented with sufficient clarity and distinctness. I felt, therefore, that the sheer descriptive task had to come before all other considerations. (*The Divided Self*, p. 18)

However, it is not merely a matter of emphasis. He makes much more far-reaching claims for his method as against, for instance, Freudian metapsychology. Like many others he regards this part of Freud's theory as philosophically inadequate and inessential to Freud's real discoveries (Herbert Marcuse on the other hand believes that precisely this part of Freudian theory which is furthest removed from practice and is therefore least corrupted by the conformist pressures of bourgeois society, contains the greatest critical insights into that society—see his *Eros and Civilization*).

What is the content of Laing's criticism? He rejects Freudian metapsychology (along with certain other psychiatric theories) as involving a

verbal and conceptual splitting that matches the split up of the totality of the schizoid being-in-the-world ... we have an already shattered Humpty Dumpty who cannot be put together again by any number of hyphenated or compound words: psychophysical, psychosomatic, psycho-biological, psycho-pathological, psycho-social, etc., etc.

If this is so, it may be that a look at how such schizoid theory originates would be highly relevant to the understanding of schizoid experience. (*The Divided Self*, p. 20)

These theories are rejected as schizoid by Laing because they are said to 'depersonalise' the people who are the object of their study. This occurs in two ways:

(1) These theories treat people not as unitary wholes, but as made up of various elements (e.g. ego, super-ego, id) which can be known only through science, not through our ordinary ex-

perience of people (in particular, of ourselves). That Laing directs this criticism not only at the body/mind dualists alluded to in the above passage, but also at Freud, can be seen from p. 19 of *The Divided Self* where he says: 'Instead of the original bond of I and You, we take a single man in isolation and conceptualize his various aspects into "the ego", "the superego", and "the id".'

(2) They do not treat people as 'persons' i.e., as conscious responsible agents, but as 'things' or 'complexes of things'.

I hope to show that the first of these criticisms is true but no criticism, and that the second is unclear. If this is so, why are they seen as criticisms by Laing? It is striking that the fear of 'depersonalization' and the belief that knowledge, or threats to the autonomy of consciousness, constitute depersonalization, are characteristic of schizoid individuals. Could it be that so far from Freudian theory representing a reflection of schizoid states, this might be true of Laing's theory itself?

First of all it is necessary to ask whether Laing's criticisms of the application of these scientific methods to psychology are justified.

Take then, the point about the psyche or personality as a unitary whole. This is a concept Laing uses (on p. 19) in the following context:

. . . we cannot give an adequate account of the existential splits unless we can begin from the concept of a unitary whole, and no such concept exists, nor can any such concept be expressed, within the current language system or psychiatry or psychoanalysis.

The psyche or personality of a non-psychotic person certainly has some degree of unity in it; the components within it (e.g. the individual's sexuality and his ideas, his phantasy life and his personal relationships) are related to each other in their essence, not merely accidentally. To a greater or lesser extent, a person's psyche is unified by his conscious purposes and intentions; the failure to achieve this conscious organisation of one's personality into a unified whole is one of the fates befalling the patients Laing describes. However Laing quite correctly speaks of this unity as an achievement,[7] the end product of a process of inter-action between the individual and his immediate human environment. Hence Laing is not at all justified in talking as if we were concerned here with an original unity, which cannot be broken down into components, even in thought. The bits of Humpty Dumpty which Laing fears can never be put together once taken apart are in fact the components out of which Humpty Dumpty has been produced in the first place. So if we are to understand the human psyche, we must analyse it into these elements, some of which pre-existed the unity of which they form part.

In other words, the psyche is not a *unitary* whole of which the parts merely express a single principle—the 'autonomous' consciousness. It is a *unified* whole, which has achieved a more or less stable equilibrium under the direction of consciousness, but which has other (unconscious) elements which may obstruct this direction, which may act on and determine consciousness independently of its knowledge or volition, which may in turn be acted upon by consciousness, etc. Hence the possibility of this unity breaking down in schizophrenia.

We have here two quite different conceptions of the unity of the psyche; according to one—which appears to be assumed by Laing in passages like the last quoted, and is certainly Sartre's—consciousness directs the psyche with godlike autonomy and omnipotence; nothing in the psyche exists independently of it or could exercise any force upon it. The psyche is therefore unitary in essence; the unity can break down only by conscious choice or by being smashed from outside, or from some combination of these—i.e. a choice of breakdown in response to the hostility of the outside world; there is no possibility of breakdown through the interplay of internal forces, for there are no such forces except insofar as they express the essentially unitary principle of the psyche. On this view, understanding the psyche must consist of tracing its various phenomena—particularly acts, desires, wishes etc.—to a single conscious central core, the self, of which they are expressions.

According to the other conception, that of Freudian psychoanalysis, this unity is the result of the interplay of various—often conflicting forces. The original instinctual endowment of the child undergoes various vicissitudes as the result of relations with his family etc.; the 'institutions of the psyche', ego, super-ego and id, are produced by this process; the unity of the adult psyche is less a godlike order than a political one, that of a state, itself a product and to some extent servant of social forces, maintaining order yet beset with difficulties, sometimes insuper-able, and opposition, which can sometimes only be held down by savage repression; there is always the possibility that a shift in the balance of social forces may cause the state to break down in civil war or be overthrown and replaced in revolution.

In the Freudian theory, no phenomenon of the breakdown of the unity of the psyche can be understood without an account of the relations between these institutions of the psyche, and the specific nature of each of them in the individual concerned.

Two reasons for preferring the Freudian to the Sartrean ac-count have already emerged: given that the unity of the psyche is the result of a process, the elements unified in it may be ex-pected to retain some independent being; it is inconceivable how a unity that cannot be broken down even in thought could come about. And the fact that this unity can break down in reality without this breakdown being necessarily either total or final, indicates that it is a complex and relative unity, not an absolute and simple one.

However there is a further point that can be made about the whole methodology implied by these two notions of totalities—unified or unitary wholes. Both Freud's and Sartre's theories may be said to be dialectical, in the sense that they study totalities and unearth contradictions in these totalities—that is, they find that two (or more) elements or aspects of some totality (in this case, an individual psyche), while both being intrinsic parts of that totality, are in conflict. For instance, a man may combine an attitude of extreme tenderness and respect towards women with violent and sadistic impulses towards them; a Freudian account would be that the respect is a reaction-formation against the sadism, one of the defence-mechanisms by which the conscious ego protects itself against the unacceptable impulses of the id. So that, while the original phenomenon of respect/sadism cannot simply be resolved into two conflicting attitudes which happen to be co-present—the respect and the sadism are intrinsically connected—it is nevertheless the case that in the first place two conflicting wishes (perhaps infantile wishes in relation to the mother) have been operative in producing this contradictory attitude. The Sartrean account on the other hand must trace all mental phenomena to a single centre of the individual mind in question, a single consciously chosen way of being-in-the-world. All particular desires or attitudes or wishes would be aspects of this single (though complex) choice. Hence all apparent conflicts in the psyche will, on closer investigation, turn out to be unreal; if all one's desires are aspects of a single conscious project, how could two desires conflict? One might of course have a self-contradictory desire, such as to officiate at one's own funeral, but this is contradictory in the sense of its fulfilment being a logical impossibility, it is not a real conflict between elements within a totality.

We have here two concepts of the dialectic: (1) The unifying principle of the totality determines the entire totality; hence, 'contradictions' which appear, do so in a totality which is originally and essentially one; they are ultimately only 'apparent' contradictions; complete knowledge of the totality leads to their disappearance; therefore they can be overcome in pure thought. Thought proceeds from a contradictory appearance to a unitary reality. (2) The totality and its unifying element are products of the interplay of forces; these forces, not being mere aspects of a unifying principle, may be in real conflict, which it is not in the power of the unifying element to iron out. But the *appearance* of unity may be produced (in the case of Freudian theory, one of the characteristics of conscious mental phenomena is their tendency to consistency, while contradictory desires or beliefs can co-exist in the unconscious). It is the task of science to pierce through this appearance of unity, if it is to achieve knowledge of the underlying contradictions in the totality which is the object of its study. So in this case, thought proceeds from the unitary appearance to the contradictory reality; the contradictions cannot be resolved by thought, but only by practice.[8]

If one wishes to seek venerable ancestors for these two concepts of dialectics, the former may be traced to Parmenides, the latter to Heraclitus. But in more recent times, the former is the idealist dialectic found in classical German philosophy (Kant, Fichte, Hegel) and in Sartre, the latter the materialist dialectic used by Marx and Freud.[9]

The question we must ask here is: Which is the dialectic as used by Laing? In the most concrete (and best) parts of his work —for instance the family case histories in *Sanity, Madness and the Family*—I think the answer is undoubtedly the materialist dialectic. (Here, though, the totalities studied are families, not individual psyches. There is a tendency in Laing to stress interpersonal contradictions at the expense of intrapersonal ones.)

However, Laing has been strongly influenced philosophically by Hegel and Sartre, and his theoretical formulations, such as those I have been discussing in which he rejects any theory which breaks up or explains the 'unitary whole' of the psyche, show this influence.

In the cases discussed in *The Divided Self*, the 'splitting of the self' is experienced by the subject as a splitting into 'true self' (inner self), which has all the qualities of the mind according to idealism—autonomy, unity, invulnerability—and the 'false self', which is the only part of the self to have relations with the 'outside world' and which is totally given over to the control of other people. Any breach of the autonomy and unity of the 'true self' is feared like the plague, but the 'false self' on which the inner self is dependent for its relations with others, its supply of ideas etc., is neither unitary nor autonomous. Now Laing— as the title of his book itself suggests—clearly does not take the 'true self' as the whole self; the self is composed of both fragments. The resolution of the contradiction in the self would involve recognition of the impossibility of the sort of autonomy pursued by the inner self—a recognition that 'The self can be "real" only in relation to real people and things'. (*The Divided Self*, p. 142)

A genuine autonomy would mean the ability to relate to other people in ways in which one wanted to, not freedom from the need for satisfying relationships. In Laing's patients we notice (1) the absence of and need for a real (but relative) unity and autonomy of the personality, based on acceptance of one's own psychic needs and dependence on freely developed relationships with others, and (2) the defence of an idealized unity and autonomy, based on rejection of any dependence of the conscious self on anything else, whether others, or its own unconscious and body. Any challenge to this autonomy and unity, whether theoretical or practical, is feared and resented.

Now Laing, as I have pointed out, is insistent on the self-defeating nature of the idealized, unreal autonomy of the schizoid person. Yet in his theoretical formulations, Laing seems to be unduly influenced by considerations resembling the schizoid fear of depersonalization. Any theory which would understand people in other than 'personal' terms, i.e. in terms of the autonomy of consciousness, of responsible agency, of self-experience as self-validating, is seen as depersonalizing in the sense that the schizoid individual fears, and this depersonalization is equated with the real lack of self-direction suffered by the schizoid.

It seems to me that what is occurring here is a case of a frequent kind of mistake: that which associates the theoretical with the practical assertion of some value, as if by saying that something is the case one contributes to bringing it about that it becomes the case. Take the example of the concept of human equality. When the philosophical cults of hellenistic and Roman times asserted the essential equality of men, that every man has the same essential humanity and capacity for happiness, this might appear very 'democratic' compared with Aristotle's view that, since ethics was concerned with the pursuit of happiness, it was only a suitable study for the small élite who had some chance of attaining it. Yet the latter view, by recognizing that a share of this world's goods is a necessary condition of happiness is a theory which would be revolutionary in the hands of classes deprived of those goods. On the other hand the cynic-stoic view that all are free and equal 'inside', serves to reconcile the deprived to their condition as it holds out illusory possibilities of happiness within this (actually miserable) condition. Ideologies which are flattering to the oppressed may have an appeal to them for that reason, and indeed may arise spontaneously amongst them as a slave-morality of sour grapes, as Nietzsche suggests, but as long as these hold sway amongst them, they will remain oppressed. When an oppressed class or group becomes acutely aware of its oppression and the possibility of its liberation, it contemptuously rejects these ideologies.[10]

Laing's sympathy or 'empathy' with the schizoid condition may have led him to accept too much of the schizoid world-view, to the detriment of the therapy which aims at overcoming the miseries of this condition. This may also be the case in connection with his criticism of the accepted concepts of sanity and madness (see below, Ch. 5).

If the world view of the schizoid person is inextricably bound up with his condition, it must be a necessary part of therapy to dissolve this world view; a therapy which accepts its concepts cannot hope to do more than console. This is the danger in Laing's in many ways admirable tendency to 'use the same words as the other person'. The belief that the mind is independent of the body, that the self is independent of the external world, that all relationships threaten 'loss of self', these are symptoms of the schizoid condition. The understanding of these concepts is necessary to any adequate description of what it feels like to be ontologically insecure, and such a description is a necessary prerequisite to understanding and analytic therapy of schizoid sufferers. But these concepts must be taken as symptomatic of this highly unhappy mode of self-experience. They have a mystifying function within that mode of experience, and cannot be used to acquire knowledge of it. If a patient tells an analyst that to be understood or loved by others would 'depersonalize' him, or destroy his autonomy, the analyst must accept that this is how the patient experiences relations with others, but he cannot accept it as a true account of personal relations in general. The patient may fear for his 'autonomy', meaning thereby his independence of the 'external world' including other people and possibly his own body; the analyst can by no means reassure him about such autonomy; it is an illusion which he will have to shed in the course of cure.

This certainly does not mean that an analyst should be brutal in his effort to break down schizoid defences (and sometimes perhaps 'treating the patient as a person' means no more than being nice to him);[11] but to leave these defences intact would be to leave the patient in the misery which, presumably, led him to seek help. The way in which an analysis contradicts the analysand's self-experience as it breaks down his defence-mechanism is certainly painful, but it cannot be avoided as part of the analytic cure.[12]

Laing's reluctance to admit the full force of the way in which the analytic process contradicts the previous self-experience of the analysand is understandable when we look at some of his findings about the way in which certain parental behaviour can induce schizoid or schizophrenic conditions. A persistent theme in Laing's writings is the role of *cognitive denial* in producing these conditions; for instance, puritanical parents may tell their daughter, not merely that she should not act on her sexual desires, or even that she ought not to have them, but that she does not have them. This point looms so large in the case histories in *Sanity, Madness and the Family*, that it led Trevor Pateman to say that what these patients needed was not a psychiatrist but an epistemologist.[13]

In these cases it appears that the patient had originally had—and in some respects still had—a truer perception of the realities of her family situation than did the other, 'sane', members of the family. They had induced doubt about her own capacity for correct observation by persistent and collusive denial. It appears to be psychologically impossible to retain one's grip on reality when one's own perceptions are constantly contradicted by those on whom one is emotionally dependent.

However it is not the case, as is sometimes alleged, that the schizophrenic patients studied were really perfectly sane, that they had merely been labelled mad because of their position as minorities of one within the family group. Their situations in their families may explain their symptoms and make them intelligible, but it is not claimed that they are thereby shown to be no symptoms at all, but sane and rational responses. An analogy Laing has used is that of seeing a formation of planes with one missing, and also a stray plane, (the one missing from the formation) and assuming that the stray plane is lost; then one discovers that the formation was itself lost, and assumes that the stray plane was on course. However in reality all the planes are lost.

If the 'stray plane' (the individual who has been diagnosed as schizophrenic) has any advantage relative to his or her family (along with the manifest disadvantages in terms of suffering, inability to cope with life, etc.) it is that, as the 'lostness' is more obvious, it is more likely to receive treatment. This of course might be a disadvantage at the hand of some psychiatrists— (who would merely reinforce the parental judgments)—but presumably not Laing's.

Given the importance of the role of the disconfirmation of experience in the background of neurosis and psychosis, it is understandable that Laing stresses the need for confirmation of experience by the analyst. But this can mean no more than that the analyst takes the patient's side against those who have mystified him. It certainly does not mean that he can accept the self assessment of the patient. This may seem too obvious to need stressing, and I do not think Laing falls into this mistake in most of his concrete histories; but he does take a viewpoint about the nature of consciousness, of autonomy, of the unity of the psyche, etc. which can be seen as reflecting the experience of the schizoid person, and consistent only with the schizoid experience of the world.

This may be illustrated by reference to 'case I', described by Laing in the chapter of *The Divided Self* on ontological insecurity (pp. 54–58). Mrs. R. was a woman of twenty-eight living with her father after the break-up of her marriage; she suffered from agoraphobia.

An insensitive application of what is often supposed to be the classical psycho-analytic theory of hysteria to this patient might attempt to show this woman as unconsciously libidinally bound to her father; with, consequently, unconscious guilt and unconscious need and/or fear of punishment. Her failure to develop lasting libidinal relationships away from her father would seem to support the first view, along with her decision to live with him, to take her mother's place, as it were, and the fact that she spent most of her day, as a woman of 28, actually thinking about him. Her devotion to her mother in her last illness would be partly the consequences of unconscious guilt at her unconscious ambivalence to her mother; and her anxiety at her mother's death would be anxiety at her unconscious wish for her mother's death coming true. And so on.

However, the central or pivotal issue in this patient's life is not to be discovered in her 'unconscious'; it is lying open for her to see, as well as for us (although this is not to say that there are not many things about herself that this patient does not realise).

The pivotal point around which all her life is centred is her *lack of ontological autonomy*. (p. 56)

No argument is presented by Laing to show that the Freudian explanation in terms of the unconscious is inapplicable. Rather it is seen as unnecessary because there is an explanation ready to hand. But this would not be surprising from a Freudian point of view, for rationalizations of behaviour the real motives of which have been repressed is to be expected; the rationalization is also likely to be a desexualization, as in this case. Laing's departure from psychoanalytic orthodoxy here consists in the replacement of sexual themes by ontological ones, and in conjunction with this, the acceptance of the conscious self-experience of the patient as giving the true explanation.

One cannot transpose her central problem into 'the unconscious'. If one discovers that she has an unconscious phantasy of being a prostitute, this does not explain her anxiety about streetwalking, or her preoccupation with women who fall in the street and are not helped to get on their feet again. The unconscious phantasy is on the contrary, to be explained by and understood in terms of the central issue implicating her self-being, her being-for-herself. (p. 57)

But if this whole process takes place in consciousness, it is not clear how it could produce such strong irrational fears.

Furthermore, it is clear enough how e.g. castration-anxiety and fear and repression of sexuality can come about; and that in conscious experience this anxiety might, as a defence, be 'ontologized' (i.e. experience as fear of loss of being); but it is unclear what the equivalent phenomenon would be if ontology were primary in the way Laing suggests. Why should one find it ontologically threatening to meet strangers in the street? It is precisely this that needs explanation.

It may be said that it is because one has not achieved ontological autonomy; but how much is implied in this formula? It seems to be suggested by Laing in this chapter that in order to find relationships with other people gratifying (and specifically, sexual relationships), one must first have achieved ontological security and autonomy 'in oneself'.

This recalls the social contract theories of politics: first there are independent individuals, then they voluntarily associate for some mutual advantage. It has often been pointed out that social contract theories ignore the material and social interdependence of people in any society, their original involvement in social relations not of their own choosing, and the fact that the economic autonomy of e.g. the bourgeois is not independence of these relations, but the product of an advantageous position in and successful manipulation of them. It is astounding that many ideologists of the left recognize this yet fail to apply the same insights in the area of personal relations and psychology; that people are necessarily emotionally interdependent, that everyone finds themselves originally involved in dependencies not of their own choosing—on their parents; that autonomy cannot mean independence of others, but only the achievement of satisfactory relationships of one's own choosing, and dependence on these in place of the parents or 'internalized parents'.

Now one of the strengths of Laing's work is the emphasis he places on analysing interpersonal processes, not just the psyche of the individual in isolation. So it might be thought, he, less than anyone, can be accused of this micro-social contract theory. His account of ontological insecurity also stresses the self-defeating nature of the cult of isolation to which it leads. His account of his psychiatric work shows a concern to create a real autonomy in patients whose experience of dependence on their parents has prevented this from developing; but the personalist ideology of autonomy in terms of which he describes this situation often leads him to treat people as already autonomous and hence to take their self-experience at face value and operate with an essentially schizoid ideal of autonomy—i.e. of an original unity and independence on the part of the self, which can first achieve autonomy, and afterwards relate to other people. This by no means always distorts Laing's concrete descriptions, but sometimes, as in the above case, it does. In many of his theoretical formulations moreover, he criticizes other theories from the standpoint of this personalist ideology, in a way which, if legitimate, would invalidate much of his own work.

It is important to distinguish at this point different opponents in the psychiatric world against whom he directs his personalist polemics.

On the one hand, it is directed against various ways of treating psychological disturbances by purely physiological methods—drugs, electric shock treatment, brain surgery and the like. Given that physical illnesses can have psychological effects, and vice versa, I do not think one can object in principle either to such treatment of neurosis and psychosis, or to psychotherapeutic treatment of physical illness (psychosomatic medicine). Laing does not object to operating to remove a brain tumour which is causing psychiatric symptoms. But Laing has a very good case to make against the almost exclusive reliance on drugs and ECT in most English mental hospitals. A doctor does not normally refer a patient with physical symptoms to a psychiatrist until he is fairly sure that he has exhausted his search for a physical cause, and one might expect that a psychiatrist would likewise be cautious about using physical treatment until the possibilities of a psychosocial explanation and cure had been explored.

It is quite possible to express this criticism of conventional psychiatric methods by saying that they fail to treat people as people (or even 'persons') because mental life is something that people possess and other beings do not. The same applies to behaviour therapy, based as it is on a theory which seems better adapted to white rats, and which aims at conditioning people's emotional responses by means of physical stimuli; particularly when it takes the form of aversion therapy, which is obviously by definition unpleasant for the person concerned.

Laing's colleague David Cooper writes:

One illuminating bit of the horror story is the diagnosis and treatment of 'homosexuals' by aversion methods. Men who, the psychiatrists complain, are complaining of homosexual wishes have a gadget attached to their penises that measures the strength of erection by the blood volume in the penis. They are shown a series of nude men interspersed with a series of nude women. When they respond to the nude men by erectile increase they are given an electric shock, when they respond to nude women they are given the 'reward' of a non-shock. (*The Death of the Family*, p. 114)

Here, in addition to the unpleasantness, it is a prejudice of existing society—its discrimination against homosexuals—which is being conditioned into men who, for all we know, might be quite happy as homosexuals if society were less repressive.

But I think it is highly unfortunate that Laing expresses his criticisms of orthodox psychiatry in personalist terms (rather than e.g. in terms of its refusal to recognize the peculiar nature of mental processes and of disturbances in mental functioning, as contrasted with physical processes and physical illness—terms which on the face of it look very similar to Laing's). It is unfortunate not only because it suggests a false conception of the autonomy of consciousness, but also because it lumps those psychoanalytical schools which reject this conception (i.e. Freudian ones) together with non-psychoanalytical psychiatry. Yet all the above criticisms of behaviour therapy, exclusive reliance on drugs and so on, are as much Freudian as Laingian.

There is an extraordinarily widespread belief among politically radical critics of psychiatry that Freudian psychoanalysis is not essentially different from orthodox psychiatry. One even hears the same people criticizing Freudian psychoanalysis both from a personalist standpoint derived from Laing and his collaborators, and from that of orthodox psychiatry, which claims that analysis is less effective than drugs. No doubt such inconsistency indicates the presence of a resistance rather than a rationally held position, but I feel that the form of Laing's criticisms must be partly responsible for this misconception.

It is necessary to point out then that psychoanalysis cures purely by increasing self-awareness, and therefore cannot in principle be used in a manipulative way as behaviour therapy can, despite the fact that subjectively, many analysts no doubt, like Freud himself, have relatively conformist values.

Laing's own theory and practice cannot be understood except as a version of psychoanalysis, however unorthodox; it is also worth remembering that many 'existential' versions of psychoanalysis, unlike Laing's, attack Freud precisely in the name of the official values of bourgeois society, which they defend in personalist terms.

The personalist ideology has other effects—theoretical, therapeutic and political—in Laing's later writings. However, in no two books is the relation between the psychoanalytical and the existentialist and personalist elements in his thought quite the same, although the tension between them persists.

What is perhaps worth remarking on by way of conclusion to this chapter on *The Divided Self* is a sort of circular reinforcement between aspects of Laing's theory and therapy. The personalist ideology carries with it a partly methodological and partly moral imperative that one should treat people as conscious, responsible agents who know what they are doing. This restricts the method of investigation of people to a phenomenological description, which takes people's self-experience at its face value. When applied to schizoid people, this leads to taking their 'existentialistic' world view as a datum. This world view in turn dictates personalism. Thus the circle is complete: personalist ethic—phenomenological method—uncritical description of schizoid experience—existentialist world view—personalist ethic.

The weak link in this chain, from the scientific point of view, is precisely its point of contact with reality—the description of schizoid experience: not because that description is inaccurate, but because it is limited to schizoid experience, and tells us nothing about other forms of experience, or of the unconscious origins of schizoid experience itself.

But if this theoretical circle were all that there is to Laing's work, that work would not be what it is—an important contribution to contemporary knowledge of people and their problems. The circle is no more than a 'knot' in which Laing gets tied at certain points in his theoretical ruminations.

Chapter 2

Social Phenomenology and Psychoanalysis

The same personalist ideology which makes its appearance in *The Divided Self* affects Laing's conception of scientific method in his later writing as well. Hence he often describes his work as a contribution to the Science of Persons, of experience or of inter-experience. If the criticisms I have made at the end of the last chapter are valid, it may be asked: can there be such a science; would it really give us new knowledge about people; can a therapeutic practice be based on it?

In the first place it seems to me Laing has accomplished a very valuable descriptive task. His writings have an important place in the literature to which one should turn if one wishes to understand what it is like to be schizoid or, so far as such understanding is possible, to be schizophrenic. Such description is invaluable from a scientific point of view as well as from that of therapy itself or of a layman's attempt to understand himself and his fellow creatures better. However, it is not itself science; a biography or a novel might serve the same purpose.

But I think that Laing has contributed more than this. He has investigated areas neglected by traditional psycho-analytic theory and has contributed to the scientific knowledge of them.

41

This raises new questions. What is the status of his investigations; do they constitute a new science, and if so, what is its object? Perhaps the best way of clarifying this is by examining the relation of Laing's theoretical work to traditional psychoanalytical theory.

I shall attempt this clarification with regard to the following topics: (a) the problem of defining the object of social phenomenology as a theory laying claim to scientific status, and the relation of this object to that of orthodox psychoanalysis; (b) the role of meaning and of causality in each of these theories—in particular, the question whether the search for meanings in these areas is compatible with, or perhaps even requires, the search for causes; (c) the Sartrean notion, sometimes used by Laing, of making something intelligible (finding meaning in it) as 're-solving process into praxis'—and the contrast between this and psychoanalytical explanation; (d) the relation between the role of the individual's past history, and of his or her present situation, in accounting for experience and behaviour. Finally, (e) I shall try to locate the legitimate place of social phenomenology in relation to psychoanalysis on the basis of these discussions.

These topics are inter-related, and though I devote a separate section to each, there will be some unavoidable overlapping of the discussions. The concept of the unconscious, and its specific differences both from the conscious and from the non-mental, will be at issue throughout.

(a) The objects of social phenomenology and psychoanalysis

If we ask what psycho-analysis is the theory of, what its object as a science is, the most satisfactory answer is that it is the science of mental processes whether conscious or unconscious. It cannot claim to be a science of persons. It is a science which tells us about people but so do Human Anatomy and Physiology, as well as Linguistics, Economics, etc. It does take experience as part of its object but in this case, only a part: as a science of mental processes it does describe and explain experience but not only experience. In talking of a science of persons or of experience then, Laing is distinguishing his own theoretical work from that of psychoanalysis, not only in its method, but in its object. By 'persons' he actually means not simply human individuals but human individuals viewed in a certain way dictated by a personalist ideology, i.e., as conscious, responsible subjects. This would seem to indicate that the relation of his own theory to Freud's is one of radical revision. If people really are persons in this sense, Freud's method would be quite inappropriate, but more than that, almost all his findings would have to be rejected as false, for the theory of the unconscious, if well founded, deals a death blow to all ideas of the autonomy of consciousness. In which case, the high terms in which Laing speaks of Freud are incomprehensible. For instance,

The greatest psycho-pathologist has been Freud. Freud was a hero. He descended to the 'Underworld' and there met stark terrors. He carried with him his theory as a Medusa's head which turned these terrors to stone. We who follow Freud have the benefit of the knowledge he brought back with him and conveyed to us. He survived. We must see if we now can survive without using a theory that is in some measure an instrument of defence. (*The Divided Self*, p. 25)

Here Laing seems to conceive the necessary task to be the revision of Freud's philosophical premises while retaining his discoveries. Laing seems here to belong to that large class of neo-Freudian revisionists who see Freud as a great scientist but philosophically naive and hence needing his terminology revising. The revision in question would be, in Laing's case, that Freud's concepts would have to be given a phenomenological sense: the unconscious would have to be interpreted as not really unconscious but a particular area of conscious experience. A good example of Laing in his role as a post-Freudian revisionist is his attempt at a phenomenological restatement of the nature of the unconscious at the beginning of *Self and Others*. The problems discussed in this book are posed in terms of communication, primarily in terms of the way people's phantasy life affects their relations with others. According to Freudian theory much

phantasy is unconscious, and this is accepted by Laing to the
extent that he does not assume self knowledge in respect of
phantasy. However he sees a philosophical problem in talking
about unconscious phantasy.

Is it a contradiction to speak in terms of 'unconscious experience'? A
person's experience comprises everything that 'he', or 'any part of
him', is aware of whether 'he' or every part of him is aware of every
level of his awareness or not. (*Self and Others*, p. 22)

It is assumed here that unconscious phantasy must really be an
experience of some kind: this is understood to mean the subject
is aware, i.e., conscious, of it. How then can it be unconscious?
But this way of setting up the problem itself derives from
phenomenology. Laing tells us:

The situation is not assisted by the fact that the concept of unconscious phantasy has received very little scrutiny from an existential
and phenomenological perspective. (*Self and Others*, p. 17)

But this is not surprising for phenomenology cannot speak of
such things. Of course it does not follow that phenomenology
rules out the possibility of other disciplines speaking of them but
Laing is suggesting in this chapter that only a phenomenological
account will be adequate:

Let us distinguish two usages of 'unconscious'. First, the term 'unconscious' may refer to structures, functions, mechanisms, processes that
are meant to explain a person's actions or experiences. Such structures, functions, mechanisms or processes are outside experience but
are used to 'explain' experience, whether called conscious or unconscious. These concepts lie outside experience but start through inferences about experience. If these inferences are incorrect, everything
built upon them is completely wrong.
    In the second place, 'unconscious' might signify that the user of the
term is claiming that he or the other is unaware of part of his own experience, despite the apparent absurdity of this claim. (*Self and
Others*, p. 21)

What Laing wants to do is to establish a coherent account of
the second sense of 'unconscious' within phenomenology and

the implication is that this will do the work which the Freudian account, which is clearly concerned with the unconscious in the first sense, was supposed to do. He sets up a phenomenological account in terms of his model of communication and breakdowns in it. Thus,

> *The 'unconscious' is what we do not communicate, to ourselves or to one another.* We may convey something to another without communicating it to ourselves. Something about Peter is evident to Paul but is not evident to Peter. This is *one* sense of the phrase—Peter is unconscious of . . . . (*Self and Others*, p. 32)

It certainly is, but can this sense replace the Freudian one?

It is no doubt a common phenomenon for anyone who is at all reflective about their experience to recall their experience of some incident and say something like, 'Of course, I felt such and such, I knew I did all along, but I did not recognize it at the time.' Such cases seem to answer to Laing's description and nothing is easier than to assimilate the psycho-analytic experience of becoming conscious of some previously unconscious idea to this familiar pattern. However, this is not an accurate account of the psycho-analytical concept of the unconscious. It is closer to Sartre's idea of self deception (*mauvaise foi*).

The point about the unconscious idea in the Freudian sense is that the most thorough and honest self examination possible fails to make it conscious, conspicuously misses it, avoids and circles round it. It is this conspicuous avoidance by which the analyst can locate the resistance to the repressed idea becoming conscious. The unconscious idea may explain the neurotic behaviour of the subject and his resistances. This sense of unconscious clearly does not fit Laing's description.

In addition to this, the concept of unconscious mental processes in Freud has other features than that one is not aware of what is unconscious. The unconscious is governed by different laws and has different kinds of content than the conscious. It is not a unified system in quite the way that consciousness is and its contents obey laws of primary processes etc. In Laing's account, however, the two parts of the mind which fail to communicate with each other are more or less on even terms. One is unconscious only relatively to the other. Neither is pre-eminently a representative of the instincts or of the power of the past over the present, though both of these characteristics apply to the unconscious in the Freudian sense. They can be seen to apply also in certain cases cited by Laing.

What then does Laing regard as unsatisfactory about the concept of the unconscious as 'dynamic structures, functions, mechanisms, processes that are meant to explain a person's actions or experiences'. One possibility is suggested by Laing's statement: 'Meta-psychology must begin from somebody's experience but it is seldom clear whose experience or what experience'. (*Self and Others*, p. 25) Concepts of things which we experience, it is implied, are clearly valid, but things we do not experience we must, nevertheless, infer from experiences, and we may make mistakes in making the inferences.

Certainly we may, but in the first place the appearance can notoriously be deceptive and it may be rational to hold to well founded inferences even when they contradict our experiences. The earth appears to be flat and the sun appears to rise. If I experience pink rats scurrying about my kitchen, then I am wise to trust my inference and lay off the gin, rather than to trust my experience and set rat traps.

Meta-psychology in the Freudian sense, theories about instincts and repression, conscious and unconscious, pleasure principle and reality principle, ego, super-ego, id, and so on, presumably starts from experience. In the first place the experience is that of the person being analysed, then of the analyst who perceives patterns in his experience which he is unaware of, e.g., the phenomenon of circling round a repressed idea, which I mentioned before. Later the experience is again that of the analysand, as unconscious material becomes conscious.

What I suspect in the unstated objection to psychological concepts which do not correspond to anything directly experienced is the notion that only concepts derived directly from experience correspond to reality. Concepts derived from inferences or other forms of theoretical reflection are thought to be in some way fictions, things that we put into the facts or invent rather than discover. This view of knowledge can be seen as a continuation of Berkeley's idealism according to which only what is perceived is real and the connections and laws behind the phenomena are merely practically convenient fictions.

One conclusion drawn from this idealist position is that experienced facts, and logical constructions are different categories and hence that nothing which is known in one of these ways can be known in the other; it is said to be a category mistake to identify something known by inferences with something experienced. But this is clearly wrong. The existence of the planet Pluto was discovered by inference from the movements of already known planets before it could be seen through the telescope. Genes were postulated to explain the transmission of physical characteristics from parents to children, before they were 'discovered' and identified as D.N.A. molecules.

The existence of different routes to knowledge of the same object is an important test of their reality in science. This is stated by Maxwell's criterion of scientific reality,

If a concept can be embedded in the network of laws such that together they yield alternative definitions of the concept, couched in logically independent terms, not built into its original definition, then we feel that the concept tells us something about reality, that is, that the concept itself is in some sense 'real'. (As cited by Michael Ruse in his paper 'Definitions of Species in Biology', *Brit. J. Phil. Sci.* 1969)

Now, to consider the case in psycho-analysis. The analyst infers from the analysand's account of his conscious experience the presence of certain ideas in his unconscious, using psychoanalytic theory in making the inferences. Having done so in the course of the analysis he brings these ideas to consciousness in the analysand. Cure is not affected unless they are made conscious. Telling the analysand that he has these ideas as unconscious ideas and getting him to believe it would not be effective according to Freud; but of course if the experienced and the inferred are regarded as different categories of being, the merely inferred unconscious idea could not later become experienced any more than the merely inferred planet Pluto could later be seen through the telescope. It may be objected at this point that in arriving at the conclusion that a certain individual has a certain unconscious idea the analyst is using a theory, Freudian meta-psychology, and that the origin of this, in experience, must be traced. This would be based on an intuitively plausible but incorrect inference: from the correct proposition that all scientific knowledge is derived from experience, to the incorrect one, that there must be some scientific knowledge which is derived directly from experience without the aid of any pre-existing scientific knowledge. But this is exactly analogous to the argument that because all machines have been produced from natural resources, there must be some machines which were produced without the aid of machinery.

It seems from what has been said here that in those places where Laing suggests that psycho-analytic theory needs revision along phenomenological lines, he is mistaken. He is likewise mistaken if he believes that phenomenological psychology can stand as an independent and autonomous discipline alongside psycho-analysis. But the supplementation of psycho-analysis with a social phenomenology is a different matter. Here, what is new and valuable is not the phenomenological element, for in so far as this is legitimate it is implicit in psycho-analysis anyway, but the social nature of the phenomenology.

I think that whenever Laing confronts Freudian theory head on, what he wishes to do is not to reject it in favour of an incompatible alternative but to reinterpret its concepts in a phenomenological sense. Whether this is possible without sacrificing its essential discoveries is a question to which I shall return. Laing clearly thinks it is. However, this confrontation of Laing and Freud takes the form of philosophical criticism of an established body of knowledge. What is of more interest in Laing is his investigations of areas neglected by traditional psychoanalysis, i.e., of the immediate social situation of neurotic and psychotic patients, the network of inter-personal relationships in which they are enmeshed.

Laing is not the only psychiatrist or psychologist to turn his attention to these matters but he has done so with great insight and, like Freud, extended his discoveries outside the clinical situation in which they originated to enlarge our knowledge of the internal dynamics of human relations generally. This side of Laing's work as developed in *Sanity, Madness and the Family, Self and Others, Inter-personal Perception* and *The Politics of the Family* seems to me his most important contribution. In this part of his work Laing's relation to Freudian psychoanalysis seems to be that he is not disputing its truth (in fact he may even be assuming it), but that he is working in different and independent territory. At the same time there is a criticism of psychoanalytical practice implicit in this work: that in treating its patients without interviewing the other people with whom they have relationships, psychoanalysis ignores facts of prime clinical importance.

This sort of relation of Laing's work to orthodox psychoanalysis is perhaps best seen from the introduction to *Sanity, Madness and the Family*. Three methodological points may be noted from this text.

(1) The families of patients who had been classified as schizophrenics were interviewed; in each case members of the family, including the patient, were observed together. An intuitively plausible justification is given for this:

If one wishes to know how a football team concert or disconcert their actions in play, one does not think only or even primarily of approaching this problem by talking to the members individually. One watches the way they play together. (p. 21)

It is claimed that we can only understand the behaviour of individuals if we observe the groups in which their psychologically significant everyday experience and behaviour takes place.

(2) The description of the ways the members of this group (the family) experience each other remains untainted by explanations which might involve attribution of unconscious motives, casual accounts, etc. These two points can be encapsulated in the phrase 'Social Phenomenology' which is what Laing often calls his method.

He does not claim that this method rules out psychoanalytical explanation or causal accounts generally; indeed he specifically asserts that such explanation is valid:

Undoubtedly, in our view, in all these families the fantasy experience of the family members and the motives, actions, intentions, that arise on the basis of such experience, are mostly unknown to the persons themselves. Thus, it is not possible to deal adequately with such a central issue, for instance, as sexuality in these families without being prepared to attribute to the agents involved fantasies of which they are themselves unconscious. However, in this volume, we have not undertaken to do this. (pp. 25/26)

He makes it quite explicit that he leaves such explanation undone because of a restriction which he places on himself, i.e., the phenomenological method. The way for an explanatory account is deliberately left open:

Here, then, the reader will find documented the quite manifest contradictions that beset these families, without very much exploration of the underlying factors which may be supposed to generate and maintain them. Subsequently we hope to go much further in interpreting data. (p. 26)

In a footnote to one of these studies Laing says:

For reasons given in the introduction, we are limiting ourselves very largely to the transactional phenomenology of these families' situations. Clearly, here and in every other family, the material we present is full of evidence for the struggle of each of the family members against their own sexuality. Maya without doubt acts on her own sexual experience, in particular by way of splitting, projection, denial and so on. Although it is beyond the self-imposed limitation of our particular focus in this book to discuss these aspects, the reader should not suppose that we wish to deny or to minimize the person's *action on himself* (what psychoanalysts usually call defence-mechanisms), particularly in respect of sexual feelings aroused towards family members, that is, in respect of incest. (p. 42)

(3) It might seem from this as though the intention was to do nothing but describe; however, Laing does intend something else which seems akin to explanation. He seeks to make the

experience and behaviour of the members of the family 'intelligible', particularly that of the schizoid or schizophrenic, as this is what might otherwise be regarded as unintelligible.

(b) Meanings and causes

It is this concept of intelligibility as distinct from causal explanation in terms of factors of which the people concerned are not conscious which forces us again to raise the question of the relation of social phenomenology to psycho-analysis, rather than simply accepting a division of labour between the social phenomenologist and the psycho-analyst such as might be suggested by the above quotations. For the psychoanalyst is also looking for intelligibility in behaviour and experience which might otherwise be unintelligible. However, his enquiry does concern unconscious processes, unconscious meanings, residues of the childhood of the individual concerned, and so on. Social phenomenology constitutes a possible threat to psychoanalytic therapy insofar as it might quite possibly seem to make a bit of behaviour intelligible too easily, and thereby prevent its psychoanalytical investigation.

In part, Laing's use of the concept of intelligibility may be seen as an insistence on looking for explanations of phenomena in terms of their current inter-relations before examining their origin and past history.[1] But the concept is a loose one if it is to be distinguished from causal explanations. In a number of places Laing repudiates the intention of putting forward any theory of the origin of schizophrenia. How seriously are we to take this disclaimer?[2]

The case histories described by Laing and Esterson give a strong impression of being accounts of what family circumstances made the patients act and experience the world in the way they did. A particular kind of action, at first unintelligible will become intelligible once seen to be a response to certain actions of others. But then those actions of the others plus the emotional disposition of the agent explain the actions of the original agent. This explanation is, among other things, a causal one. In general, explanations of the part in terms of the whole do not replace causal explanations; there must be a process governed by causal laws connecting the behaviour of the part (the explanandum) with the structure of the whole (the explanans).

It is quite likely that there is at this point in Laing's argument another legacy of existentialist thought: a suspicion of causal explanation of human behaviour. Yet Laing does not rule out such explanation; at most he believes himself to be giving a different kind of explanation, one which, while not seeking to replace causal explanations, makes behaviour intelligible independently of them.

This immediately raises problems about the validity of Laing's project which comparison to Freudian psychoanalysis can best bring out. With regard to the intelligibility of human behaviour and experience Freudian psychoanalysis is, as it were, two-edged. By explaining in terms of the unconscious it at once shows that behaviour which had previously seemed completely unintelligible, as well as apparently random or accidental actions, and symptoms thought previously to be purely physical, could be shown to have a meaning in a manner in some ways parallel to conscious intentional acts. Thus Freud and Breuer's *Studies in Hysteria* showed that certain paralyses could only be understood if referred to ideas, as shown by the fact that an arm, for instance, could be paralysed whereas it would be expected from the physiological structure of the arm that the paralysis would affect not a limb as such but a section of the body corresponding (as an arm does not) to definite elements in the nervous system. Bizarre acts of neurotic patients are likewise shown to be quite intelligible in terms of unconscious wishes and connections made by the mind, and in *The Interpretation of Dreams, The Psycho-pathology of Everyday Life,* and *Jokes and Their Relation to the Unconscious,* Freud shows that aspects of normal life, previously regarded by scientists as without great significance, mere nonsense, actually have unconscious meanings and play a role in the economy of the psyche.

But the other edge of the psychoanalytical knife is the explanation of much conscious and apparently intelligible behaviour in terms of the unconscious. Conscious intentions are shown to be rationalizations of unconscious motives. The unconscious gains explanatory importance at the expense both of the non-meaningful and of the conscious and apparently meaningful. However, the conscious has to have its own intelligibility whether the real explanations of its phenomena are conscious or not.

We are not used to feeling strong affects without their having any ideational content, and therefore, if the content is missing, we seize as a substitute upon another content which is in some way or other suitable, much as our police, when they cannot catch the right murderer, arrest a wrong one instead. (Freud: *Collected Papers*, Volume 3, p. 314)

The rationalization here makes the action or emotion intelligible: that is its function. But it is a false intelligibility. It does not give the real explanation of that action or emotion.

This makes clear the first danger of looking for an intelligibility distinct from causal explanation: that one might stop looking for explanations too soon and accept the deceptive intelligibility by which consciousness hides its real motives from itself. The notion of the real and secondary (rationalizing) motives here is clearly a causal one. The real motive causes the act and the rationalization does not. Thus psychoanalytical explanation involves both intelligibility in the sense of making clear the meaning of an act or experience, its motives and relations to the subject's own beliefs, wishes, etc., and causality. A necessary condition of an act being fully conscious and rational will be that the account of its intelligibility will also give its causal explanation.

This leads to a second mistake which Laing's method puts him in danger of committing, though I think it is far more often committed by his readers. This is the mistake of thinking that when the experience or behaviour of a patient has been made intelligible, it has been shown to be rational and not at all neurotic. Once he has shown that the symptoms of a young schizophrenic are an intelligible response to his family situation it is easy to jump to the conclusion that the patient was sane after all and only received treatment because he or she had been labelled mad by a sick family. I shall return to this point in Chapter 5; enough here to note that while Laing does not in the bulk of his work endorse the patient's view of things to that extent he does lay himself open to systematic misinterpretation of this kind in a way that Freud (who likewise rendered intelligible behaviour previously considered merely mad), does not. This is because in the absence of causal concepts to connect unconscious meanings of acts with those acts and reveal the conscious meaning as more or less epi-phenomenal, the relation of intelligibility to rationality becomes unclear and the two are likely to be confused. It becomes unclear what is wrong with the intelligibility of a rationalization.

It is perhaps necessary here to refer to a familiar philosophical objection to Freudian theory (though one which is sometimes presented as an interpretation of that theory). There is a difference, in this view, between giving a causal explanation of an action or a symptom, and giving an interpretation of its meaning. The psychoanalyst, it is said, must choose which he is doing, for he cannot legitimately be doing both.

Now it is certainly true that there is a relation other than a causal one between a motive or reason for an action and that action, or between a symptom and the unconscious wish that it expresses. This relation is often referred to in the philosophical literature as a logical one, though the term 'intentional' (in the phenomenological sense) would be more accurate. In any case, it is a relation of meaning rather than of causality; giving a motive or reason for an action does not or not only explain the action causally, it makes it 'intelligible'. (Of course, it may be shown psychoanalytically that, in a given case, the conscious reason does *not* explain the action causally at all, but is a rationalization. But this notion would be impossible if a reason could not in principle be the cause of an action, just as there could be no illusions if there were no reality.)

But many British analytical philosophers not only make the

distinction between these two types of relation ('logical' or intentional relations, and causal ones), but also deny that phenomena that are related in one of these ways can be related in the other. (An example of this position in the context of the philosophy of psychoanalysis, can be found in Alasdair MacIntyre's book *The Unconscious*.)

So far as the philosophical refutation of this view is concerned, I see no need to add to the excellent arguments raised against it within analytical philosophy (see for instance Donald Davidson's paper 'Actions, Reasons and Causes' and David Wiggins' 'Freedom, Knowledge, Belief and Causality', neither of which is specifically concerned with psychoanalysis or the unconscious, but which are completely consonant with Freudian theory).

But it is worth mentioning that this doctrine that causal and intentional relations are mutually exclusive, if combined with the acceptance of physical determinism, can only lead to regarding both actions and the mental states which motivate them as mere epiphenomena of physical processes. When on the other hand the denial of mental causality is intended anti-deterministically, as it is by Sartre, it rests on the equation of the meaningful with the freely chosen (Sartre explicitly equates these); but this is exactly what Freud refuted by demonstrating the reality of unconscious meanings.

Either way, the exclusion of causation from mental life would entail the rejection of such central psychoanalytic concepts as overdetermination, displacement and rationalization. The psychoanalyst explains a symptom causally *by* making it intelligible in terms of unconscious meanings.

(c) Process and praxis

Is there then any criterion by which Laing can know when a pattern of experience and behaviour has been made intelligible, and distinguish real from spurious intelligibility? After all, thunderstorms can be made intelligible by saying that Thor is angry but that is probably not the real explanation. Laing does in one

c

place give a clear definition of what it is to make something intelligible. He does so in terms of concepts derived from Sartre, not in his existentialist phase (*Being and Nothingness*) but in his neo-Marxist one (*Critique of Dialectical Reason*).

When what is going on in any human group can be traced to what agents are doing, it will be termed *praxis*. What goes on in a group may not be intended by anyone. No one may even realize what is happening. But what happens in a group will be *intelligible* if one can retrace the steps from what is going on (process) to who is doing what (*praxis*). (p. 22)

At this point, however, Laing appears not as doing something different from (but complementary to) Freudian psychoanalysis, but rather as doing exactly the opposite; for Freudian explanation, like Marxian explanation of the wider canvas of history, is essentially concerned with revealing process where there had appeared to be praxis, unconscious motives, unintended consequences, where there had appeared to be deliberate decisions, conspiracies, and so on. If, as Althusser claimed,[3] the essential point learnt by Marx from Hegel is that history is a 'process without a subject', one could have hoped that a psychologist of inter-personal relations should have learnt from Freud that family life and human interaction generally is also a process without a subject.

The notion of making a social process intelligible by resolving it into individual praxes is also expounded by Laing in his account of Sartre's *Critique of Dialectical Reason* in *Reason and Violence* and in an article, 'Series and Nexus in the Family' in *New Left Review* No. 15 (May–June 1962). As formulated in these texts it seems to involve a sort of methodological individualism (the doctrine that statements about societies, groups, structures, etc., are only meaningful if they can be translated into statements about individuals), which is in sharp contradiction to his characteristic insistence on the need for knowledge of the social context. On the one hand he wishes to make individual practice intelligible in terms of social practice and processes, on the other to reduce all these to individual practices.

Structure is the quite specific relation of the terms of a reciprocal relation: the structure, as Sartre puts it, *is existed* by everyone, in and through each and every relationship. Once more, the structural mediation of each relation is *in each*, as the unity of interiorised multiplicity, and *nowhere else*. (*Reason and Violence*, p. 146)

This seems to reduce social phenomenology to taking account of the effects of *other people* on an individual, which is different from taking account of a *structure of a group*. In *The Politics of the Family* Laing is insistent that it is the latter which the individual internalises, as well as the former, and puts this forward as a gain over traditional psychoanalytical theories.

Not that he anywhere denies that the group structure is real for the members of the group, but he sees it, it seems, as a sort of illusion which gains objective reality only because of people's subjective belief in it. Or better still, processes, structures, etc., are seen as ossified praxes. This is seen as having highly undesirable effects.

Processes without agents, production without producers, synthetic unifications of multiplicities of human beings (into coloured, Jews, hysterics, terrorists) appear as part of the socio-historical *mise-en-scène*, as self-perpetuating and self-fulfilling prophesies, self-actualising phantasies, seeming to have a demonically autonomous nomadic life. The beings of this realm are divorced from the intentions or praxis of any single person yet they seem to determine, control, condition, individual and group behaviour. Group actions appear to be generated without anyone's expressed desire and without anyone being able to see the possibility of an option, much less to exercise it. The social 'forces', 'structures', 'facts', 'processes', without authors seem to operate according to natural laws, frequently destroying, undermining, corroding, killing, eating away at praxis like a plague.

Laing seems both to recognize the 'illusion' as having real effects and to insist that to understand it, one must resolve it into the reality of many individual praxes.

Now there is a certain obvious sense in which Laing is quite right in saying that all that really exist are individuals.

The existence of social structures, relations and laws—of all that, in reality, corresponds to the abstract concepts of scientific theories—logically presupposes the existence of material objects, some of which are persons. For any family to exist there must be individual members of it. For any collective myth to arise in that family, there must be individual phantasies, actions, etc., which constitute that myth. Likewise, for an economic crisis to occur there must be many individual acts of e.g., selling shares, sacking workers, collecting debts, putting up prices, etc.

But if one wishes to explain these events, and know why they occur, one must have recourse to structural laws. It is no doubt necessary against the excesses of holism and structuralism to insist that structural laws operate only through actions by the bearers of social positions and presuppose certain facts about the nature of those bearers. But even so, it must be remembered that it is largely not to intentions or to any notions of the conscious agency of individuals that this dependence of structure on bearers refers, but to often unconscious and unintended actions themselves determined by the effects of the structure on the individual bearers.

Laing is, it seems to me, unclear as to whether he means only that the group can only act through individuals, or that the group does not exist except in the minds of its members.

We have seen that the group has no way of acting except in and through the individuals who compose it; and this is possible because group action exists in each individual praxis as interiorised unity of multiplicity. (*Reason and Violence*, p. 147)

The effect of attempting to trace process back to praxis rather than vice versa is regressive both theoretically and practically. Theoretically because a bit of praxis, a conscious decision, is precisely what is most in need of explanation in terms of unconscious as well as conscious motives, sources and meanings. It is a primitive sort of intelligibility that gives no further explanation once a conscious decision has been discovered. Practically the consequence of discovering praxis in place of process is that instead of seeking to act on and transform the processes which give rise to pathological effects, a culprit, subject of the pathogenic praxis, is searched for. Laing warns against the danger of the investigation of the family circumstances of schizophrenic patients leading to witch hunts against the mother, but a strong impression is created in many of Laing's writings that a moral rather than a therapeutic solution is called for. (I shall say more about this in Chapter 6.)

Once again however, it is possible to see the attractiveness of Laing's idea of 'process into praxis' by examining the connections of Laing's practical (therapeutic) and theoretical stand points. The typical patient described by Laing is a young adult who has failed to break away from his or her parents. They have not become capable of taking their own decisions but still allow their lives to be lived for them by their parents. Laing is a psychiatrist who has the courage to take sides with the adolescent against his or her parents. He therefore is seeking to promote the patient's capacity to take conscious action rather than to be governed by forces outside consciousness—the parents, the collective phantasies of the family, the internalized parents, and so on. Indeed, the slogan, 'replace process by praxis', has wider application than this in psycho-therapy. It could be seen as a translation into Sartrean language, of Freud's maxim of the international psychoanalytical association: 'That there should be ego where there had been id'—the bringing of unconscious mental processes into consciousness where they can be dealt with by conscious decision instead of acting blindly. There is here a concept of freedom akin to that expressed in the doctrine that 'freedom is the knowledge of necessity' as expounded by Marxists. This is *not* the view that freedom is recognition of and *submission* to external necessities but that it is knowledge of the causal laws governing our life which enables us to consciously utilise those causal laws. 'Necessity is *blind* only *insofar as it is not understood*'.[4] If one wishes to call conscious choice based on self-awareness and a correct assessment of reality 'praxis', and unconscious processes, 'process', then the transformation of process into praxis is a reasonably accurate account of the aim of psychoanalysis. However, the attainment of this aim is dependent on previous analysis of praxis into process which shows the unconscious sources of conscious acts. A view which simply consists of saying 'praxis good, process bad', could result in a merely *theoretical* transformation of process into praxis, i.e., the assertion that process is really praxis after all. This would render that *therapeutic* transformation of process into praxis unnecessary. Once again, one should not assume that Laing has made such a crude mistake. What he in fact seeks to do in *Sanity, Madness and the Family*, is to understand the intra-family social processes involved in the production of certain symptoms; and the only role of the process-into-praxis schema in the case histories is the implication that this understanding, if possessed by the patient, could transform his or her existence from blind process to a conscious praxis. The idea that the understanding itself consists of redescribing these processes as praxes makes its appearance in the 'Introduction' but could not have been guessed from the cases themselves.

The terms 'process' and 'praxis' themselves are sometimes used in these histories, but generally in a non-mystifying way— i.e., deliberate action is called 'praxis' (without there necessarily being any implication about what caused it), and compulsive and otherwise less than fully conscious behaviour is called 'process'. Even here, however, some confusion is caused by the terms. For instance, in Esterson's *The Leaves of Spring*, which is an extended account of one of the case histories in *Sanity, Madness and the Family* (that of the Danzigs and their daughter Sarah) a confusion of process and praxis is attributed to the parents. This is because when Sarah acted according to their wishes and in ways dependent on their judgements they saw her as a responsible agent, and when she tried to act on her own desires, this was attributed to her 'illness'. They were also confused about whether she could be blamed for behaviour which they believed she was not responsible for. This point is an important one, though I think it could have been made quite adequately without the Sartrean terminology.

The confusion caused by this terminology can be seen in the following fact: as already mentioned, a characteristic of most of the histories described by Laing and his collaborators is that the patient was seen by his/her family as having been through three stages—good, bad and mad. In Sarah's case, she had spent a great deal of time in bed, and this had been seen by her parents, during the period when they regarded her behaviour as 'bad', as sheer laziness. Later they came to see it as a symptom of her 'illness'. Now the impression is created by Esterson's account that there was no illness, and this development in her parents' view of Sarah was simply a new stage of mystification. Be that as it may, the tendency of the majority of families is to resist to the last minute the conclusion that a member of the family is 'mentally ill' and continue indefinitely to regard behaviour they cannot accept or understand as perverse, wilful, in short 'bad'. Most people love to have someone to blame, and we can be sure that responsible agency is incorrectly attributed more often that it is incorrectly denied. It is sometimes alleged that this view is better because it shows more 'respect' for the individual concerned— e.g., Laing says of Julie in *The Divided Self* that 'Only her father, in a curious way, treated her as a responsible person. He never admitted that she was mad. To him she was wicked.' (p. 193) This 'curious' form of respect led him to twist her arm when he visited her, to get her to snap out of it.

To prefer such a view seems to me perverse. There is no such thing as laziness, and if someone prefers to lie in bed rather than get up and do things, there is something amiss emotionally, and it is best that this should be recognized. That the parents may be the cause of the trouble, and may misuse the recognition that there is something wrong other than 'laziness' to score points, is another matter. Certainly there is a *misuse* of the attribution 'mad' by the Danzigs and other parents described in Laing and Esterson's histories, but this is not in that they see process where there is praxis, but that they see an 'illness' that just happens, like measles, where they should see an intelligible process, one which is laden with meaning. That they cannot do so is no doubt to do with their refusal to see their own part in its causation.

It is worth noting that Esterson does not actually resolve process into praxis in his account of family interaction. For though what happens to Sarah is explained in terms of what the other

members of the family do, this 'praxis' itself is shown to have unconscious determinants in the parents' phantasies concerning
bowel control, and their unconsciously assigning Sarah the
meaning 'uncontrolled bowel'. The total development from the
parents' defences in relation to anal functioning to Sarah's hospitalization can be seen as a process, in which there are moments
of praxis which, however, explain nothing if taken by themselves.

In the histories recounted in *Sanity, Madness and the Family*,
there generally occurs a statement to the effect that the 'illness'
can be made intelligible in terms of the family process and praxis.
This is for the most part not a matter of resolving process into
praxis, but of shifting the symptom from the individual to the
family. For instance, in the case of the 'Irwins', Laing and Esterson talk of, 'Further evidence, showing that such catatonic behaviour was praxis'. There follows an account of how the
'patient', Mary, was able to snap out of her catatonic stage to be
bridesmaid at her sister's wedding (though not without an inter-
vening suicide attempt). I take it that Laing and Esterson do not
think that this proves that the catatonic behaviour was a ruse;
yet if 'praxis' means more than that behaviour is intelligible in
terms of meaning (as opposed to purely physical illness), this is
what the term suggests. The meanings are presumably unconscious, not deliberate intentions. It is in every way like the cases
of hysterical paralysis analysed by Breuer and Freud. The new
point is rather that this (unconsciously motivated) behaviour
was a response to (no doubt equally unconsciously motivated)
behaviour on the part of the parents.

(d) Past and present

It is legitimate therefore, to ignore the possibility of confronting
the methods employed by Laing and by Freud in terms of process
and praxis and take another methodological point of Laing and
Esterson as the basis for the discussion of what is new in *Sanity,
Madness and the Family*. Page 27 of *Sanity, Madness and the
Family* reads:

In this book, we believe that we show that the experience and behaviour of schizophrenics is much more socially intelligible than has
come to be supposed by most psychiatrists.

We have tried in each single instance to answer the question: to what
extent is the experience and behaviour of that person, who has already
begun a career as a diagnosed 'schizophrenic' patient, intelligible in
the light of the praxis and process of his or her family nexus.
We believe that the shift of point of view that these descriptions both
embody and demand has a historical significance no less radical than
the shift from a demonological to a clinical viewpoint three hundred
years ago.

In relation to Freudian psychoanalysis this shift of viewpoint
involves two things, an extension and a restriction of the scope of
investigation (remembering that the possibility of a traditional
Freudian account *also* having an explanatory role to play is not
ruled out). The restriction is that within the limits of the investigation there is to be no explanation in terms of the unconscious
or the infantile experiences of the subject. The extension is that it
is not only the patient who is studied but the patient's relations
with family members as well as family inter-relations.

This turn towards explanation in terms of the social nexus
rather than of the unconscious is one of the things which immediately strikes most readers of Laing; it connects in fairly obvious ways with his radicalism and determines the subject matter
of the texts discussed in this and the following chapter: forms of
human inter-action in general and two scenes of such inter-action
in particular—the family and the doctor/patient (or analyst/
analysand) situation. This re-orientation, incidentally, indicates
a certain move away from the existentialist position of *The
Divided Self*; despite appearances, this is also a move towards
Freudian psychoanalysis. Although Laing's prime concern in
The Divided Self was with the individual patient and his self-
experience (which would appear to be close to that of Freudian
psychoanalysis) whereas he later moved into new territory (the
social nexus), precisely, this move meant (a) that he was no
longer confronting Freud head on, demanding new concepts in

order to understand the same subject matter, but rather was in most places assuming the main Freudian discoveries but breaking new ground and (b) that the fate of the individual self and its needs came to be seen far more to lie in its experiences of the family situation than in some primary ontological insecurity. This takes Laing back close to Freud's ideas about the causation of neurosis. Although, as I have already pointed out, Laing is never wholly existentialist even in *The Divided Self*, and never wholly escapes existentialist influence, this influence is far less marked in his social phenomenological writings, even in their theoretical parts (which owe more to the neo-Marxism of the later Sartre and to structuralism than to existentialism). The concrete studies in these writings are almost wholly free of existentialist influence and are, I believe, the strongest part of Laing's work.

One way in which Laing's social approach is often contrasted with more individualistic versions of psychoanalysis is in terms of the relative power of the past and of the present situation in producing neurotic symptoms. Laing is seen as stressing the present relationships and the attitudes of others in the present social nexus of the patient, whereas Freudian psychoanalysis explains neurosis primarily in terms of patterns laid down in infancy. There is some truth in this but with reservations. In the first place, Laing has never minimized the effects of past experiences, and if he has stressed adolescence more than many psychoanalysts, he has not neglected the importance of infancy either.

For instance, at the beginning of *The Politics of the Family* he discusses the relations between 'the family and the "family" '. Where 'family' is used to mean the internalized pattern of family relations in the individual. He announces

It is to the relation between the observable structures of the family and the structures that endure as part of the 'family' as a set of relations and operations between them that this chapter is addressed. (*The Politics of the Family*, pp. 3/4)

His difference from classical psychoanalysis here is not over the importance of the past or of the mechanism of introjection and projection but over what is internalized and projected. 'The "family" is not the introjected object but an introjected set of relations.' (p. 6)

The re-projection of the 'family' is not simply a matter of projecting an 'internal' object on to the external person. It is superimposition of one set of relations onto another: the two sets may match more or less. (p. 9)

This does not really involve such a radical break with psycho-analytical theory for the oedipal situation is essentially experienced as a triad, father-mother-self, and the particular relations experienced between the elements of this triad determine the nature of the Oedipus complex in any individual according to Freudian theory. Thus, for instance, Freudian psychoanalysts have noted the 'need for injured third party', in many people, i.e., the need in forming any relationship with a person of the opposite sex to oust an existing sexual partner. This can be traced to an attempt to reverse the oedipal situation in which the child is ousted by the parent of the same sex from its relation with the parent of the opposite sex.

Compare the following brief case history given by Laing:

A man felt destroyed by a woman. He felt, when thirty, that she behaved just as his mother had done when he was three. This was not the first, nor was it to be the last time he felt that way.

The prototype was brought to light through an analysis of its transference onto the present, then checked against collateral evidence from parents and others.

Prototypical sequence
1. He is with the woman he loves (his nanny).
2. His mother returns, sends nanny away,
3. and then sends him away to boarding school,
4. while father does not intervene.
5. Mother vacillates between him and affairs with men.
6. He runs away from boarding school and is returned by the police.

Repeating scenario as an adult
1. He falls in love with A.

2. He leaves A for B,
3. and breaks up with B.
4. C does not intervene.
5. He and B vacillate between each other and affairs with others.
6. He tries to escape but can't.

The main difference between the two sequences is that in the latter *he tries to do what was done to him*. He leaves A. B does not take him away. He drives B away. In making B leave him, he seems to be in control. But he experiences each repeat of the scenario as though he is the victim of B, and finally of the scenario, for which mother is held responsible. B took him away from A, then deserted him, then forced him into the wilderness. I looked on like his father.

The drama, 'internalized' and re-enacted with a semblance of control, is experienced as his destruction at the hands of a woman. (*The Politics of the Family*, pp. 10/11)

There is no playing down of the power of the past here. Indeed, once the effect of the internalized family is understood in its full force, it becomes clear that any attempt to understand, e.g., the problems arising in a relationship in terms of the current issues in that relationship would be sheer mystification; one must understand an individual in terms of his relations with others, but by no means only or even primarily others who are still around.

Of course, there is something metaphorical about the expression which I have used: 'the power of the past'. The past as such is no longer operative, only the effects of it which exist in the present; the point at issue is the power of *survivals* from the past. But the notion of a survival from the past is not something peripheral to psychoanalytical explanation, but something absolutely central to it. The unconscious is that which has survived relatively unchanged from the infantile self because, as repressed (excluded from consciousness) it has not been subjected to the 'weathering' of reality (Freud uses the analogy of objects preserved by their burial in Pompeii, which began to be destroyed only after they had been dug up; see his *Collected Papers*, vol. III, pp. 314–15).

The point is that these survivals are every bit as present and real as the new situations confronting the individual; and indeed, survivals are operative in the interpersonal sphere as well as in the individual unconscious.

At the same time it is not true of Freudian psychoanalysis that it ignores the effect of current situations on the individual. Freud originally divided neuroses into two groups: psychoneuroses and actual neuroses. The 'actual neuroses'—neurasthenia and anxiety-neurosis—are caused by current disturbances in the sexual life, e.g., abstinence, masturbation, coitus interruptus, stimulation without release. Psychoneurosis (e.g., hysteria, obsessions) are caused by infantile experiences, also of a sexual nature (in the broader sense of 'sexual'). Strictly speaking, only psychoneuroses can be analysed; in them, each symptom has an unconscious meaning which can be made conscious by analysis. When the meaning, together with the feelings associated with it, is made conscious, the symptom disappears. Actual neuroses on the other hand can only be cured by removing their cause, i.e., by the achievement of a satisfactory sex life.

However, actual neuroses and psychoneurosis cannot be rigidly separated. Freud recognized (e.g., in his *Introductory Lectures on Psychoanalysis*) that any psychoneurosis must draw its energy from somewhere; and if neurotic symptoms—as Freud alleges—constitute the sex life of the patient, it is implied that he or she is not getting normal sexual satisfaction. Hence every psychoneurosis has an actual-neurotic element. At the same time, under most conditions, the fact that someone's sex life is unsatisfactory needs explanation. The explanation may be partly in terms of reality, i.e., of external conditions over which the individual has no control, but most often it will be at least partly due to inhibitions, irrational anxieties, etc., which are themselves psychoneurotic in nature, i.e., they derive from the repressed infantile wishes of the person concerned.

So it is not altogether true that psychoanalysis can do nothing about actual neuroses—it can remove the psychoneurotic element, and thus enable the patient to establish satisfactory sexual relations. At the same time, if psychoanalysis succeeds in resolving the psychoneurotic problems but, for some external reasons, the patient is unable to achieve such relations, it is to be expected that the frustration of his or her sexual needs will lead to regression, and psychoneurotic symptoms—perhaps new ones—will again occur.

This aspect of Freudian theory—the 'economic' principle that something must happen to sexual energy, and if it is not expressed in normal sexual activity it will express itself in neurotic symptoms—is strongly emphasized by Reich, but it follows logically from Freud's metapsychology, and Reich did not revise Freudian theory in this matter, but upheld it against revisionists. This is a good example of the phenomenon noted by Marcuse, of Freudian metapsychology retaining its critical potential, while psychoanalytical practice has often adapted to the norms of bourgeois society. In fact few psychoanalysts now believe that sexual frustration of itself causes neurosis,[5] although this must surely be the most easily empirically verified of Freud's discoveries. Freud himself, although in a number of places he attacks the sexual repressiveness of the society of his time (see e.g., his paper 'Civilized Sexual Morality and Modern Nervousness', in his *Collected Papers*, vol. II.), sometimes talks as if psychoanalysis could be successful without issuing in a satisfactory sex life, and that someone might even find an alternative solution to their problem in analysis rather than in sexual fulfilment. Thus in his 'Observations on "Wild" Psychoanalysis' (*Collected Papers*, vol. II) he takes a colleague to task for the advice he gave to a woman suffering from anxiety-states, in the following terms:

Oddly enough, the three therapeutic alternatives of this would be psycho-analyst leave no room for psycho-analysis. This woman can only be cured of her anxiety by returning to her husband, or by satisfying her needs by onanism or with a lover. And where does analytic treatment come in, the treatment which we regard as the first remedy in anxiety-states? (p. 301)

Freud in his embarrassment is repudiating a conclusion that the 'would-be psychoanalyst' had quite correctly drawn from Freud's theories—that the woman's anxiety-state, an actual neurosis, could not be cured while her sexual needs remained unsatisfied.

The view that all neurosis has a sexual origin, with its implicit assertion of the value of sexual fulfilment, and criticism of the cultural denial of sexuality, was one of the most unacceptable parts of Freudian theory, and to a large extent still is. For the cultural denial of sexuality is not primarily a question of 'morality' in the narrow sense of what actions are permitted and what condemned by society. Specific prohibitions may have been relaxed in the so-called permissive society, but the low cultural valuation of sexuality remains. The attribution of sexual motives or pre-occupations is regarded as lowering, so that people still find the importance given to sexuality by Freud 'reducing'. In everyday talk, a compliment concerning a person's sexual being is often seen as an insult; and sexual words used out of their etymological sense always express annoyance or aggression. So it is not surprising that the psychoanalytical movement should from the outset have been subject to great social pressure to adapt to our anti-sexual culture by eliminating this scandal.

However this has involved an inversion of Freud's evaluation of what he calls 'autoplastic' and 'alloplastic' behaviour. According to Freud[6] there are two ways of reacting to the conflict between some psychic need and the world which must be altered if it is to be satisfied; one can try to change the world and adapt it to one's needs, or one can try to change oneself—to adapt one's needs to existing conditions, to resign oneself to their frustration, to repress them, etc. The former type of behaviour Freud calls 'alloplastic', the latter 'autoplastic'. Alloplastic behaviour—the effort to change the world in accordance with one's desires—Freud regards as characteristic of normalcy, while autoplasticity is characteristic of neurosis. Psychosis consists in changing one's image of the world, i.e., retreating into fantasy to the point of hallucination.

Now if the economic principle and the importance of current disturbances in the sexual life are taken seriously in investigating the origins of neurosis, psychoanalysis, though it certainly does aim at helping the analysand to change himself, has a primarily alloplastic aim. It aims at removing the inner obstacles to changing the world and achieving gratification. Of course the psychoanalyst himself cannot remove the external obstacles. If he is trying to help a young adult who cannot break away from the domination of his or her parents (the typical situation in Laing's case-histories), he cannot physically remove the patient from the parents' clutches. But to do so, the Freudian might argue, is not necessary, for what is in need of analysis in such cases is the inability of the person in question to leave home. That he or she does not is evidence enough that there is an internal obstacle to doing so. If these can be removed by analysis the young person will be able to leave home and establish independent relationships. So although a psychoanalyst can only treat an individual in isolation from, no doubt, objectively oppressive and pathogenic circumstances, he can enable the analysand to deal with those circumstances—by getting out of them. There is no reason why a Freudian psychoanalyst should regard the problems of his clients as all 'in the head'. They may be occasioned by the behaviour of others. But he is nevertheless only in a position to deal with these problems which are 'in the head' (i.e., the psychoneurotic rather than the actual-neurotic element). And this fact does not worry him, because he expects the analysand to be able to cope with reality-problems once his psychoneurotic problems have been resolved. In the case of child psychoanalysis, where the patient is really not in a position to bring about a change of circumstances, the success of the treatment does largely rest on influencing the parents' behaviour towards the child.

However this aim of enabling the analysand to change his or her objective circumstances still comes up against problems of reality in existing societies. The badly treated wife may not be able to leave her husband for financial reasons, however much she may be emotionally free to do so. Reich, while taking a somewhat puritanical view of any sexual activity which fell short of his ideal of genital love, did a real service in focusing attention on *social* obstacles to fulfilment. He saw that once one had settled accounts with one's neurotic inhibitions, reality might still present insuperable obstacles. He pointed out that among the Viennese proletariat, bad housing conditions often made a normal sex life impossible for sheer lack of privacy. He drew the conclusion that when psychoanalysis had done its best for its individual patients, it had to criticise the social and sexual status quo, and hand over the torch to Marxism.

Faced with this alternative, if it was to consistently carry out its alloplastic mission, it is not surprising that the psychoanalytical movement preferred, by and large, to compromise with the dominant ideology of the society in which it emerged. This meant that it must aim at helping the patient to adjust to reality rather than change it. Such an alteration of the therapeutic task is not a mere sell-out; after all, a psychoanalyst has the task of relieving the suffering of his patients, and this may well be connected with their inability to adjust to circumstances which there is no chance of altering. The psychoanalyst cannot wait for the revolution before he can help, however much he personally may deplore existing conditions.[7]

Such tactical compromises *need* not lead to revision of principles. But it can scarcely be questioned that they have:

Even as late as 1949, the American psychologist Ernest Hilgard declared before a meeting of the American Psychological Association that the mechanisms of adjustment were the feature of Freudian theory that were domesticated earliest into American psychology. This is an astonishing statement, if one remembers that the theory constructed by Freud (in this context it is perhaps necessary to distinguish it from 'Freudian theory') did not in the slightest degree make adjustment either a basic issue or a therapeutic goal. (No such word even appears in the indexes of Freud's works.) In Europe we feel that Hilgard would have been more accurate if he had said, 'the concept of adjustment was the first that American psychology injected into the Freudian theory in order to *domesticate it*'. (Octave Mannoni, *Freud: The Theory of the Unconscious.* p. 182)

This tendency in psychoanalysis though should not be seen as forced on the movement by American imperialism. It is a very common assumption that no conditions that one is likely to encounter in reality in modern western societies are so bad that a healthy person cannot adapt to them. The whole concept of actual neurosis and the harmful effects of disturbances in the sexual life has been dropped in practice, and the aim of analytical psychotherapy becomes 'adjustment'. Almost every revision of psychoanalytic theory has consisted in playing down sexuality in one way or another, as a pre-condition of making adjustment the goal of therapy. (Jung and Adler, 'ego-psychology' and the 'cultural school' etc.)

In order to defend such a position, the post-Freudian revisionists have generally tried on the one hand to sever all the links which connect psychoanalysis with the biological sciences, and on the other, to break down the barriers which divide it from linguistics and social science. Some psychoanalytical theorists share this latter tendency, while rejecting what seems to me the ideological retionale of it (i.e. the denigration of sexuality and the advocacy of adjustment). This seems to be Laing's position (and also that of Lacan and his followers).

For although Laing shares some theoretical positions with the post-Freudian revisionists (he does not, for instance, use the 'economic' principle of sexual instincts), one of the really liberating and radical aspects of his work is his uncompromising partisanship of alloplasticity. On this point, Laing is a rescuer rather than a reviser of Freudian insights. In stressing the origin of mental disorders in the social nexus, he points out the need for the victim, e.g. of a bad family scene, to get out. Repeatedly his work insists that adjustment to insane conditions is no criterion of sanity. And although sexuality does not seem to have the same central theoretical role within 'social phenomenology' as in psychoanalysis, Laing never plays down the sexual aspect of the pathogenic conditions in the way that the other schools of 'existential psychoanalysis' (Frankl, etc.) do. Indeed Laing has become for many the symbol of the liberation of young people from parental oppression, and this oppression consists above all in the prevention or domination of the young person's sexual relationships. If other revisionist schools of psychoanalysis have used their concepts of the sociality of human existence to justify the domination of the individual by conventional norms, Laing has used it to expose the conventional norms for the miseries they cause individuals to suffer. In this matter Laing has been perhaps the foremost continuer in our time of Reich's work in emphasizing the critical and revolutionary insights of psycho-analysis in relation to bourgeois society and the patriarchal family. All those of us who believe in the importance of those insights should be thankful for this.

Freud introduced the concept of a reality-principle, by which the individual perceives how the world is without the admixture of wishful thinking so that he can then act on it to secure real fulfilment of his wishes. This reality-principle serves the pleasure-principle because it enables the individual to pursue the line of greatest advantage instead of the line of least resistance, i.e., to gain satisfaction of his desires by manipulating reality rather than to satisfy them in fantasy and perceive reality through a veil of wishful thinking. But the content of the reality perceived will of course depend on circumstances and will not be part of the object of psychoanalysis. Thus psychoanalysis can allow for the fact that although all mental phenomena have their psycho-logical causes, some are adequately explained by the external reality with which the person in question is confronted and there-fore do not have to be interpreted as symptoms. This saves psy-choanalysis from the relativism often attributed to it according to which view it can only judge ideas as symptoms and not in relation to their truth value (just as Marxism is rescued from such relativism by its distinction of science from ideology).

However, in investigating psychic conflicts, psychoanalysis is restricted in its scope by the impossibility of taking into account conflicts imposed by reality itself. It is to these conflicts that social phenomenology draws our attention. In placing itself under a restraint against investigation of the unconscious of the individual patient, it investigates instead the possible sources of conflict from the reality-principle of that individual. Whereas in the case of most Freudian analysis, the analyst is in no position to deal with the human environment of the analysed, Laing wherever possible, has made a study of the others, the people with whom the patient has his or her closest and most emotion-ally significant relations. The result is that the behaviour of the patient, which in most cases has been diagnosed as psychotic rather than neurotic, becomes intelligible. I have already expressed doubts about the clarity of Laing's elucidation of this concept of intelligibility. I think if it is to be useful it must be a causal concept. But there is no reason why it should not be, and were it not for Laing's explicit disclaimers I think anyone would interpret it as such.

I do not think the responses of the patients, for instance, in *Sanity, Madness and the Family*, can be regarded as perfectly healthy; the rational thing for any of these young women to have done would no doubt have been to have left home and escaped the social nexus which made their symptoms intelligible. They were not able to do this; even those of them who had lived away from home had clearly not escaped domination by the parent within. It would be true but unhelpful to say that their problem was inside them in that they could not break free from their parents' influence. The trouble had started at an age when this solution was not possible and now their ability to cope with reality was too shattered for them to achieve the necessary independence of their parents without first being removed from their influence and given the support needed to develop this independence. Laing nowhere suggests that the problem was all outside the patient; but his description of these cases does show that it was a response to problems which were in each case already there in the relations between the members of the family of which the patient was one, before the patient became a patient. So the conflict which needed to be resolved would seem to be in the inter-personal sphere not within any one person, before they came to a head in one person, the victim of the family social nexus in question.

In his paper on 'The Obvious' read at the Dialectics of Liberation Conference at the Round House, Laing spoke of this kind of displacement of the problem in the following terms:

As we begin from micro situations and work up to macro situations we find that the apparent irrationality of behaviour on a small scale takes on a certain form of intelligibility when one sees it in context. One moves, for example, from the apparent irrationality of the single psychotic individual to the intelligibility of that irrationality within the context of the family. The irrationality of the family in its turn must be placed within the context of its encompassing networks. (*The Dialectics of Liberation*, p. 15)

The location of the conflicts which led to one person being hospitalized is seen to be, in the first place, in the set of relations between the members of the family rather than within the hospitalized individual. The breakdown of intelligibility in the behaviour of one individual is transformed into the breakdown of intelligibility in the social context of that individual.

As I have suggested, a psychoanalytical understanding of the unconscious determinants of experience and behaviour cannot be dispensed with by concentrating on the social phenomenology: and Laing does not dispute this. But the phenomena to be psychoanalysed are not those which appear unintelligible at first; it is no longer the paranoid delusions of the patient, which may turn out to be well-founded insights into family conspiracies, but on the one hand, the inability of the patient to escape the family and on the other, the peculiar behaviour of the other members of the family.

One patient, Cathy, a girl of seventeen, was engrossed in a struggle to leave her parents. She could not do so in a real way, but developed a manic psychosis in which she 'left' her parents in a psychotic way by denying that her parents were her real parents. In a mental hospital, she ran away from the hospital repeatedly *in order to run home*, where she would arrive at any hour of the day or night and have to be dragged away again. For as soon as she got home she screeched and screamed that her parents were not letting her lead her own life, that they were dominating her in every possible way. Meanwhile the hospital was doing all it could to arrange for her to live away from home outside the hospital. The only reason she was in hospital was the disturbance she made when she got home.

She began to see me daily in hospital. Far from feeling that I might help her to gain her freedom, or to make use of the opportunities placed before her, she quickly began to attribute to me the same power-crazed drive to dominate and destroy her that she attributed to her parents. But she did not avoid me. On the contrary, in order to make her point she would follow me around shouting at me that I would not let her alone. (*Self and Others*, p. 149)

This indicates the degree to which the inability to break free of the parents remains an internal problem even in those who are most oppressed by parental stifling.

As to the need for psychoanalytical explanation (and the desirability of treatment) for the behaviour of others in the family, there are the places quoted above where Laing mentions the unconscious sexual desires evidenced by certain parents, and also comments like the following concerning statements made by the mother of a patient about the father:

They may or may not be true. If they are not true, Mrs. Blair is probably psychotic. If they are, then her husband probably is, or both of them. (*Sanity, Madness and the Family,* p. 58)

In short, if one asks why people go mad and answers that it is because other people drive them mad, that still leaves the unanswered questions, why do people want to drive each other mad and why do people go on living with people who are driving them mad? Both these questions, if they are to be answered at all, must be answered psychoanalytically, but these answers will not be the same as the answers which a psychoanalyst might have offered to the original question, why a particular individual went mad.

(e) The place of social phenomenology

The place of social phenomenology in relation to psychoanalysis then, can be formulated in this way: social phenomenology does not give an alternative explanation of psychological disturbances; but it changes the set of phenomena which stands in need of explanation.[8]

To give a crudely obvious example, if you saw a woman cowering in terror every time her husband came near her, you might think, on the supposition that her husband was a decent enough man, that this behaviour was a neurotic symptom in need of psychoanalytical explanation and treatment. If you then discovered that her husband regularly beat hell out of her, you would want something different to be explained and treated, firstly her husband's sadistic tendencies and secondly, her failure to leave him.

There remain a few questions about the status of social phenomenology: the first concerns its scientific status. Its value may have been established in locating the phenomena in need of analysis—in this respect it is not the phenomenological part of social phenomenology which is new, for this corresponds to the phenomenological element already in psychoanalys, i.e., it is the free stream of experiences of the analysand which is analysed. It is the social part which is new; that it is the stream of experience of a group in their relations that is the original datum. Thus social phenomenology might be seen as the extension of a preliminary part of an existing science.

This is true enough, but it is worth pointing out that one important objection to the scientificity of phenomenology does not apply to social phenomenology as practiced by Laing and his collaborators. It is, in general, true that phenomenology, because it restricts itself to an account of appearances, is unable to pierce beneath those appearances. It is in this sense one-dimensional. If an experience is deceptive it cannot know anything of this deception. Thus, if someone acts in a certain way with an unconscious motive and has a conscious rationalization of this act, phenomenology knows only the rationalization and is always in danger of taking it for the reason.

This one-dimensionality is no longer present in social phenomenology. It is still the case that unconscious motives may be missed if conscious phenomena are taken at their face value, but it is no longer the case that there are no signs in the phenomena themselves of some discrepancy between appearance and reality. The signs are present in a discrepancy between the experiences of various individuals in their mutual relations. Phenomenology is one-dimensional because it operates within the transparency of consciousness. But the consciousnesses of different individuals are notoriously not transparent to each other.

Precisely this opacity of one person's experience to another's is made the object of systematic study by Laing and his col-

laborators. He has created a notation for inter-personal perception for this purpose and has set out questionnaires for
investigating phenomena of shared and discrepant experiences.
Definite results were obtained from this: married couples whose
marriages were disturbed showed less perceptiveness and more
misinterpretation of each other's experience of each other than
did the control group of non-disturbed married couples. This is
not surprising, of course, but it is a starting point for investigation (although within the book *Inter-Personal Perception* itself,
misunderstandings seem to be taken at face value as different
expectations based on different past experience rather than as
symptoms of any more deeply-rooted problems).

Another charge of unscientificity is often levelled against
Laing on account of his conclusions from his case histories, on
the ground that he has not used control groups. He himself regards these criticisms as based on a mistaken conception of what
he is trying to do and hence irrelevant:

Such criticism would be justified if we had set out to test the hypothesis that the family is a pathogenic variable in the genesis of schizophrenia. But we did not set out to do this and we have not claimed to
have done so. We set out to illustrate by eleven examples that if we
look at some experience and behaviour without reference to family
interactions they may appear comparatively socially senseless but
that if we look at the same experience and behaviour in their original
family context they are liable to make more sense. (*Sanity, Madness
and The Family*, p. 12)

It is important to separate Laing's repudiation of the use of
causal concepts from his denial that control groups would have
been relevant in the sort of investigation that he was carrying
out. As I have already indicated I think the accounts Laing gives
of the social intelligibility of schizophrenia do involve causal
concepts and do contribute to knowledge of the origins of the
phenomena described. However, that is not the only relevant
point about them. They also tell us something about the meaning of these phenomena. There is certainly a place for such
accounts of meaning as well as causal accounts in psychology

and psychoanalysis; as we have already seen, Freudian theory makes reference both to meaning and to cause in its central concepts. Take for instance the concept of over-determination. According to Freud a symptom or dream image may express more than one unconscious idea. These unconscious elements cause the over-determined phenomena, and the unconscious thus kills two birds with one stone and economizes its use of energy in gaining admission to consciousness for its representative. But if this set of relations were a purely causal one the idea of over-determination would be superfluous: after all, if it takes more than one weight hung on a rope in order to break the rope, the breaking is not thereby over-determined. This concept is only justified because the relation of the over-determined phenomenon towards its determinants is not only a causal (quantitative) one, but also one of meaning or representation. Over-determination means multiple symbolic relations but these relations are also causal. It is not simply that the overdetermined phenomenon has more than one meaning; its presence may be causally explained by the economy of energy effected.

Now if Laing is indicating meanings while leaving their other causal aspects unanalysed he is doing something legitimate and valuable but also something that could hardly be verified by control groups. It may well be that the sort of interaction described in *Sanity, Madness and the Family* does go on in all families (including those in which no one is classified as mentally ill); this would not invalidate the conclusion that these interactions tell us the meaning of (render intelligible) the symptoms of schizophrenia. It would simply indicate that there must be other causal factors missing from the majority of families. In principle, there would be no objection to the conclusion that given the generality of these forms of interaction it is the non-schizophrenia of the majority of people that requires explanation.

Another question about the status of social phenomenology relates to its therapeutic value. No doubt the insight it gives us into the way a patient experiences his or her family situation is itself valuable—some have argued that this is the only value of such insights. But in displacing the site of conflict from the individual to the family, social phenomenology transforms the problem of treatment as well. Psychoanalytical treatment assumes in the first place voluntary choice of analysis as a form of treatment and secondly a degree of insight into one's real situation and one's problems. The others in the families of the patients described in *Sanity, Madness and the Family* for the most part did not meet either of these conditions. The task was therefore rather removal of the individual from the family situation and the creation of a supportive environment to enable them to build up the confidence and independence necessary for the establishment of a life of their own.

Furthermore the practice of interviewing families together rather than (or as well as) the patient alone seems in practice to be invaluable in the case of young adults whose problem-causing relationship with their family is still in existence. And abreactions of feelings repressed in earlier years may be more successful in the presence of the objects of those feelings—particularly when the effects have been continuously active. Many of these practices are quite widespread—not restricted to Laing and his colleagues.

I have tried in this chapter to untangle a cluster of dualities, which are easily mistaken as different aspects of the same duality: unconscious/conscious; survival of past/present situation; intrapersonal/interpersonal; process/praxis. At first sight it may seem that, by the same token, Laing upgrades the second of each of these pairs in relation to the first.

In relation to all these issues I am asking: in what way, if any, does Laing want to revise Freudian theory? Does he need to do so in order to justify his work? Is he correct in doing so? I conclude that: (1) although Laing does in places try to reformulate the conscious/unconscious distinction, his reformulations are not essential to his project, and are in fact incorrect; (2) contrary to what is commonly believed, Laing does not argue that neurotic and psychotic states are explicable without reference to the past and its survivals in the unconscious of the patient and the others; (3) the real locus of Laing's revision insofar as it is legitimate is the pair intrapersonal/interpersonal. Laing takes interpersonal relations, not only individual experience and behaviour, as the raw material of analysis. (For another example of such a 'socialization' of psychoanalysis, see *Group Psychotherapy* by Foulkes and Anthony—a book which is in intention Freudian methodologically, though with a certain bent towards biologism and holism.) (4) Laing's idea that 'praxis' is somehow more fundamental than process in human relations seems to me a false path, though the real transformation of process into praxis is a legitimate formula for the therapeutic task.

Along with these four dualities, there is the false opposition between causality and intelligibility or meaning. Cause and meaning are not of course the same thing, but neither are they characteristic of two, mutually exclusive fields of discourse. That mental life is characterized by relations both of meaning and of causality is a basic premiss of Freud's, against which I have never seen a cogent philosophical or empirical argument.

(Perhaps, to avoid a possible misunderstanding, I should mention here that in speaking of 'causality', I am not referring to 'genetic' *as opposed to* structural explanations (see the quote from Lévi-Strauss, above.) Structural explanation—at any rate in the psychological sciences—is a species of causal explanation, not an alternative to it. There may be purely semiological sciences in which structure is *constitutive* of its elements, but psychoanalysis is not one of them. 'The effectivity of a structure on its elements' must be defined differently within each science, and in psychoanalysis refers to causal interaction between mental processes.)

The therapeutic advance made over traditional psychoanalysis by supplementing it with social phenomenology can be summarized as follows:

(1) It enables the therapist to locate the problem better—something that had appeared to be a neurotic symptom may be seen to be normal and rational while something which had appeared normal may be seen as neurotic (e.g., the young woman's belief that her parents are plotting against her may turn out to be justified; her desire to live at home may thereby be revealed as insane).

(2) It enables the therapist to intervene in the pathogenic situation either by increasing the self awareness of the others in that situation as well as of the patient or by assisting the removal of the patient from that situation. (I do not mean to imply that such removal is possible or desirable in every case.)

It must remain however a supplementary discipline to psychoanalysis—it is not an autonomous new science, still less a rival alternative to psychoanalysis. So much for the status of social phenomenology as a method; it must justify itself by the concrete new knowledge and practice it makes possible. This brings us to the findings of Laing's social phenomenology; the situations it analyses and the concepts it uses to understand them. The next chapter is devoted to the consideration of these questions.

Chapter 3

Social Phenomenology—
Concepts and Applications

(a) Transpersonal defences

Most defences described in psychoanalysis are intrapsychic defences
—for instance: splitting, projection, introjection, denial, repression,
regression. These defence mechanisms of psychoanalysis are *what a
person does to himself*. They are not actions on the external world, on
others, or on the world of others.

Persons do manifestly try to act on the 'inner' worlds of others to preserve their own inner worlds, and others (so-called obsessionals, for
instance), arrange and rearrange the *external* world of objects to preserve their inner worlds.

There is no systematic psychoanalytic theory of the nature of *transpersonal* defences, whereby self attempts *to regulate the inner life of the
other in order to preserve his own*, nor of techniques of coping with
such persecution by others. (*The Politics of the Family*, pp. 12/13)

Psychoanalysis has provided a vocabulary and a theory for
understanding intrapsychic defences. This, I believe, is a necessary condition for understanding what goes on in interpersonal
relations. Without such understanding a large number of statistically normal patterns of human interaction might appear per-

verse and unintelligible. That is to say, they would appear so were there not a whole armoury of false explanations ready to hand. These range from question-stoppers such as original sin, male or female nature, etc, to the entire vocabulary of 'attitudes', which are seen as at once completely comprehensible and completely gratuitous ('laziness', 'greed', 'lust', 'ego-tripping' etc.). The effect of the psychoanalytical account, if taken seriously, would be to eject these words from the dictionary and replace them by genuinely explanatory concepts.

However, it is possible to go further: once individuals with their various defence mechanisms are situated in relationships with each other, interactions between these defences occur, and qualitatively new phenomena arise: interpersonal or (as Laing calls them here) transpersonal defences. Relations between people can reinforce and modify the defences of each; and obviously enough, internal defences originate in the relation of the child to his/her parents and brothers and sisters. After a discussion of the various defence mechanisms described in traditional psychoanalytical literature in his essay 'Operations' in *The Politics of the Family*, Laing writes:

The operations I have alluded to are operations on one's own experience. They are done by one person to himself or herself. But they would be unnecessary unless the rules of the family required them: and ineffectual unless others co-operated. (p. 99)

Laing and his collaborators provide us with a set of concepts which can be applied in analysing this area of transpersonal defences. They are not for the most part concepts used in traditional psychoanalytic theory (though not necessarily invented by Laing—Bateson originated the notion of 'double bind', and much of Laing's theory in this area is indebted to Sartre's later writings). A particular intrapersonal defence mechanism is not necessarily a product of the same mechanism in the parent. In order to understand how particular parents with their own defences induce particular—often quite different—defences in their children, these mediating concepts of transpersonal defences are necessary.

Once inserted into this psychoanalytical context to provide new knowledge within that theory but in an area traditionally neglected, these concepts *must* be interpreted as involving causal notions. It is no longer enough to assign them descriptive tasks. They explain various pathological formations, and in this context I shall from now on simply discount Laing's disavowals of explanatory intent. If individual psychoanalysis is allowed to use causal concepts, and if social phenomenology is allowed to instruct psychoanalysis about which phenomena are pathological, then social phenomenology as a supplementary discipline must be able to use causal concepts as well, so that its explanations can as it were cohabit with psychoanalytical ones.

Anyway, if the denial of causality is connected as it usually is with the attribution of personal responsibility (and the 'personalist' elements in Laing's thought might suggest this), then it goes strangely with his concern for social context. How many parents, afraid of seeing their son's or daughter's 'illness' as caused in any way by themselves, have insisted that he or she could have avoided it with a little effort. When one hears attributions of responsible agency, one should understand that it is meant 'the buck stops there'. (I am not of course suggesting that the buck should stop anywhere.)

The transpersonal defences are no more conscious than are intrapsychic ones.

The most common situation I encounter in families is when what *I* think is going on bears almost no resemblance to what anyone in the family experiences or thinks is happening, whether or not this coincides with common sense. Maybe no one knows what is happening. However, one thing is often clear to an outsider: there is concerted family *resistance* to discovering what is going on, and there are complicated strategems to keep everyone in the dark. (*The Politics of the Family*, p. 77)

In *Self and Others* Laing shows how phantasy—a phenomenon of individual psychology—enters into interpersonal relations and becomes an integral part of the structure of the group, with far-reaching effects for the dynamics of the group, and for the

fate of the members of the group as it develops, and as they perhaps find themselves trapped by it.

The capacity to distinguish objective reality from one's phantasy is an important part of sanity, and the breakdown of this
capacity is madness. This capacity—the reality-principle, in
Freudian terms—is not however something that grows automatically in human individuals, or that is always perfected in
statistically normal adults. The objective world is also the public
world, and the process of learning to distinguish objective realities from subjective appearances takes place with the aid of other
people—their confirmation of an experience induces belief in its
veracity, their disconfirmation throws doubt on it. From this
follows the possibility of a *false objectivity* arising from agreement about what is real and what is not, when the agreed position is mistaken. Even for a thinking adult it is extremely easy to
persist in the most absurd beliefs when one lives in a community
which shares them, and very difficult to hold on to beliefs, however well-founded, when they never convince other people. Much
more so for a child, whose main sources of knowledge are precisely those people on whom he is emotionally dependent.

Now phantasy, though an unsatisfactory mode of experience
in the long run, is in general a form of wish-fulfilment, and therefore a pleasanter mode of experience than much reality.[1] So that
a situation which can make possible the indulgence of a phantasy
—the misrecognition of it as reality—in a 'normal' individual
without leading to a total collapse of practical relations with
reality, is highly tempting from the point of view of the pleasure-
principle. This situation is possible given that the phantasy can
be shared with, or fit in with the phantasies of, a close group of
other people. The commonness of collective phantasies which
are taken for realities by 'normal' people is therefore not surprising.

The human tendency to seek out people of like mind is no
doubt partly a matter of giving a pseudo-objectivity to our phantasies. In any small and close social group (the family is obviously the group most widely used in this way) there is likely to be
a network of shared phantasies, and this is true not only because

these groups are conveniently ready to hand to function as con-
firmers of individual phantasies, but also because, insofar as
phantasy is a determinant of behaviour, unshared phantasies will
lead to discordant behaviour.

All groups operate by means of phantasy. The type of *experience* a
group gives us is one of the main reasons, if not for some people the
only reason, for being in a group. What do people want to get from
the experience of being *in* a particular set of human collectivities?

The close-knit groups that occur in some families and other group-
ings are bound together by the need to find pseudo-real experience
that can be found only through the modality of phantasy. This means
that the family is not experienced as the modality of phantasy but as
'reality'. However, 'reality' in this sense is not a modality, but a
quality attachable to any modality. (*Self and Others*, pp. 39/40)

Some of the most important phantasies of any individual concern the family; within a family therefore shared phantasies will
be to a great extent shared misperceptions of that family itself. It
is as if within each member of the family there is an image of the
family, and (in the case of a shared phantasy) these images correspond to each other, but not necessarily to the real family. In
analysing this phenomenon, Laing uses the notion of mapping.
He calls the internalized family the 'family', and speaks of mapping the 'family' onto the family. There are a number of mapping
operations which can be performed here: first one's family of
origin is internalized as a child; this is of course fundamental to
any psychoanalytical theory, though Laing lays particular emphasis on the idea that 'the "family" is not an introjected object,
but an introjected set of relations'. (*The Politics of the Family*
p. 6)

These relations are not necessarily between persons: 'Elements may be persons, things or part-objects'. The sexual relation between the parents as envisaged by the child 'holds a sort
of nuclear position in every internal "family" '. (*The Politics of
the Family* p. 4)

The 'family' is mapped back (projected) onto the family, but
also onto later relationships. In a family with a shared phantasy
of its own structure, it is to be expected that, in the first place, the

D

'families' of the parents, derived from their experiences of their own families of origin, will form the core of the new 'family' which the children will be under pressure to internalize. The pressure on another person to adopt one's own phantasy is what Laing calls 'induction'.

> Suppose I projected my mother onto my wife . . . . I may or may not *induce* her to embody my mother. The operation of inducing her to embody my projection is what I am calling *induction*. Projection is done by one person as his *own* experience of the other. *Induction* is done by one person to *the other's* experience. (*The Politics of The Family*, p. 119)

Children will be particularly subject to induction by the parents of their own phantasy-structures.

Once we have a family with a shared phantasy, transpersonal defences really come into their own. The phantasy has to be defended against conflicting 'maps' of the family—including more accurate ones. Anyone who ceases to share the phantasy, or the child who has never properly internalized it (perhaps has internalized the 'real' family instead) is perceived as a threat. Confirmation of the shared phantasy is reinforced, disconfirmation of it is punished. The function of transpersonal defences in relation to intrapsychic ones is clearly enough illustrated in the essay 'Persons and experience' in *The Politics of Experience:*

> If Jack succeeds in forgetting something, this is of little use if Jill continues to remind him of it. He must induce her not to do so. The safest way would be not just to make her keep quiet about it, but to induce her to forget it also.
>
> Jack may act upon Jill in many ways. He may make her feel guilty for keeping on 'bringing it up'. He may *invalidate* her experience. This can be done more or less radically. He can indicate merely that it is unimportant or trivial, whereas it is important and significant to her. Going further, he can shift the *modality* of her experience from memory to imagination: 'It's all in your imagination'. Further still, he can invalidate the *content*. 'It never happened that way.' Finally, he can invalidate not only the significance, modality and content, but her very capacity to remember at all, and make her feel guilty for doing so into the bargain. (p. 31)

In an essentially unequal relationship, such as the mother-daughter relationship described in the chapter on 'The Churches' in *Sanity, Madness and the Family*, such invalidation is going to wreak systematic havoc on the daughter's experience. The mother asserts that she and her daughter have always got on well together. The daughter's account of this is that this is because the mother is a domineering character, and she (the daughter) preferred to submit rather than argue. Her mother replies that 'When you *are* an organizer in business' (as she is) 'you sort of carry it a bit into the home as well . . . but we seem to have got on very well throughout the years' and that 'you (the daughter) never like a lot of fuss do you?' Without actually denying the facts as seen by the daughter (indeed her reply confirms them) she is redefining them such that the problem disappears: we no longer have on the one hand a domineering character and on the other one who finds it easiest to submit, but rather an efficient organiser, and someone who does not like a lot of fuss; how admirable! At the same time the mother reasserts her view ('we got on very well'), and is putting the ball back in the daughter's court. Laing comments:

We wish to emphasize here not so much the mother's evident *intra*-personal defences but that she has to defend herself from the evocation in her of her own feelings by acting on Claire to muddle *her* up, to render *her* speechless, to obliterate *her* memory—in short by inducing a disorganisation *in her daughter's* personality. That Mrs. Church's actions serve this function does not of course mean that they necessarily have this intention. (pp. 94/95)

It is this invalidation of the individual's experience of reality by virtue of the transpersonal defences existing in that individual's social nexus, which *is* the social intelligibility of individual 'madness'.

Thus in the case of Maya Abbott,

An idea of reference that she had was that something she could not fathom was going on between her parents, seemingly about her. Indeed there was. (*Sanity, Madness and the Family*, p. 40)

Her parents constantly communicated with each other in non-verbal ways about her, while denying to her that they did so. As a result of this, she

could not know when she was perceiving or when she was imagining things to be going on between her parents ... Much of what could be taken to be paranoid about Maya arose because she mistrusted her own mistrust.

In an interesting article already referred to ('Sanity, Madness and the Problem of Knowledge' in *Radical Philosophy*, No. 1, 1972), Trevor Pateman argues on the basis of this case: (1) that it is from our parents that we learn the criteria of truth and falsehood; (2) that possession of these criteria—'cognitive autonomy' —is a necessary condition of general independence of one's parents; (3) that some parents (e.g. Maya's) prevent their children from learning these criteria. What is wrong with Maya is her lack of 'cognitive autonomy'. Trevor Pateman sees in this 'some sort of empirical illustration of the philosopher's thesis about the connexion between freedom and knowledge' (*Radical Philosophy* No. I, 1972, p. 23). There are certain problems about this notion of cognitive autonomy. Pateman describes lack of it as not having learnt to tell true from false (on analogy with the notion of learning to tell right from wrong). This can not mean that e.g. Maya does not know what truth and falsehood are— Maya does make judgements of facts, and sometimes with insight. Likewise when someone is said to be unable to tell right from wrong, what is meant is presumably not that they do not value or disvalue anything, but that they have no ability to see what considerations are relevant in making practical judgements. But knowing the *criteria* of truth and falsehood presents no less problems for, as Kant pointed out, it is easy to define truth (i.e. as the correspondence of thought to reality) but impossible to give a criterion or an exhaustive set of criteria for truth and falsehood; different criteria are relevant in dealing with different subject matters.[2] What Maya's parents confuse her about is the cognitive content of her *experience*, by insisting that what she thinks she perceives and remembers (cognitive modes of experience), she actually only imagines. They are able to do this because, as Pateman points out, she has no objective means of checking her own experience other than her parents' confirmation of it (that, *as a child*, no one has such independent means of checking the veracity of their experience is precisely why it is inevitable that the parents are the epistemological authorities.[3])

In the light of this discussion it is possible to reformulate the notion of false objectivity. There is no knowledge without objective checkability; there are no objective checks available to a child concerning its experience of its family apart from the views of members of the family themselves; so where there is a shared phantasy of the family in the minds of its members, a child, though it may come to doubt the veracity of that phantasy on the basis of its own experience, can have no knowledge of the family, and hence no consistent orientation towards it in practice, unless it be on the basis of accepting the phantasy as reality.[4] It is for this reason that the 'disturbed' member of a family is often closer to the truth than the others (not perhaps in perceiving reality, but at least in doubting the collective phantasy), though practically at a disadvantage, through not having a coherent picture of the situation, which the others have (though it is a false one).

To this account however must be added the emotional dependence of the child on the parents, which places in their hands a powerful weapon with which to punish any doubts about their phantasy-family. I think Laing's writings constitute a convincing case that this situation of false objectivity with emotional sanctions is of the first importance in understanding the sort of psychotic phenomena he describes.

The degree of insight and of delusion on the part of the 'disturbed' member of the family varies greatly from case to case. In *Interpersonal Perception*, where the interpersonal perception method is set up for testing the accuracy of the perception of the viewpoints of others with whom one has relationships of some sort, it is stated that Laing's guesses concerning the mutual perceptiveness of schizophrenics and their families were as follows:

The schizophrenic sees the mother's point of view better than the mother sees the schizophrenic's.
The schizophrenic realises that the mother does not realise that he sees her point of view,
and that she thinks she sees his point of view,
and that she does not realize that she fails to do so.
The mother, on the other hand, thinks she sees the schizophrenic's point of view,
and that the schizophrenic fails to see hers,
and is unaware that the schizophrenic knows that this is what she thinks, and that she is unaware he knows. (p. 47)

Of course such a cognitive advantage on the part of the schizophrenic does not preclude him or her from having experience which is discrepant from reality in ways more obviously pathological.

A person in an alienated false position within a social phantasy system, who begins partially to apperceive his position, may give 'psychotic' expression to his partial apperception of the actual phantasy state of affairs by saying that he is being subjected to poisons concealed in his food, that his brains have been taken from him, that his actions are being controlled from outer space, etc. *Such delusions are partially achieved derealization-realizations.* (*Self and Others*, p. 39)

One can imagine such a person having a far better understanding of what is going on in the family than his/her parents; at the same time the delusions about poisoned food are more far-fetched than the delusions suffered by the parents, which may nonetheless explain them.

This can be illustrated from the case of 'John', discussed by Laing in *Self and Others*, (pp. 95–97). John's father, a naval officer, had brought him up with the idea that his identity as his father's son depended on what he did—on his success at doing certain things. When John's naval career came to nought, his father told him he was not his son. Biologically speaking, this could have been true, as his mother was a prostitute. John's 'psychosis' took the form of the belief that he could become whoever he wanted by snapping his fingers. Laing comments:

What his father had taught him was: 'You are my son if I say you are, and you are not my son, if I say you are not.' He replaced this by: 'I am who *I* say I am, and I am not who *I* say I am not.' (*Self and Others*, p. 96)

The root error of his psychosis was in the soil of his pre-psychotic assumptions. His psychosis seemed to be not so much a *reductio ad adsurdum* of these assumptions, as a conjuring with the absurdity already present. Namely, that he was who his father said he was. He negated this by: 'No, I am who I say I am.' True sanity lies at the other side: the negation of the psychotic negation of the original false promise. I am not what they say I am, nor what I say I am. (p. 97)

In this example, we can see (i) that the element of unreality in the psychosis derives from unrealistic (though non-psychotic) assumptions made by the father; (ii) that the father used this (unrealistic) assumption about his control of his son's identity to reinforce his real control of his son's life; (iii) that the son's revolt against this control at first took place within the false assumption; the son had therefore moved from acceptance of real domination (neurosis) to unreal rejection of domination (psychosis); (iv) cure consisted in recognition of the falseness of the original assumption, not only in the form it took in the son's psychosis, but also in the form it took in the father's mystification; this made possible real revolt against the real domination of the son by the father as well.

The cases in *Sanity, Madness and the Family* also manifest some variety in the degree of insight and of delusion in the family and in the patient. In addition to this, it is often difficult for the reader to tell in a given case whether Laing and Esterson think there was not much wrong with the patient, or that what was wrong was socially intelligible. In some cases it is clear: that of the Fields for example. In this case it seems that there can be little doubt that what was originally regarded as symptomatic of madness by the mother—expressions of independent thought and action by her fifteen-year-old daughter, June—was nothing of the kind. During this period, neither June's schoolteachers nor her father and sister, nor two doctors her mother consulted, saw anything wrong with her. By the time she was admitted to hospital however, she was more clearly seriously disturbed than most of the patients referred to in the book—she was admitted in a catatonic stupor, and had delusions of being poisoned, of having destroyed the world etc. In other words, the attribution of madness may have been instrumental in fulfilling itself (as it was certainly instrumental in impeding recovery, used as it was by June's mother to prevent her taking independent initiative). The concept of a self-fulfilling prophecy or attribution, which is dangerously mystifying both on the macro-social scene (e.g. when politicians accuse the opposition of 'talking the country into a crisis') and in individual psychology (the idea that 'you are only unhappy because you think you are', and the whole power-of-positive-thinking syndrome) seems to have authentic application in the area of family interaction, precisely because parents are 'epistemological authorities' and are in a position to impose emotional sanctions against the son or daughter who belies their attributions.

The case of 'the Golds' in *Sanity, Madness and the Family* is perhaps a classic case of the sort of progress from family conflicts to hospitalization that most readers of Laing see as the typical case in his accounts—i.e. one in which there does not seem to be anything wrong with the daughter, Ruth, at all. She wanted to go to a drinking club, mix with 'beatniks', wear unconventional clothes, etc. and her parents, who had a clear picture (with no basis in current reality) of what sort of person she was, feel that this was all alien to her, and must be the result of 'illness'. She did not think she was ill at all. The account as written up by Laing and Esterson ends:

Interviewer: But do you feel you have to agree with what most of the people round you believe?

Ruth: Well if I don't I usually land up in hospital. (*Sanity, Madness and the Family*, p. 175)

(b) Complementary identity

Every relationship implies a definition of self by other and other by self. (*Self and Others*, p. 86)

The concept of complementary identity as used by Laing is a good example of the demystification of existentialist concepts which has already been noted as a feature of his work. One of the most striking sections of Sartre's *Being and Nothingness* is the account of relations between people. This is contained in part III of that work, in the section on 'the look' and the chapter entitled 'Concrete Relations with Others'. One's reaction to this account (speaking for myself at least) is that it contains many striking insights, but leaves one with the feeling—not wholly induced by the pessimism of the account—that human relations are not always quite like that. Closer examination reveals that there are internal mistakes in Sartre's argument, and that indeed it is not ontologically necessary—as Sartre seems to think—that things should be as he describes; but in that case it becomes inexplicable that people should be so perverse as to behave in the ways Sartre so accurately describes. Laing's discussion of complementary identity gives empirical content to much of Sartre's speculation, and at the same time provides some indication of why the pattern of human relations in question is so often encountered. I shall discuss Sartre's account first, and then look at what Laing does with it.

Sartre's account of interpersonal relationships begins, significantly enough, in the context of a refutation of solipsism—i.e. of the notion that one's own consciousness is the only existing consciousness. Sartre believes that there are certain forms of self-experience of which we can only make sense on the assumption that other consciousnesses exist and experience us. Shame is the clearest case of this mode of self-experience. In shame, one is aware of one's body as an object for another person. One is not aware *of* the other's consciousness—that, according to Sartre, is impossible; nor is one aware *of* one's own body in the way that one might be when examining it in a mirror, or telling a doctor 'where it hurts'. The experience that Sartre describes is rather one in which consciousness, from being concentrated on certain intentions or happenings outside one's own body, suddenly 'flows back' onto the perimeter of the body as a possible object for others. Sartre's example is as follows:

Let us imagine that moved by jealousy, curiosity or vice I have just glued my ear to the door and looked through a keyhole . . . My consciousness sticks to my acts, it *is* my acts; and my acts are commanded only by the ends to be attained and by the instruments to be employed. My attitude, for example, has no 'outside'; it is a pure process of relating the instrument (the keyhole) to the end to be attained (the spectacle to be seen), a pure mode of losing myself in the world, of causing myself to be drunk in by things as ink is by a blotter . . .

But all of a sudden I hear footsteps in the hall. Someone is looking at me! What does this mean? It means that I am suddenly affected in my being and that essential modifications appear in my structure . . . all of a sudden I am conscious of myself as escaping myself . . . (*Being and Nothingness*, pp. 259–260)

Not only one's body but the objects in one's world which were hitherto organized around one's aims, now 'turn toward the other a face which on principle escapes me.' (p. 261). One's own world which was centred around one's project is now de-centred, because the other appears in it with aims and an experience of the world which are opaque to one. Thus if one is walking alone through a park, and then another person comes on the scene, one's awareness that the park is also organized (differently) around the other's consciousness, and that the nature of such organization escapes one, changes one's own experience of the park. It 'flows away' into that hole—the other's consciousness. Sartre refers to this as an 'internal haemorrhage' in one's world.

Now Sartre holds that one cannot simultaneously experience the other as an object in one's own world and oneself as an object for the other.

The objectivation of the Other would be the collapse of his being-a-as look . . . the Other's look is the disappearance of the Other's eyes as objects which manifest the look. (p. 268)

Hence being an object for the other is always a loss of one's own consciousness, one's own possibilities. Sartre falls here into the mistake, which Marx already criticized in Hegel, of identifying objectification with alienation, i.e. of seeing the fact that one's being, activity and products have objective being in the world of others as involving the robbery by the others of one's true being, and the assigning of alien values, meanings and uses to that being. This 'alienation' however is only one form of objectification—it presupposes that the 'others' are antagonistic. Objectification in itself is obviously highly desirable—its absence would be precisely solipsism. Laing recognizes this and never assumes that the Sartrean model of interpersonal relations works unless (for some independent reason) others are really antagonistic or are experienced as antagonistic. For Sartre on the other hand even a positive form of objectification, such as pride, is seen as being built 'on the ground of fundamental shame or shame of being an object' (p. 290).

This account so far has been concerned primarily with a particular kind of relation to others, i.e. those in which the consciousness of the other is not essential to one's own aims, but accidental to them. Thus in most encounters between unacquainted people in everyday life, the other person figures as an instrument towards some goal which has nothing to do with that person's consciousness. For instance, if someone goes into a shop to buy a packet of cigarettes, the shopkeeper is an 'instrument' with regard to one's intention of getting the cigarettes; a vending machine would have served the same function. The difference (according to Sartre) is that another person is a particular kind of instrument, an 'explosive' one. This means that at any moment the other person may be transformed into the 'subject' for whom oneself is an 'object'. (It is not simply a question of the relative unpredictability of people as opposed to machines; indeed in the example cited, a shopkeeper is probably more predictable than a cigarette-machine.) So that Sartre can conclude:

Thus the Other-as-object is an explosive instrument which I handle with care because I foresee around him the permanent possibility that they are going to make it explode and with this explosion I shall suddenly experience the flight of my world away from me and the alienation of my being. Therefore my constant concern is to contain the Other within his objectivity, and my relations with the Other-as-object are essentially made up of ruses designed to make him remain an object. (*Being and Nothingness*, p. 297)

I have already suggested (in Chapter 1) that this aspect of Sartre's thought (and echoes of it in Laing) is somewhat schizoid.

On the basis of this view, Sartre goes on to give an account of those interpersonal relationships in which the consciousness of the other is an essential element—relationships in other words in which a non-human instrument could not serve as a substitute. For Sartre, the motivation of such interpersonal relationships is that: 'The Other holds a secret—the secret of what I am.' (p. 364) What one tries to grasp in one's relations with others is the other's perception of oneself. One tries to determine the other to have a definite mode of consciousness of oneself (the question whether that consciousness is love or hate, fear, contempt or sexual desire etc. is *secondary* for Sartre).

It is at this point that Sartre's ontological pessimism appears at its most pronounced—i.e. his doctrine that certain features of human experience are both intrinsically undesirable and could not conceivably be otherwise. For he thinks that our relations with others—insofar as they are not purely instrumental—are necessarily motivated by the desire to secure an identity between what one chooses to be and what one is for the consciousness of the other. Yet he also believes that it is ontologically impossible to realize this desire, for it involves the consciousness of the other being simultaneously a free consciousness and a determined object.

More than this, one's aims in regard to the other are essentially hostile, for they are directed towards enslaving the other. Hence: 'Conflict is the original meaning of being for others.' (p. 364). Relations with others appear as essentially unpleasant (cf. the conclusion of Sartre's play *Huis clos* that 'Hell is other people').

Marcuse, in his review of *Being and Nothingness*, reprinted in his *Studies in Critical Philosophy*, suggests that Sartre's account of sexual desire holds out the possibility of a 'good reification', but despite the fact that Sartre is certainly no prude, and writes of sexual experience with great phenomenological acuteness and feeling for its importance in human life, it nonetheless seems that he sees sexual relations as essentially an attempt to dominate the consciousness of the other, and finds the unsatisfactory thing about desire to be precisely that it is satisfiable.

Laing uses the insights obtained by Sartre in this account of interpersonal relations, but discards the metaphysical wrappings. He starts from the observation that there are a large number of roles in which people find themselves or in terms of which they define themselves, and which depend for their existence on another person, i.e. to be a mother one must have a child, to be a husband one must have a wife, to be dominated one must have a dominator. Laing is inquiring about the importance of this in terms of one's self-conception, one's image of 'who one is'. This must be stressed because it is obviously true also, for example, that in order to make love one must have a sexual partner; but this is not the point. We are not directly concerned here with desires of which the other person is the object, but self-conceptions which logically involve reference to one's being-for-others.

Intense *frustration* arises from failure to find that other required to establish a satisfactory 'identity'.

Other people become a sort of identity kit, whereby one can piece together a picture of *oneself*. (*Self and Others*, p. 87)

It is being accepted here that people have a need for some kind of 'identity'. Laing does not however simply take this for granted; in the first place, it is something that can be experienced in more ways than one:

This complementarity can be central or peripheral, have greater or less dynamic significance at different periods of one's life. At some point a child rebels against the nexus of bonds which bind him to these parents and siblings which he has not chosen; he does not wish to be defined and identified as his father's son, or sister's brother. These people may seem strangers to him. Surely, he has affinities with parents who are finer, wiser, more exalted. Yet, this nexus of complementary bonds is an anchor that others long for. (*Self and Others*, p. 86)

The original sense of our own identity then must be understood as a complementary one—we are our parents' children. The search for an identity may be a way of denying the original definition of the self in relation to the parents.

This search must substitute others for the parents, for 'a person's "own" identity cannot be completely abstracted from his identity-for-others.' (p. 86). These others may be real or phantasied.

The 'family romance' is a dream of changing the others who define the self, so that *the identity of the self can be self-defined* by a redefinition of the others. It is an attempt to feel pride rather than shame at being the son or daughter of this father and this mother. (*Self and Others*, p. 95)[5]

Phantasied others, however, will not meet the requirements very well unless they can be embodied in real others; whether real or phantasied, the other will be in large part a projection of one's ideal image of one's parents, which is a relic of one's infantile experience, and which has been set against one's actual parents in the process of emancipating oneself from their authority.

If this is a correct account of the origin of the pursuit of power over others' definition of oneself, two features of that pursuit become clearer. The first is the ambivalence involved in the desire for an identity in the eyes of others. This can be illustrated by the fact that most people like filling in 'personality questionnaires', or wearing badges, yet also resent 'being labelled'. Generally when a remark is made about someone's characteristics that person—assuming the remark is not a clear case of a compliment or an insult—will feel a mixture of pleasure at self-recognition and dislike of being labelled. Sartre sees this as a basic feature of human existence—that we both seek to define ourselves—and this requires being defined by others—and seek to be free and hence escape any definition. Laing on the other hand does not take this ambivalence for granted, and although he does not put forward an explicit theory of it, I think it is implicit in his work that the schizoid fear that any objectification is enslaving must be seen in the context of a failure of the schizoid person to free himself or herself from the parental definition, so that that person's only experience of definition by the other is an enslaving one.

The other point is that the nature of the role in which the others through whom one seeks definition are cast, i.e. the role of embodying one's ideal image of one's parents, is going to be a rich source of interpersonal conflicts and transpersonal defence-mechanisms.

Much of Laing's account of interpersonal behaviour is an account of conflicts between different 'identities' possessed by the same person, e.g. identity as seen or desired by oneself and identity as conferred by others, real and illusory identities, identities for different others, and contradictory assignments of identities made by the same other person.

We can already see from this discussion of complementary identity what possibilities there are in this area both of conflict between people who each demand of the other that they play roles necessary to their own identity, when the people involved have incompatible ego-ideals, and of the pseudo-objectivity inherent in the arrangement of complementary roles when this is possible.

(c) Confirmation, disconfirmation and collusion

Any human interaction implies some measure of confirmation, at any rate of the physical bodies of the participants, even when one person is shooting another. (*Self and Others*, p. 98)

Confirmation, disconfirmation and collusion can be seen as responses to such aspects of the human condition as complementary identity, and the fact that we are not, even in adult life, completely 'epistemologically autonomous', i.e. that we need our own conception of the objective world to coincide with—or at least not to be too discrepant from—the world as seen by others. If in the discussion of complementary identity the elusion of unwanted identities imposed by others looms largest, we are here more concerned with the positive need for some kind of 'objectification' in the eyes of others, and the deleterious effects of the lack of such recognition, or of spurious forms of it.

We can already see from the above quote that confirmation does not mean or imply agreement; the case (which is clearly desirable) in which two people confirm each other's being or experience is not the case in which they form a 'mutual admiration society'. It is necessary to make this clear, as total mystification would result from the idea that it is healthy for people e.g. to always accept other people at their own assessment of themselves.

There are, Laing points out, degrees of confirmation and disconfirmation, and shooting someone is certainly a relatively low degree of confirmation. But it is not therefore without point to call it confirmation; to take an example from literature, when Cathy shoots Adam in the shoulder (in Steinbeck's *East of Eden*) what hurts him most is that she did not shoot to kill, out of hate (which would imply a degree of confirmation), but in indifference, simply to remove an obstacle from her path.

A confirmatory response is *relevant* to the evocative action, it accords recognition to the evocatory act, and accepts its significance for the evoker, if not for the respondent. A confirmatory reaction is a direct response, it is 'to the point', or 'on the same wavelength' as the initiatory or evocatory action. A partially confirmatory response need not be in agreement, or gratifying, or satisfying. Rejection can be confirmatory if it is direct, not tangential, and recognize the evoking action and grants it significance and validity. (*Self and Others*, p. 99)

As against such direct, confirmatory responses, there are, for instance, 'tangential responses', of which Laing gives a classic example—that of the boy with a worm, running to his mother and saying, 'Mummy, look what a big fat worm I have got', and getting the reply, 'You are filthy—away and clean yourself immediately.' There are other forms of disconfirmation, as when an opinion is invalidated rather than contradicted—treated as worthless, not merely false.

The importance of confirmation and disconfirmation depends on the issues involved.

Some areas of a person's being may cry out for confirmation more than others. Some forms of disconfirmation may be more destructive of self-development than others. One may call these schizogenic. (*Self and Others*, pp. 99–100)

Probably most people have found at some time or other that the discrepancy between the self's and the other's way of seeing a given situation is so great as to induce the feeling: one of us must be mad. In part, it is no doubt a technique of interpersonal aggression (not necessarily or even usually conscious) to disconfirm the other's experience. When there is enough mutual aggression in the relationship, one person can often be fairly sure that anything he/she says will be contradicted by the other and made to seem stupid, even if it is only 'London is bigger than Birmingham'. Such a tactic is often reinforced with a familiar pattern of 'double bind': if A makes a statement B automatically contradicts it; if B turns out to be right, A is a fool; if A turns out to be right, A is a pretentious know-all, or it is useless and boring information anyway. In this case, we may assume that the disconfirmation is based on a pre-existing hostility, but it need not be that way round. The fact that everyone's experience is different can itself be a disturbing factor in relationships, as each wants their ideas based on their own past experience reinforced. In a society as pluralistic as ours, basic assumptions can be quite radically different, and each partner can have invested a great deal of emotion in his or her own assumptions, so that to accept them as questionable or even simply as not universally held can be painful. These problems are of course problems arising in adult relationships, not in the relation of a child to its parents. Disconfirmation in the latter situation is different in principle as, in the relation of the child to its parents, the child brings no 'past' with it into the relationship.

Another possibly pathogenic phenomenon of disconfirmation might be that in which quite different qualities are attributed to a person by two groups of people. For instance a person may be thought by one group of acquaintances to be very witty, and may rely on this 'social skill' in order to maintain his relationships

with people in this group. If that person finds that among
another group he is regarded as quite devoid of wit, his capacity
to cope socially may be seriously impaired. Very often a person
who is somewhat ill at ease in social situations will rely on some
single social skill, and become totally 'ontologically insecure'
when this skill goes unrecognized.

Disjunctions between self-experience and other's experience of
oneself are the object of study in *Interpersonal Perception*. Reading that book, incidentally, is a useful corrective for anyone who,
either dismissively or in a spirit of discipleship, regards Laing as
a guru rather than a serious scientist. For the 'interpersonal perception method' (IPM) set forth in that book uses such tools as
a technical symbolic notation, and the matching and statistical
analysis of questionnaires, in order to discover information un-
available to the experience of any individual—i.e. information
about discrepancies in interpersonal perception.

The method is simple in principle: two people who are in some
mutual relationship are each asked how they rate themselves and
the other on various counts, how they think the other would
answer the same questionnaire, and how they think the other
would think they had answered, e.g.:

A. How true do you think the following are?
   1. She makes up my mind for me.
   2. I make up her mind for her.
   3. She makes up her own mind.
   4. I make up my own mind.

B. How would SHE answer the following?
   1. 'I make up his mind for him.'
   2. 'He makes up my mind for me.'
   3. 'I make up my own mind.'
   4. 'He makes up his own mind.'

C. How would SHE think you have answered the following?
   1. She makes up my mind for me.
   2. I make up her mind for her.
   3. She makes up her own mind.
   4. I make up my own mind. (p. 145)

And likewise for a whole series of other attributions—deceiving, blaming and being afraid of the other person and oneself, and so on. Typical discrepancies might be as listed on p. 11:

I act in a way that is *cautious* to me, but *cowardly* to you.
You act in a way that is *courageous* to you, but *foolhardy* to me.
She sees herself as *vivacious*, but he sees her as *superficial*.
He sees himself as *friendly*, she sees him as *seductive*.
She sees herself as *reserved*, he sees her as *haughty and aloof*.
He sees himself as *gallant*, she sees him as *phoney*.
She sees herself as *feminine*, he sees her as *helpless and dependent*.
He sees himself as *masculine*, she sees him as *overbearing and dominating*.

However the most important and interesting feature of Laing's account of confirmation and disconfirmation is not the idea of disconfirmation as schizogenic when it relates to fundamental enough aspects of one's self-image but his idea that confirmation of a false self or a partial and peripheral aspect of the self at the expense of other aspects may be a form of disconfirmation and, more significantly still, a means of inducing the development of that false self.

Thus, a man who has developed an exaggerated intellectuality as a compensation for social inadequacy may find it disconfirming in the extreme when he is complimented precisely for his intellectual abilities; he may feel on the one hand that he is being put on a pedestal and therefore subjected to demands he cannot meet, and on the other hand that it is being implied:

Yes, you have a first rate mind, *but* . . . you are not physically attractive, good company, sensitive or practical . . . .

He may feel that he is being put in a false position by being admired for something which is not the essential thing, but only a compensation for its lack, and by being an object of admiration, he is more likely to be considered fair game for criticism in other respects; he feels disconfirmed and threatened precisely by the confirmation of this aspect of himself.

However confirmation of a false self may be *experienced* as fulfilling, while it is actually complicity in self-deception—i.e. what Laing calls 'collusion'. Collusion may be a 'solution' to the problem of disconfirmation.

Collusion is always clinched when self finds in other that other who will 'confirm' self in the false self that self is trying to make real, and vice versa. The ground is then set for prolonged mutual evasion of truth and true fulfillment. Each has found an other to endorse his own false notion of himself and to give this appearance a semblance of reality. (*Self and Others*, p. 111)

The foregoing discussion of false objectivity in connection with transpersonal defences, and of complementary identity, should already have made clear what is going on in confirmation, disconfirmation and collusion. Laing's work is rich in concrete examples.

There are three points it is worth making about these phenomena of confirmation, disconfirmation and collusion, as described by Laing. The first concerns the formalism of these concepts, despite the many concrete examples in Laing's works. The formalization of the theory of interpersonal perception is deliberate; of the patterns described in *Knots*, Laing says:

I hope they are not so schematized that one may not refer back to the very specific experiences from which they derive; yet that they are sufficiently independent of 'content', for one to divine the formal elegance in these webs of *maya*. (Foreword to *Knots*)

At times, I think, explanatory power is sacrificed to this formal elegance. For instance, questions about the desirability or otherwise of the attributes over which there is confirmation, disconfirmation or collusion are left on one side in discussing these phenomena abstractly. One wry instance of this has been noted and commented on in Peter Sedgwick's essay in *Laing and Anti-Psychiatry*:

The IPM questionnaire sheets completed by the Jones couple established (a) that she does not love him, and (b) that he is conscious of the fact that she does not love him. But these (on the face of it plausible) indicators of marital rupture need not be taken as definitive, since they are drawn only from the first windings of the perceptual spiral. They matter less than the fact that Mr and Mrs Jones are in considerable agreement at the higher, more indirect levels of attribution: thus, she correctly perceives him as perceiving her as feeling disappointed in him, and so on. The Jones' perspectives on one another may be at odds, but their meta- and meta-meta-perspectives concur: they may be out of love, but *they at least know it*. And on the strength of these disillusioned, bitterly refracted awarenesses, the authors conclude that the unloved Mr Jones, and the unloving Mrs Jones have a hopeful marital prognosis, with 'a good capacity to work with and contain their conflicts'. It needed an awful lot of statistics to produce that avuncular twinkle. (p. 33)

Another example of this same formalism occurs in Laing's comparison of a pair of conversations—one of them hypothetical— between a mother and daughter:

M (to fourteen-year-old daughter): You are evil.
D: No, I'm not.
M: Yes, you are.
D: Uncle Jack doesn't think so.
M: He doesn't love you as I do. Only a mother really knows the truth about her daughter, and only one who loves you as I do will ever tell you the truth about yourself no matter what it is. If you don't believe me, just look at yourself in the mirror carefully and you will see that I'm telling the truth. (*The Politics of the Family*, pp. 121–22)

Laing suggests that we substitute the word 'pretty' for the word 'evil' in this conversation. He tells us:

The *technique* is the same. Whether the attribution is pretty, good, beautiful, ugly or evil, the *structure* is identical. The structure is *so* common that we hardly notice it unless the attribution jars . . . I suggest that we reflect on the *structure* of the *induction* not only the content thereof. (pp. 122–23)

But structure and content are not quite that independent. There are real differences between the two cases which are relevant to the cognitive issue which Laing is raising. The relations between loving someone and finding them pretty are very different from the relations between loving someone and finding them evil. One might love someone because she is pretty, or find her pretty because one loves her; it is hardly possible to substitute 'evil' for 'pretty' here. So that to say 'I know you are evil because I love you' is to put someone into a sort of double-bind situation which does not apply in the other case.

The other two points are special cases of this relation between form and content. Most relationships which are close enough to involve significant phenomena of confirmation, disconfirmation and collusion take place within families, and are relationships between members of different sexes and/or different generations. The importance of this is obvious. I will discuss it in the next chapter.

The other point concerns the occurrence of confirmation, disconfirmation and collusion in the relations between the analyst and the analysand. Laing has often stressed the necessary role of the analyst in confirming the experience of many patients who have lost the capacity to trust their own perceptions under constant pressure of disconfirmation from their families. So it is perhaps necessary to point out that he is no less aware of the danger of collusion between analyst and analysand and that he insists that a therapeutic relationship must not be collusive.

It is in terms of basic frustration of the self's search for a collusive complement for false identity that Freud's dictum that analysis should be conducted under conditions of maximum frustration takes on its most cogent meaning.

It is worth examining the 'place' of the therapist in such a group, and the 'place' the persons within the group feel themselves to have in relation to him.

One basic function of genuinely analytic or existential therapy is the provision of a setting in which as little as possible impedes each person's capacity to discover his own self.

Without beginning to enter into a full discussion of this, one can comment on one aspect of the therapist's position. The therapist's intention is not to allow himself to collude with the patients in adopting a position in their phantasy-system: and, alternatively, not to use the patients to embody any phantasy of his own. (*Self and Others*, p. 123)

One important phantasy that the therapist has to see through and help the others to see through, is that he has 'the answer'.

Destroying these phantasies will involve painful disconfirmation of the patients' experience. Psychoanalytical responses are notoriously 'tangential'. If someone consults an analyst because he/she is depressed at not being able to find the meaning of life, the analyst cannot say 'I will tell you what the meaning of life is', or even (what a philosopher might justifiably say) 'life is not the sort of thing that has a meaning; it is not a sign'. The analyst will simply not take the question seriously as a question, but only as a symptom. 'Therapy without collusion cannot help but frustrate desires generated by phantasy'. (*Self and Others*, p. 124)

(d) Double bind and other untenable positions

The concept of double bind is derived from Bateson, who introduces it in terms of Russell's Theory of Logical Types. The Theory of Types distinguishes (among other things) first order statements (which do not themselves *refer to* statements) and second (and higher) order statements (which do). This solves some problems concerning certain apparently self-referring statements, e.g. 'I am now telling a lie'. On the surface, this appears to be true if it is a lie, and a lie if it is true. According to Russell's theory, it remains a lie, as it must be interpreted as meaning 'I am now making a false first order statement', which is a false second order statement (as there is no first order statement involved). Russell encountered this paradox (which had puzzled the Greeks in connection with the case of Epimenides the Cretan, who is supposed to have said that all Cretans lie whenever they speak) in his work on the foundations of mathematics (set theory), but the paradox does present itself in everyday life from time to time. For example, my father once saw a notice on an airport information board, saying: 'Please ignore all information on this board, as it is out of order'.

Bateson's view is that children who later become schizophrenic had been repeatedly put into a position (generally by the mother) in which conflicting demands were made of them at different levels (logical types). He concludes 'There will be a breakdown in any individual's ability to discriminate between logical types wherever a double bind situation occurs', and that just this breakdown is involved in schizophrenia.

Laing seems to be sceptical of the relevance of the Theory of Types here, and I think justifiably. Bateson himself, having introduced the concept in terms of this theory, goes on to mention cases in which the conflicting demands are imposed by different individuals (e.g. mother and father), rather than by one individual in different orders of discourse. Even where only one individual is doing the 'binding', what is often involved is information conveyed by word of mouth on the one hand, and by bodily expression on the other, as when a girl tells her would-be lover 'no' and indicates clearly enough that she means 'yes'. These are certainly different types of communication, but scarcely different logical types in Russell's sense. They can only be assimilated to the latter by taking the non-verbal communication to be a comment on the verbal one, as when an ironic expression indicates that what is being said should be taken with a pinch of salt.

In the original presentation of the double bind hypothesis (which Laing quotes at some length from Bateson), there is the additional element of an injunction to prevent the victim from escaping from the field. This Bateson admits is 'in a formal sense' unnecessary. There is no doubt that this pattern is recognizable. For instance, a woman who no longer loves a man but has not admitted this fact to herself, may completely cease to express affection for him and reject his attentions, while denying that this is so when he mentions it, saying that they still have a very good relationship, and that he is imagining things, but that if he does not stop fussing her, she really will leave him. This is a double-bind situation alright, but if he does not see what is happening, or act on what he sees, his complicity in the situation needs explaining. It is not enough to say that she is preventing his escape, one wants to know why he accepts this. In any adult double-bind situation an injunction not to escape is insufficient explanation of the victim's failure to escape, while in the case of double binds imposed on children by their parents, it is unnecessary. As Bateson himself says, 'if the double binds are imposed during infancy, escape is naturally impossible'.

In certain cases, the double bind in the strict sense (the Theory of Types model) does apply, notably where a prohibition imposed by a parent is denied to exist. Indeed, second order denials of first order assertions play a considerable role in ordinary speech, as in: 'I don't want to be uncharitable about Mrs. Hughes, but . . . ', which invariably precedes an act of being uncharitable about Mrs. Hughes.

Laing gives an example of a schizogenic double bind of this form in the chapter on 'The Churches' in *Sanity, Madness and the Family:*

What Mrs. Church says she says is bewilderingly incongruent with what she says. She repeatedly maintains, for instance, that she forgets things and lets bygones by bygones, advising Claire to do the same. But she 'forgets' things in a peculiar way. She recounts them at length and qualifies her account by saying that she forgets them. After one such story from twenty years back, she said, 'I think of those things, Claire—I mean I forget it and let it pass'.

Unless one has a vantage point outside this relationship, it must be very difficult to know where one is. She says 'I am doing X'. She then does Y; then she says she had been doing X, and expects Claire not to perceive that she had done Y. (p. 87)

Another common way of imposing conflicting demands without contradicting oneself is that in which one mode of behaviour is approved in general, and the opposite in every concrete instance, as in the case in which a girl is told she should have more friends, while all her actual friends meet with disapproval. (e.g. 'The Golds' and 'The Lawsons' in *Sanity, Madness and the Family*).[6]

Laing tells us that 'the double-bind hypothesis contains a number of sub-hypotheses, some of which seem more sound than others'. This I think is true. It is very easy to apply the concept to a whole range of situations once one has learnt it, simply on the basis of a 'family resemblance' to strict cases of double bind.

These turn out to have little in common apart from there being conflicting demands on one, which cannot both be met. Rather than try to assimilate all these to the double-bind model, it seems to me more profitable to use the term 'untenable positions', as Laing does, and recognize double bind as one source among others of such positions.

Such situations are not necessarily imposed by another person, and certainly not in any way that would lead us to regard that person's behaviour as odd. For instance, Laing points out the possibility of a two-way double bind, and also suggests that it may be the result of an instinctual dynamic:

One must remember that the child may put his parents into untenable positions. The baby cannot be satisfied. It cries 'for' the breast. It cries when the breast is presented. It cries when the breast is withdrawn. Unable to 'click with' or 'get through', mother becomes intensely anxious and feels hopeless. She withdraws from the baby in one sense and becomes over-solicitous in another sense. Double binds can be two-way. (*Self and Others*, p. 147)

An interesting possibility is the link-up of this type of theory [i.e. Bateson's] with recent biological theory.

A child runs away from danger. In flight from danger it runs to mother. At a certain stage, flight to the mother and clinging to her may be a pre-potent behavioural pattern in reaction to danger. It is possible that 'flight' and 'clinging' to the mother are compounded of component instinctual response systems in the child that can be modified at certain stages only to a limited extent.

Let us suppose a situation wherein the mother herself is the object that generates danger, for whatever reason. If this happens when the pre-potent reaction to danger is 'flight' *from* the danger *to* the mother, will the infant run *from* danger or *to* mother? Is there a 'right' thing to do? Suppose it clings to mother. The more it clings, the more tense mother becomes; the more tense, the tighter she holds the baby; the tighter she holds the baby, the more frightened it gets; the more frightened, the more it clings. (p. 148)

This presents the possibility of 'double bind' where at least one of the 'demands' is of instinctual rather than social origin. If the concept of double bind is extended this far, it comes to include repression in the strict Freudian sense, which anyway is structurally similar—its elements being (1) a wish, (2) the prohibition of that wish, (3) the refusal to both wish and prohibition of admission to consciousness, and (4) the persistence of both the wish and the defence against it in the unconscious. In this connection, Laing's paper 'Operations' in *The Politics of the Family* is very interesting as showing the parallelism between intrapersonal and transpersonal defences.

It is important to stress this in view of the tendency to excise the instincts from psychoanalytic theory and reduce the psychological to the social. The original contradiction may not be within the family, but between the family and the child's instinctual requirements. This seems structurally and effectively equivalent to double bind, but there is no binder—though sometimes God has been cast in this role, and conflicts between instinct and morality seen as the conflicting injunctions of God as creator and as law-giver. This view is expressed in Fulke Greville's poem 'Chorus Sacerdotum';

Oh wearisome Condition of Humanity!
Borne under one Law, to another bound:
Vainely begot, and yet forbidden vanity,
Created sicke, commanded to be sound.

Sometimes this theological double bind is explicitly recognized and used to reinforce the familiar ones. According to the puritan ideology of the Jones and Head families, described in the chapter on 'The Heads' in *Sanity, Madness and the Family*,

Passion must be suppressed before marriage, and outside marriage, and to a large extent inside marriage, but sufficient passion must be left, and sufficient potency effectively preserved, to beget children. One must think only clean thoughts, yet one must handle dirty children. . . . (the Jones) expressly define their spiritual-carnal human condition as a double-bind. (pp. 179–180)

If one is to understand this kind of untenable position without introducing God into the discussion—and incriminating him—one must give up the idea of accounting for all untenable positions as positions we are put in by someone.

One particular kind of untenable position—and one which is closely linked to the sort of cognitive oppression which Laing is so remorseless in unearthing, is that which results from attributions which are covert injunctions (see the chapter 'Attributions and Injunctions' in *Self and Others*). Here we have a confusion between two kinds of speech act, in order to disguise an imperative, (just as according to Freud a prohibited wish may be expressed in consciousness by a fear—e.g. 'Wouldn't it be terrible if my father stepped under a bus?'). Here it works at the level of transpersonal defences. There are plenty of—more or less harmless, if sometimes irritating—such transformations in polite usage, such as 'Would you like to do the washing up?' or 'What are the potatoes doing on the draining-board?' But more serious are the cases already mentioned of a son or daughter being told he or she does not have certain desires, as a means of being told not to have them.

Of course the person doing the attributing no doubt believes in the truth of the attribution, but often against all the evidence. They repress the thought of the truth about the other's desires in themselves, and attribute the opposite to the other person, inducing the other to perform a similar operation of repression of those desires. Thus everything is as if there were only one person involved, who was disavowing certain desires, yet in fact the disavowed desires are those of a separate individual from the one who originally felt compelled by his/her own ideals to disavow them.

Thus in the case of Jean Head (*née* Jones), her parents, who objected on fundamentalist religious grounds to their daughter wearing lipstick, going to the cinema and dances, going out with boys outside their denomination etc., could not admit to themselves that she wanted to do these things, and by assuming and when necessary asserting that she did not want to do them, induced her to feel guilty about them. This could have led to her repressing these desires, though in fact she did indulge some of them, though at the expense of splitting her personality.

We have seen that one crucial concept used in extending the notion of defences to transpersonal contexts is that of induction;

an attribution of the requisite qualities to induce a defence in another, backed up by emotional rewards for fitting the pattern and punishments for failing to live up to it. Thus:

A father says to his son who was being bullied at school and had pleaded to leave: 'I know you don't really want to leave, because no son of mine is a coward.' (*Self and Others*, pp. 154–55)

This mechanism of induction by attribution has a history of theoretical justification, as well as being so prevalent at the every-day level. The classical idealist philosophical justification of morality has been 'become what you are!': an ideal self (Kant's 'rational being') is set up (without any basis in the actually existing self); it is then asserted 'this (ideal self) is what you *really* are; live up to it!'—to which the correct answer is 'first thou tellest me a lie, then thou givest me an order'.

Likewise, educational theorists have urged that children should first be treated as responsible agents (i.e. punished) so that they will then become responsible agents—which really gives the game away about the justification of punishment in terms of responsibility.

A similar attribution occurs in the case of Jean Head. Her father says:

I think that's the one good thing that can emerge out of this experience. I mean people say, 'Now you've got to help youself,' and all this that and the other, well that may or may not be the case, but in *this* matter, I believe that the power to prevent it occurring again is in Jean's hands.

Laing comments:

The attribution of autonomy to someone who clearly is completely alienated from her autonomous self, by persons who are perpetuating this alienation, albeit unwittingly, is surely most mystifying. (*Sanity, Madness and the Family*, p. 186)

It is now possible to outline a typical Laingian case history of a young person who has been diagnosed schizophrenic and whose symptoms Laing shows to be socially intelligible. This

will enable us to pass on to an examination of the critical implications of Laing's work with respect to the family as it exists in
contemporary western societies, and the definitions of sanity and
madness prevalent in the psychiatric profession.

The typical victim is a young person who has not escaped his
or her family of origin—although in a number of cases the victim
has left home, and even been married. The disturbing factor has
always been conflicts arising from the nature of the internalized
family, and these can be made socially intelligible by relating this
'family' to the real family, and to the collective myths prevalent
in that family.

The family of origin has from the outset established a collusive
harmony—a shared self-image which has acquired a false objectivity, and disbelief in which is 'punished' in various interpersonal
defensive operations. The harmony as to familial self-image by
no means requires harmonious relations between members of
the family. In many cases the family was fraught with bitter
conflict; yet this conflict takes place in the context of shared
illusions, one of which might be that there is no conflict taking
place.

Each new member of the family—notably of course the future
patient—has been socialized into the world as defined by this
collective phantasy from birth on. An identity and role has been
pre-ordained for each recruit, which is a function of the collective self-image of the family. Various things contribute to the
defining of this identity—the projection of the unrealized possibilities of the parents onto the child, the mapping of a parent's
own relation to his or her own parents onto the relation with the
child, the identification of the child with a previous member of
the family (the child's uncle or grandparent), the substitution of
the child for an unsatisfactory marital partner, and so on.

Insofar as the child conforms to the pattern laid down for it
by the unconscious phantasies of the parents, it is rewarded by the
confirmation of its experience; insofar as its experience is discrepant with the family myths, it is disconfirmed. In this way,
systematic epistemological confusion is induced—the child is
taught to identify the real with the family myths, and is prevented

from developing the capacity to assess critically for itself the realities of the situation.

This mystifying socialization is fairly successful. But there remain desires which conflict with the induced self-image, and perceptions which conflict with the induced image of the family. The onset of puberty and the need for relationships independent of the family of origin sharpen this conflict—without achieving insight and independence of action, the young person's desires for a social and sexual life will be thwarted. But the road to such insight and action is blocked by mystifications, double-bind situations, etc. The desires which disturb the collusive equilibrium are dealt with by the family by denying their existence. Attempts by the victim to come to terms with these desires are disconfirmed. The attempts to break out of this unlivable situation are seen as 'bad' by the family. As the forms of expression of the excluded desires become less direct and more fantastic, this attribution (bad) gives way to 'mad'.

It is worth looking in greater detail at the typical progression of the victim as seen by the family through three stages 'Good—Bad—Mad'.

We must bear in mind that this is a process that has two sides to it: real changes in the behaviour of the individual concerned, and changes in the way this behaviour is interpreted by the family (this interpretation always having, among other functions, the function of preventing the destruction of the collusive self-image of the family). The real changes in the individual's behaviour are not necessarily the only causes of the change in the family's perceptions of them, and are often partly their effects.

'Good' here, as already noted, is used in that peculiar negative sense in which e.g. a good dog is not a lively, healthy specimen of a dog, but a lifeless creature which does not budge from its box except for a daily walk at the heel of its master. This use of the word 'good' is quite a common one in our culture, particularly when referring to children.

Julie was never a demanding baby. She was weaned without difficulty.

Her mother had no bother with her from the day she took off nappies completely when she was fifteen months old. She was never 'a trouble'. She always did what she was told.

These are the mother's basic generalizations in support of the view that Julie was always a 'good' child.

Now, this is the description of a child who has in some way never come alive: for a really alive baby is demanding, is a trouble, and by no means always does what she is told. (*The Divided Self*, pp. 182–83)

Later, 'good' will come to mean fitting into the role in the family assigned by the phantasy of its senior members. This goodness is expected to extend not only to actions but to desires. Awareness of desires in the child which are alien to this phantasy is repressed (in the strict psychoanalytical sense of 'repression', i.e. excluded from their own consciousness) by the parents, who *thereby* induce the child to repress them.

The trouble is that goodness in this sense is itself an 'untenable position'. It involves acceptance of total definition of the individual in terms of his or her relation to the family. Such acceptance is possible (though still impoverishing) for the parents in a family; for the children it means the inability to grow up, to establish separate social and sexual relationships, etc. The existence of the family obviously is dependent on the parents' having left their families of origin, but it is in certain families as if this fact has been repressed. Indeed, in several of the families described, the parents seem to have managed to found a family without ever really 'leaving home'. For the Danzigs for instance, their marriage seems to have been based on respect for their own parents rather than on the nature of their own relationship and feelings (see chapter two of *The Leaves of Spring*). Or again, Mrs. Church 'rebelled against her own mother, once' (*Sanity, Madness and the Family*, p. 91). She took a holiday alone for the first time in her life when her daughter was nineteen, despite her mother's attempts to stop her.

It is important to note the two related aspects of this 'good' phase of the child as seen by the parents (as also the equivalent aspects of the other phases)—as a parental requirement and as a parental perception. It can never be purely a realistic perception, for to be perfectly good in this sense one would have to be dead. But in overt behaviour and even in conscious experience the parents may well be able to induce this 'goodness' in a child as long as it remains a child.

At puberty it becomes necessary for the son or daughter to break out of this 'goodness', but any attempt to do so is defined as bad by the family. The needs to question the family's outlook and form relationships outside the family are seen as interlopers which destroy a beautiful harmony—not just as bad but as per-verse, evil. It is required of the children that they grow up *without changing anything*—a double-bind situation, for failure to grow up is condemned as childishness, (as when parents in Laing's accounts reproach their son or daughter for not going out and making friends while at the same time discouraging any actual attempt to do so. This is of course rationalized in terms of approving only the 'right sort' of friends, which generally turn out to be a non-existent sort, or at least a sort not acceptable to the young person.) Real attempts to act in the independent ways necessary for such growing up are precisely what is seen as bad and perverse.

The 'goodness' involved here is very close to sentimentality i.e. the refusal to recognize the contradictions within an apparent equilibrium that must disturb it and compel it to change. People who are sentimental in this sense will react with extreme, often surprising violence (for it seems out of character with their 'innocence') when their picture of harmony is upset. They see no reason why it could not go on for ever, and see the disturber as an invader to be destroyed, not as the representative of an inner necessity to develop. Sartre describes 'good people' in this way in his book *Saint Genet*, which is discussed by David Cooper in Laing and Cooper's *Reason and Violence*.

For the good people, goodness is equated with being, with that which already is, and evil with that which calls being in question, with nega-tion, non-being, otherness. The argument cannot be reproduced here in detail, but essentially it is this: the 'good man' perpetually denies the negative moment of his actions. He affirms without denying the contrary of that which he affirms. His permitted actions are to main-

E

tain, to conserve, to restore, to renew. These are the categories of re-
petition as opposed to those of change. But the spirit, as Hegel says,
is unrest, and this unrest inspires the good man with horror. He then
cuts off from his freedom its negative moment and projects it outside
himself. In this the good man becomes himself the most abstract negation, the negation of his own negation.

The wicked man is an invention of the good man, the incarnation
of his otherness to what he is, his own negative moment. All evil, for
Sartre, is projection. (pp. 72–73)

It is easy to see that such 'goodness' is parasitic on 'evil', contrary to the conventional way of seeing these matters.

Now when the necessary stage of independence from the
family of origin and the establishment of outside relationships
is reached in adolescence, the 'good' child has a particularly
difficult problem. In the first place, because the wrench from
past dependences will be greater; but also in that this process
as perceived by the parents will be different again. It will be a
sudden, inexplicable transition from good child to bad adolescent. The whole armoury of interpersonal defences will be
brought into operation against the young person. If it succeeds
in suppressing the 'badness' there is only one outcome for the
victim: he or she must achieve illusory gratification of the frus-
trated attempt to become self-determining, while actually con-
forming, in a negative way, to the parental requirements. I say
in a negative way, because the result is not always pleasing to
them. The attacks on the parental phantasy-system must still be
made, but they will themselves be within phantasy—a conflicting
phantasy, though one which is likely to have drawn its elements
from the parental phantasy-system. These mystified attacks and
illusory gratifications are the basis of the third attribution—
'mad'.

It is tempting to relate these stages, good-bad-mad, to Freud's
account of neurosis, psychosis and normalcy in his paper 'The
Loss of Reality in Neurosis and Psychosis' (*Collected Papers*,
vol. II pp. 277–82). In the case of the 'good' child, like the
neurotic in Freud's account, 'the ego, in virtue of its allegiance
to reality, suppresses a part of the *id* (the life of instinct)'. In the

'mad' stage, as in psychosis according to Freud, the ego 'in the service of the *id*, withdraws itself from a part of reality', and then tries to 'make good the loss of reality, not however at the expense of a restriction laid on the *id*—as in neurosis at the expense of the relation with reality—but in another, more lordly manner, by creating a new reality which is no longer open to objections like that which has been forsaken'—i.e. it builds an illusory 'reality'. The 'bad' stage, whose suppression by the parents has led to this last solution, coincides very well with what Freud describes as follows: 'A reaction which combines features of both these is the one we call normal or "healthy"; it denies reality as little as neurosis, but then, like a psychosis, is concerned with effecting a change in it.'

It should be clear from this that the task of the psychotherapist is not to take sides with the 'mad' behaviour of the patient, but with the 'bad' behaviour. The parents come to the doctor expecting him to restore a 'mad' young adult to the state of a 'good' child; but the real 'cure' is a restoration to the state of a 'bad' adolescent, who then stands a genuine chance of breaking away from the family phantasy and its restraints on his/her behaviour.

I think we can also see from this account that we should not interpret the attribution 'mad' as a mere change of response by threatened parents to continued 'bad' behaviour, the more effectively to suppress it; rather it is a response to a genuine change of behaviour for the worse (in terms of the subject's own rationality), which change however is a result of their transpersonal defences against healthy 'bad' behaviour.

Chapter *4*

The Contradictions of the Family

Let the ruler be ruler, the minister minister, the father father, and the son son. (Confucius, *Analects*, XII, 11)

When the great Tao is lost, spring forth benevolence and righteousness.

When wisdom and sagacity arise, there are great hypocrites.

When family relations are no longer harmonious, we have filial children and devoted parents.

When a nation is in confusion and disorder, patriots are recognized.

(Lao Tzu, *Tao Te Ching*. Quoted by Laing in *The Politics of Experience*, p. 63)

Laing and his colleagues were not the first to investigate the relation of the family to schizophrenia, or to generalize from such investigations to a theory of the role of the family in society at large. The specific characteristics of the Laingian account can be illuminated by contrasting it with that of Theodore Lidz.

Lidz, in *The Family and Human Adaptation*, also starts from an admirable awareness of the role of the family in producing personalities of a kind well suited to the form of society in question. Though he uses the term 'the scientific era' for what would better be described as 'capitalism' (for he does not discuss possible alternative societies of a similar level of technology—i.e. socialism), much of his account of society/family/individual relations cannot be faulted. What he avoids raising even implicitly however, is the question whether the fact that a given type of family is functional in a given society is necessarily a justification of that type of family.

Having put forward the (reasonable enough) view that the nuclear family is the sort best suited to the 'scientific era', he describes the strain this type of family puts on individuals, and the crisis it is undergoing. But the solution he indicates places the burden of responsibility squarely on the shoulders of individuals. The crisis is blamed on feminist wives who want the same opportunities as men, irresponsible husbands who want to relax in the evening, disrespectful children, and 'hedonists' of all ages and both sexes, who put pleasure before commitment to moral principles. The re-affirmation of sex roles and generation roles is prescribed. All this is within a liberal rather than an overtly authoritarian context; excessive authoritarianism in the family is also condemned as leading to a personality-structure dangerous to democracy. Sex roles are supposed to be equal but different. One cannot doubt that there is a humane concern for individual problems. Lidz is far closer to Laing than to the mainstream of medical psychiatry. Yet it is simply assumed that, if the kind of family best suited to our civilization is destructive of the happiness of individuals, it is the individual that must adapt, not civilization that must be changed, and hence that the requisite reform of the family must consist in individuals adapting to their roles of mother, father and child.

At times the tone does become alarmist. Decline of a civilization is said to follow 'the deterioration of its family life and the ensuing blurring of cultural traditions'. The cause and cure of this 'deterioration' are seen in moral rather than social terms.

The superego, with its moral and ethical injunctions derived from internalization of parental guidance and authority, enables long-range adaptation through guiding beyond the moment to more enduring objectives and to gaining pleasure from the esteem and affection of others. (p. 34)

At the end of the chapter, it is optimistically assumed that the crisis is not so deep that goodwill cannot overcome it.

If Laing, with his quotes from Lao Tzu and his tendency to see whatever is the result of social conditioning as evil, sometimes appears as a modern Taoist, there is a lot of justification for seeing Lidz as a modern Confucian, basing his ethics on Confucius' principle of the Rectification of Names—that a father should *be* a father, a woman should be a woman etc., i.e. that everyone should live according to their socially assigned roles. Obviously enough, this morality is an essentially conservative one—it has an aura of commonsense, even of logical necessity about it, while ruling out any radical challenge to existing values. A similar conservativism is often attributed to Freud— incorrectly. In fact one of the most striking things about reading non-radical post-Freudians after reading Freud is the unself-conscious way they use terms such as 'repression' and 'superego' as denoting highly valuable cultural achievements. For Freud these concepts had no moral connotations for or against; but they certainly denote mechanisms and structures of irrationality —perhaps necessary in the development of an individual, but involving lack of self-awareness and restrictive symptoms in adult life. An analyst would be Utopian to hope to eliminate these phenomena, but analysis can only dissolve rather than reinforce them. In post-Freudian literature on the other hand, it is just as often the absence of one of the defence-mechanisms which is lamented.

Laing on the contrary is refreshingly conscious of the fact that to promote self-awareness is not necessarily to promote a socially acceptable life-style. Indeed it often seems that the fact that a role is socially assigned is itself an argument against it in Laing's eyes.

Yet of course the fact that the nuclear-patriarchal family is the type of family best adapted to capitalism is no argument against it. One who held Lidz's view might very well reply, 'Under socialism you might develop better forms of family—well and good. But for the present, we must make the system best adapted to our present society work. To try to live as one might in a socialist society would be as quixotic under capitalism as the attempt to live like a feudal knight. And incidentally, someone whose capacity to cope with life has been shattered by a "skewed" family background will be of little use in the struggle for socialism.'[1]

Now there is nothing intrinsically wrong with this argument; the question is one of fact: is it the nuclear-patriarchal family as such that causes the damage, or only particular 'skewed' families that fail to conform to its norms?

Laing's account of family contexts of madness and of the effects of transpersonal defences in the family in general, insofar as it implies a critique of the contemporary family, does so by exposing the damage that family does to individuals, not by showing its role in the reproduction of capitalist society; and insofar as capitalism comes in for criticism, it is because it requires the existence of such families which oppress the individual. This is the correct way round: if capitalism is to be opposed, it is because it does not deliver the goods. If the nuclear patriarchal family is to be opposed, it is because it frustrates people's desires and limits their possibilities, not on extraneous political grounds.

In order to decide between the opposing views about the family, we need to answer the question whether the damage documented by Laing is due to the family-structure or to some other factor. To locate the cause is to locate the solution. Are we to trace neurotic and psychotic misery to human agency (bad parents) and propose a moralistic solution? Or to a bad system, and propose a political solution? This question has to be asked also in the context of tensions within Laing's work itself, but at present I will only be concerned with the differences between Laing and (for instance) Lidz.

But we are running ahead. For Laing actually says very little about what is wrong with 'the family' and how to remedy it. He merely documents the mess a number of families make of the lives of their members, and shows how the transpersonal defences built into these families figure in the explanation of this mess.

To show the force of this point: a friend with whom I was discussing Laing said that a book should be written on 'sanity, madness and the commune'. Now I have no doubt whatsoever that the commune as a domiciliary unit can be as oppressive and as fraught with tensions as the family, and probably, on average, communes come off worse in this respect. But communes exist in a society in which the nuclear patriarchal family predominates, and are composed for the most part of individuals raised in such families. The pathology of the commune can therefore only be understood in terms of the contemporary family. (Just as there really are families in which the mother is in all senses the dominant individual; yet the way that these work can only be understood in terms of the patriarchate. They do not refute the view that patriarchy prevails in our society, they merely illustrate the complexity of its effects.)

If, as is commonly said of Laing, his main thesis were that one's current experience of relationships—not one's past— accounts for one's psychopathology, then he would actually be in a far worse position to undertake a critique of the nuclear patriarchal family, in its specific difference from other micro-social structures, than would a purely individual-oriented psychoanalyst.[2]

While Laing's work on the family contexts of 'madness' (and of defective normality) will be useful in any critical analysis of the contemporary family, the reasons for concentrating on the *family* in this connection rather than on any other micro-social group, will lie in the more traditional concerns of psychoanalysis —the Oedipus Complex and the Unconscious. As I have said, I do not believe this psychoanalytical dimension is lacking in Laing's thought, as is evidenced most clearly by the essays collected in *The Politics of the Family*, from which I have already quoted at some length.

Now if there were nothing in Laing's account of family

pathology but a theory of the origins of schizophrenia, it would not necessarily be of much help in discussing the family as such. But in fact he implies that similar transpersonal defences to those he invokes to explain schizophrenia exist also in other families, and likewise have effects which are destructive to the happiness, insight and potentialities of the members of these families, though these members never come to be regarded as 'mentally ill'. The question which interests him most, I think, is not 'What are the relevant differences between schizogenic and normal families?', but how the same structures of transpersonal defences within families produce madness in some, and a mystified, stunted normality in others.

I have now made three points which, taken together, might lead one to ask why one should look for a critique of the prevailing form of family in Laing's work at all, i.e. (1) that this critique is not explicit, (2) that the specifically Laingian contribution to such a critique concerns the structure of small, close groups in general, not only families, and (3) that most of Laing's accounts of families are of disturbed ones.

To take the last point first: if Laing has established certain qualitative characteristics of 'disturbed' families, without which the specific qualitative characteristics of the disturbance cannot be understood, and if these characteristics can be found in other families as well, this does not vitiate his account—it merely requires some further (perhaps quantitative) factor to explain why some people are pushed over the limits into 'madness', while the rest of us remain merely neurotic. Of course Freudian psychoanalysis already has exactly the same problem, as I suspect all the 'human' sciences do. That a general problem is writ large in the most overtly 'pathological' cases means that pathological phenomena repay investigation best. An *ad hoc* theory which explained only the pathological working of a system, and took its normal functioning as not requiring explanation, would be hopelessly unscientific. Something analogous is true in the physical sciences; Newton did not assume that all the while the apple stayed on the tree, the law of gravity did not hold. What is peculiar to sciences with objects which are in part composed of meanings is that explanation is often justified even where measurement is inapplicable.

Of the second point, the following can be said: the pathology of any relationship can only be understood in terms of the phantasies through which the participants see that relationship; and in each case this phantasy is largely a mapping of situations experienced in the family of origin onto the current situation; Freud and Laing are in agreement on this matter too.

These points already take us some way towards showing what sort of critique of the present family structure can be derived from Laing. If the pathology of all relationships is the result of the structure of families, the only questions to be asked are: What structure? Of all families, or only some?

Perhaps the best way to start sorting out the critical import of various findings about family pathology is by classifying the different sorts of contradiction which occur in connection with the families described. It is possible to distinguish:

(1) Contradictions internal to the structure of a given family. These are mainly of two types, (a) contradictions between family reality and family phantasy, and (b) contradictory requirements placed on the members of the family, particularly its junior members. The latter contradictions generally stem from the former.

(2) Contradictions between family requirements and the instinctual needs of the members—e.g. the denial of the sexuality of a son or daughter.

(3) Contradictions between the values prevalent in the family and those prevalent in the 'outside world', either as it really is, or as it is in the collective phantasy system of the family.

I think I am justified in saying that both Lidz and Laing would recognize the existence and possible role in producing neurosis and psychosis of all these types of contradiction. But I think they would disagree about the cause of these contradictions, and about what could be done to resolve them.

This disagreement is at the 'political' level. But having said that I must reassert: it can only be resolved at the level of fact. It is not that Laing and Lidz are agreed about the facts but have different 'value-judgements'. It would be all too easy to say: Lidz likes people who act out their traditional roles in the family, Laing prefers those who are fairly free of such role-determined behaviour. I have no idea whether either of these statements is true, and anyway if either Lidz or Laing were led by his likes and dislikes to make statements about the cause, cure and prophylaxis of neurosis and psychosis, he would be scientifically out of court. Which 'value-judgement' is correct depends on whose assessment of the facts is correct. But the factual question at issue is a political one in the sense that it is about the social causes of disturbed families, rather than the familial causes of disturbed individuals.

For it seems to be the case that, for both these psychiatrists, the disturbing family is typically one which is turned in on itself, in which there are relations of emotional dependence between the generations, and which fosters suspicion among its members of the world outside. Both would see various inadequacies in the other family members as being at the root of the untenable situation of the patient.

Take for instance the following passage from *Sanity, Madness and the Family*:

Mrs Blair said that her husband watched over all Lucie's movements, required her to account for every minute she spent outside the house, told her that if she went out alone she would be kidnapped, raped or murdered. She tried to bring some friends home when she was in her teens, but her father snubbed them, and ridiculed her. (p. 55)

There is a footnote to this passage:

We remind the reader once more that we are fully alive to the inferences to which these facts point, namely Mr Blair's struggles with his unconscious incestuous feelings towards Lucie, her mother's jealousy of Lucie and her husband, and Lucie's own sexual attachment to her father.

Here we have dependence of the father on the daughter, requiring reciprocation, and above all the self-enclosure of the family and hostility to the outside world. This same self-enclosure can be seen in most of the families described by

Laing and Esterson. (For example, the Churches' dislike of 'crowds', i.e. social gatherings.) In effect, most of the young women in that book had been trained never to trust people outside the family. Such families are clearly dysfunctional so far as the social function of the family as an agency of socialization is concerned. A family whose progeny are trapped in the parental home, unable to mix socially, to do productive work, start families of their own and so on, is a family which has failed in the task assigned to it by the social structure.

Now a therapist confronted with a patient from such a family will attempt to restore—or perhaps build up for the first time—that patient's ability to establish a life and relationships independent of his or her family. In doing so, he is acting in the interests of society as well as of the individual concerned —whatever he may think about society; and this fact should not bother him, any more than a doctor should be worried about the fact that the worker he has cured can now go back to work and be exploited. Indeed a psychotherapist may come up against society in his service to his patients. But if *discrepancies* between familial and societal norms are, in many cases, involved in the production of schizophrenia, it will not be a simple matter of taking sides with the patient against all comers, but possibly of taking sides with those elements in the patient which would make for a satisfying life in the wider world, against those elements in the patient which would keep him or her trapped within the confines of the family.

Is the psychotherapist then to be simply another agent of socialization, a safety net for those whom the family has failed to prepare for life in society? If so, should we not accept Lidz's account rather than Laing's? I do not think so. For according to Laing, irrationalities within the family (and this must include the third group listed above) can only be understood in terms of the wider social context. If the family cannot comply with the requirements placed on it by society, that is because these requirements are themselves such that, under certain conditions, they are mutually contradictory. The family itself is put in an untenable position. So much can be inferred from Laing's own statements (e.g. that already quoted from his lecture 'The Obvious', pp. 74–75 above).

Capitalist society produces an 'enforced privatization', a self-enclosure of the family, and sometimes it does so in a way which is too successful for its own good. If the families described by Laing 'fail' to achieve the required degree of socialization in their progeny, they fail in the way that a laxative fails if it causes severe diarrhoea.

Families are supposed to rear a new generation the members of which will be deferent to their superiors as to their parents, and will compensate by dominating their subordinates and their own children; who will feel guilty if they prefer pleasure to work; and who will not be too imaginative or too critical. Yet the same people must be able to adapt to new work-situations, learn new techniques, get on with different sorts of people. A manager of a factory, explaining why he did not want university graduates working for him, said he wanted 'intelligent' people—who could learn and adapt quickly, but not 'intellectuals'—who often found mindless work boring, and were critical and spread discontent. One of the problems of contemporary capitalism is its need to produce generations of workers who have 'intelligence' (so defined) in the high degree required by modern industrial life, yet as little as possible 'intellectuality'. This is not an easy task, and some of the recent controversies about education have reflected these conflicting needs of capitalist industry. But the other great preparatory school for exploitation—the family—is placed under the strains of this contradiction as well, in a way which is no less explosive for being less conscious.

The type of family described by Laing, he calls the nexified family. Using the notions of the 'family' (internalized family) and mapping, which I have discussed in the last chapter, Laing says:

The internalization of a set of relations by each element of the set transforms the nature of the elements, their relations, and the set, into a group of a very special kind . . . Co-inherence compounded by reciprocal mapping of the 'family' of each onto the common family leads to what I have called *nexification* of the family. Such nexified families may become relatively closed systems; they are seen again and again in studying families of people diagnosed as schizophrenic. (*The Politics of the Family*, p. 18)

Now this is a description, in terms of social phenomenology, of the nuclear patriarchal family itself, in an accentuated form. A family of a more open structure, in which both generations had more 'significant others' in their lives, would presumably produce a different character-structure—less dependent on particular individuals (whether real or internalized) and hence freer (without having to resort to the narcissistic illusion of freedom from emotional dependence on *any* others). This would seem to be the prophylaxis indicated by Laing's writings. It is a programme which would come into conflict with the dominant ideology in our society, but that is another question.

It should be clear from the last chapter that a degree of nexification (as defined in the above quote) will be present in all families. In the nexified families of Laing's patients, it presumably lacks a countervailing force which mitigates its effects in other families—it is possible here to study nexification in the raw, as it were. This is another example of the methodological primacy of the pathological, a principle of inquiry which should always be observed in the human sciences. Just as Marx finds a special symptomatic importance in branches of industry without legal limits to exploitation, not for polemical reasons, but because they illustrate the economic dynamic of capitalism, in abstraction from the partial political remedies which can only be understood on the assumption of that dynamic; so the key to the understanding of the effects of nexification in the contemporary family in general can be found in the study of the families in which this nexification is manifest. The absence of laboratory conditions of experiment in the social sciences makes these cases in which the variables not under consideration are relatively weak, of particular value in defining the abstractions peculiar to those sciences—e.g. nexification.

Now the nuclear family is composed of members of two sexes and two generations. This is of course true of many other groups, but the nuclear family is constituted by this composition.

In every individual's internalized family, there will be places for mother, father, self (son or daughter), and possibly other sons and daughters (brothers and sisters). The structure of the Oedipus complex within societies with a nuclear patriarchal type of family will be determined accordingly. Relationships with parents will be mapped onto all future relationships, even though they are with members of one's own generation. The socially required dominance of the father will also be reflected in the internalized family. A major determinant of the plight of any individual will be the place of that individual on the axes of sex and generation. This applies both to one's real situation and to the phantasy through which it is seen, in which the image of the self has a definite place in the internalized family.

How are the effects of this division of mankind by sex and generation reflected in Laing's work? In the first place, by his emphasis on the family—the group in which these divisions are constitutive—rather than on other micro-social groups—an emphasis which can be justified psychoanalytically, though not within social phenomenology.

But I am concerned here with the *differences* of the effects of the nuclear patriarchal family on individuals according to sex and generation. In this connection, it can be noted that Laing's studies are in almost every case motivated by a disturbance 'in' a member of the younger generation, in relation to the relevant family. This is no accident; a parent in one of the families described in *Sanity, Madness and the Family* would have to be understood in relation to his or her parents. There is an important asymmetry between a family-context explanation of the experience and behaviour of a son or daughter, and that of a parent. For the son or daughter, explanation in terms of past history would be explanation in terms of relationships with the same people as are currently significant. Even here, these relationships as prolonged processes are not simple continuities: the parents as experienced earlier are mapped onto the presently experienced parents, who are therefore perceived through an image of past experiences of them. And neither the psychoanalyst nor the social phenomenologist has access (as a general rule) to reliable biographical data, but are rather dependent on (and concerned with) present residues of the past in the minds of the individuals. But in studying the social phenomenology of a family, one may well be able to make inferences which one could not have done from the analysis of the 'patient' alone; witness the following passage concerning the interactions between Maya Abbott and her parents in her teens:

She was frightened that her parents knew that she had sexual thoughts about them. She tried to tell them about this, but they told her *she did not have any thoughts of that kind.* She told them she masturbated *and they told her that she did not.* What happened then is of course inferred, but *when she told her parents in the presence of the interviewer that she still masturbated, her parents simply told her that she did not*! (*Sanity, Madness and the Family*, pp. 41–42)

In understanding the behaviour of parents, on the other hand, there will be far more reference to internalized others whose real prototypes are no longer in the family-unit, and possibly are no longer alive. Laing appears to become progressively more concerned about the fact that the parents' parents are no longer available for interview in many cases. (Esterson's *The Leaves of Spring* is the fullest account from this point of view which has emerged from Laingian circles.)

Very often Laing shows himself to be far from unsympathetic to the parents in the families he describes—or, for that matter, to their parents. But necessarily, the parents are generally doomed to play the villains' role, and provided that the moralistic search for a culprit is avoided, this is unobjectionable. For the parents, though equally victims of the nexified family, hold the position of its preservers and enforcers. The psychotherapist must take sides with the young person in the struggle (which often indeed takes the distorted form of the 'illness') to break free of the family; the parents cannot see this struggle as other than 'illness'—unless, that is, they see it as wicked. The process of becoming independent from one's parents is probably always painful, both for the young person and for the parents; but failure to achieve this independence is always destruction. It would therefore be quite incorrect to see Laing's advocacy of intervention in the battle of the generations against the parents as simply a romantic attitude; it is absolutely scientifically justified, and does not imply any bent for moralizing (though as I have said, the notion of 'praxis' in this context is potentially moralistic).[3]

On the division into men and women, and the assignment by our social order of different roles to them, Laing is less explicit. He has come in for criticism for blaming the mother rather than the father for the family situations he describes (e.g. the mothers are given far more interviewing time in the sessions recorded in *Sanity, Madness and the Family*). But attributing blame is irrelevant here, and it is presumably true that in society as at present constituted, the mother is assigned a greater role in the upbringing of the children, and is also, more than the father, the agent of preservation of the unity and 'nexification' of the family (though of course the father is pre-eminently the agent of authoritarian discipline, of which more later).

The specific predicaments of the sexes are not analyzed explicitly by Laing in the way that the specific predicaments of the generations are. At a purely impressionistic level, it is notable that most of the women in Laing's accounts are victims of a crowding-in process, of continuing interference by their parents at the time of treatment, of lack of breathing space in their relations with other people, whereas most of the men are socially rather isolated and dominated by internal parents rather than external ones. I do not know whether there is any statistical basis for this, but it could reflect on the one hand the fact that in our society parents are expected to 'look after' their daughters to a greater degree (and longer) than their sons, and hence that unconsciously incestuous relations between fathers and their adolescent daughters are more socially acceptable than between mothers and sons; and on the other hand the ideology of male independence (and its material basis in the greater work opportunities available to men), and the fact that men are lumbered with the role of sexual initiators, and so on.

But one should not expect to find a theoretical basis for

women's liberation and the de-structuring of sex-roles in Laing's work, for these programmes cannot be carried out purely at the micro-social level. They must be worked out also at the macro-social level of political and economic life, and at the level of the unconscious, which, while its specific structure in any society is an effect of the family-structure of that society, has a life of its own, and cannot be transformed simply by transforming micro-social structures. The effects of patriarchy and the nuclear family on the relations between the sexes are far more complex and involuted than the effects on the relations between the genera-tions. It is with respect to this latter set of relations that Laing's work helps most to theorize the struggle for self-emancipation of those trapped in unlivable family situations. Armed with a knowledge of intra-familial relations and mystification such as can be found in Laing's work, a young person will be far more able to escape from such mystification, and liberate him- or herself from parental domination than would be the case without such knowledge. In this sense, Laing's works themselves are part of the prophylaxis of neurosis and psychosis.

Women are not the only group oppressed by authoritarianism and mystification in the family, or by the nuclear-patriarchal family itself, and the feminist movement is not the only force opposed to these structures. I do not see any basis for the charges of sexism occasionally levelled at Laing, but one should not expect to find the theoretical basis for feminism in his work. His criticism of the contemporary family is not opposed to that of the feminists, but it is distinct from it.

I now come to one of the rare passages in Laing in which he explicitly raises the question of the place of the family and its effects on the individual in the society as a whole—and does so partly in direct criticism of Lidz. This occurs in the essay 'The Mystification of Experience' in *The Politics of Experience*. Un-fortunately, this is an essay not only *on* but also *in* the mystifica-tion of experience, insofar as it moves between perceptive criticism of the ideology surrounding the family, and suggestions of a cosmic disaster underlying all our problems.

Laing starts by attacking the tone of Lidz's discussion of the

family. Things are much worse than Lidz allows for: in particular, the 'normal' individual who is for Lidz the successful
product of the family is for Laing infinitely short of the potential
individual: Laing speaks of 'the frightened, cowed, abject creature that we are admonished to be, if we are to be normal',
He adds:

Behind this language lurks the terror that is behind all this mutual
back-scratching, this esteem-, status-, support-, protection-, security-
giving and getting. Through its bland urbanity the cracks still show.

In our world we are 'victims burning at the stake, signalling through
the flames', but to Lidz *et al.* things go blandly on. 'Contemporary
life requires adaptability' (pp. 54–55)

I have said that the disagreement between Laing and Lidz is
political: this is so in that Laing holds out the possibility that
human beings have far greater potentialities than are allowed to
develop by the conditioning process imposed by contemporary
society—and if we have such potentialities, this implies that
there could be a society in which these could be realized, a
society with radically different methods of socialization. On the
questions how the change is to be brought about, or what it
would entail in political terms (in the narrower sense), Laing has
little to say; there is no reason why he should say more—he is a
psychoanalyst, not a political leader. But he does have something to say about the psychological requisites of this change,
and it is important not to take these as a sufficient condition of
the necessary change. It is important that the analysis of the ill
effects of the social structures on the individual should remain
open towards the politics which could transform these structures.
On the relation of micro- to macro-politics I shall say more in
chapter 6.

There is one weakness in Laing's position, in his, in many
ways, admirable polemic against Lidz *et al.* In order no doubt to
be as provocative as possible, he says:

Lidz calls schizophrenia a failure of human adaptation. In that case,
this too is a value-judgement. Or is anyone going to say that this is an
objective fact? Very well, let us call schizophrenia a successful attempt

not to adapt to pseudo social realities. Is this also an objective fact?
(p. 57)

Certainly one should not regard Laing as urging the latter
definition on us, but the picture here and throughout *The
Politics of Experience* is of a straight fight between repressive
society and the individual seeking to escape its repression; to
the extent that one succeeds, the other fails. This is another instance, I think, of Laing slipping into an idealist dialectic, such
as I described above (in Chapter 1). The ill effects of a process
which is socially functional—the process of socialization/indoc-
trination—are seen as the success of that process; actually they
constitute a failure, though an inevitable failure given the system.
The *function* of the agencies of socialization is to produce people
who will fit their roles in capitalist society well. That this also
represses everybody and destroys some is a *side-effect*—one
which is more important from the standpoint of the individual's
happiness (with which the psychotherapist is concerned) than
from that of the well-being of 'society' (i.e. capitalism).

The possibility of a different, non-pathogenic and non-
repressive organization of micro-social structures is, throughout
Laing's work, a hope rather than a theoretically worked out
programme.

The most valuable part of Laing's contribution to the criticism
of the contemporary family is that which is implicit in his concrete family case-studies. We may not know exactly what form
of micro-social institution we want; we know it will be one
without the authoritarianism, self-enclosure, suspicion and
mystification that has been documented so thoroughly by Laing
and his colleagues.

Chapter 5

Defining Sanity and Madness

The choice of words

One of the things that 'everybody knows' about Laing is that he says that there is no such thing as madness. Like most things that everybody knows, this is not quite true; what he actually says is more complex, but also not necessarily completely clear and consistent. In the first place, his views on this matter seem to change throughout his literary career, always, it must be conceded, in the direction of greater scepticism about the distinction between sanity and madness. Secondly, there are a number of different sceptical statements, which are often taken to say essentially the same thing, but which should be distinguished.

To start with his first book, the second chapter of *The Divided Self* is called 'The existential-phenomenological foundations for the understanding of psychosis'. Throughout that book, Laing uses the terms 'psychosis', 'schizophrenia' etc. quite unselfconsciously without questioning their usefulness.

The chapter starts with the observation that the language in which psychosis is described in psychiatric literature is a 'vocabulary of denigration'—*failure* of adjustment, *lack* of insight, etc.

Laing notes that the denigration is not moralistic, does not attribute responsibility and blame. He does not, he says, entirely object to this vocabulary:

Indeed I feel we should be more frank about the judgements we implicitly make when we call someone psychotic. When I certify someone insane, I am not equivocating when I write that he is of unsound mind, may be dangerous to himself and others, and requires care and attention in a mental hospital. (*The Divided Self*, p. 27)

As against this, he sets three points; that some clinically sane people are as deluded and as dangerous as any 'madman'; that some 'delusions' of the insane may turn out to be true after all; and that 'the cracked mind of the schizophrenic may *let in* light which does not enter the intact minds of many sane people whose minds are closed'. We will meet all these points again and none of them are inconsistent with Laing's general position in this book, which accepts at least the descriptive accuracy of labels such as 'sane', 'mad', 'schizoid', 'schizophrenic'.

Yet Laing also confesses to a personal difficulty which he has as a psychiatrist:

This is that except in the case of chronic schizophrenics I have difficulty in actually discovering the 'signs and symptoms' of psychosis in the persons I am myself interviewing. (p. 28)

That the exception is to be taken seriously can be seen from his later reference to 'that uncanny "praecox feeling" described by the German clinicians, i.e. of being in the presence of another human being and yet feeling that there was no one there' (p. 195) which Laing experienced with his patient 'Julie', and which he claims is the appropriate audience response to Ophelia, who is 'undoubtedly a schizophrenic'.

But what I want to discuss first in connection with Laing's qualified acceptance of psychiatric terms relating to psychosis in *The Divided Self* is his rejection of euphemistic intent in his assertion that 'we should be more frank about the judgements we implicitly make'. For euphemism is a phenomenon of the first ideological importance, and nowhere is it more rampant

than in psychiatric matters. Furthermore, the mechanisms behind euphemism are also behind what I take to be the misreading
of Laing on this matter.

People use euphemisms, of course, to avoid insulting people.
But what is it that makes a word an insult? Generally, its *meaning*. A man will be insulted if you call him a coward, because
cowardice is an undesirable, or at least socially disapproved,
quality to have. Finding another *word* than 'coward', without
changing what is meant, will not diminish the insult.

Where there is disagreement about the desirability of a quality, there will often be more than one word for the same quality,
carrying different appraisals—e.g. differences over sexual morality are reflected in the verbal alternatives 'pure' or 'prudish', etc.
But where, in such cases, there is a purely descriptive term, its
avoidance is equally derogatory whether the intention is insult
or euphemism. Racial euphemisms for example, by avoiding
calling a member of a race by the name of that race, imply the
undesirability of membership of that race. To take an archaic
example, to call a Scot a 'North Briton' obviously implies that a
Scot is a very unpleasant thing to be, so that it would be offen-
sive to draw attention to somone's Scottishness; and it is hard to
imagine a worse insult than that.

Of course euphemism serves a useful function in politics: it is
an easy way out for the sort of politician who believes in 'human
dignity' rather than in securing the material pre-requisites of
human dignity. It is always easier to restyle old people 'senior
citizens' than to increase their pensions, or to substitute the term
'rate-aided person of unsound mind' for 'pauper lunatic' than to
improve the mental health services.

If a change in terminology does not reflect a real change in the
way we conceive of and act towards the realities to which the
terminology refers, it simply results in the new word coming to
have the old meaning. Thus when medical terms replaced moral
ones in referring to 'madness', the medical terms became charged
with moral overtones—'sick' came to be a term of condemnation. This is not because of any intrinsic moral bias in medicine,
but because of the survival of moralistic ideology among those

who use the medical terminology. Ideology is a sea which salts every stream that flows into it.

It is worth looking at some of the ways ordinary language has appropriated psychoanalytical notions and sucked them into the morass of commonsense ideology. This reflects a refusal to accept the central discovery of psychoanalysis—that a symptom's causation can be mental and meaningful without being conscious or voluntary.

The non-assimilation of this discovery is behind the popular usage of 'neurotic' to mean 'hypochondriac'—the idea that mental 'illness' is somehow a fake, that mental suffering is self-pity and deserves no sympathy. Probably the majority of people would be insulted if their doctor suggested that a physical symptom from which they were suffering had psychological causes. They would see the imputation as being, either that they were malingering, or that it was in some way their own fault. I recall a socialist comrade who, confronted with the information that the incidence of neurosis is higher in the working class than in the middle class, argued that this result must have been obtained because middle-class definitions of neurosis were used. He was simply unable to see the attribution of neurosis as other than a put-down—as for instance a recognition of an effect of deprivation.

Now insofar as the term 'illness' is never interpreted as a put-down, one can assume that people interpret 'mental illness' in this way because they assimilate it to blameworthy behaviour—thereby showing their failure to understand the vocabulary they have adopted. The solution to this is not to invent euphemisms or to blame psychoanalytical or even psychiatric terminology for denigrating people, but to carry out consistently the programme of substituting knowledge of the causes of human behaviour for condemnation of it.

But this does not take us quite far enough, because as Laing notes, there are other kinds of denigration than moral ones, and some involve no attribution of responsible agency. This can be illustrated by the anecdote told of Shaw, that a woman told him 'Sir, you're drunk!' and he replied 'Madam, you're ugly. In the morning, I shall be sober.' That ugliness is a misfortune and not a fault does not make its attribution any less hurtful. And of course neurosis and psychosis, like physical illness, are misfortunes. There is no sense in denying that. That there are misfortunes is of course unfortunate, and their elimination where possible is desirable; but they will not go away if they are ignored.

There are, of course, social reasons why attributions of particular misfortunes are taken as insults whereas those of others are not. That neurosis and psychosis are still among those which are often found insulting, itself shows that psychoanalytical insights have not been assimilated by our culture, even though its terminology has to some extent passed into common currency.

The tendency towards euphemism, often reinforced by a moralistic misunderstanding of psychoanalytical value-judgements (which are certainly not subjective judgements added to the 'facts', but objective accounts of real misfortunes) leads a lot of people to *want* to believe that neurotic and psychotic experience are just forms of experience, as good as any other forms, and that the terms 'neurotic' and 'psychotic' are just labels used to put them down. This is what many people want to read in Laing, and because they decide in advance to find it there, they miss the specificity of what he has to say.

Models of madness

At this point it might be worth mentioning an attempt that has already been made to classify Laing's different positions on the matter of the relation between sanity and madness. This occurs in a paper 'Laing's models of madness' by Siegler, Osmond and Mann (reprinted in *Laing and Anti-Psychiatry*, (eds.) Boyers and Orrill). Siegler and Osmond had previously—in their paper 'Models of Madness' in the *British Journal of Psychiatry*, 1966— distinguished seven models of madness: medical, moral, psychoalytical, family interaction, social, conspiratorial and impaired. They find two of these models in *The Politics of Experience*,

namely, the psychoanalytical and conspiratorial ones, together
with a third, original to Laing, which they call the psychedelic
model. It should be noted that only *The Politics of Experience* is
considered—Laing's most un-psychoanalytical and, in my opinion, his worst book. *The Divided Self* is also mentioned as exemplifying Laing's psychoanalytical model.

I think the article is valuable in distinguishing these models,
and correct in recognizing more than one in Laing. The value of
setting up a comparative set of models in this context is mainly
negative—eliminating conflations of ideas which are actually
distinct—rather than providing any positive theory of the contesting notions of madness. In all of Laing's writing about the
concepts of sanity and madness there is an element of criticism
of a psychiatric orthodoxy which is characterized by the belief
that the line between sanity and madness is clearer cut than
Laing thinks it is. This can lead readers to assume both that
there is one, coherent orthodoxy which Laing is attacking, and
that he himself has one coherent view of the matter. Neither of
these is the case. In the first place there are the differences between the medical and the psychoanalytic models, of which I
shall have more to say. For the moment, it is enough to note that
these tend to be conflated not only by 'radicals', but also by
behaviour therapists, who also tend to object to seeing schizophrenia as a disease or a real entity, though their favoured expression is that patients 'emit schizophrenic behaviour'. And
indeed, many psychoanalytically oriented psychiatrists, while
recognizing certain differences between mental and physical illnesses, see no problem about regarding both as illnesses in the
same sense.[1] Indeed such a position does have some *ideological*
justification in the common cause of overcoming the deadweight
of prejudice against the psychotic as a 'moral deviant' (though
this is not to say that this assimilation of psychosis to illness is
theoretically sound).

For Siegler *et al.*, the most noticeable differences between these
models seem to be the continuity held to exist between psychotic
and normal neurotic states in the psychoanalytic model, as opposed to the medical ideas of an illness that occurs unheralded;

and the suitability of the hospital as an environment for treatment according to the medical model, whilst on the psychoanalytical model, a hospital environment may be an obstacle to cure. It appears from the article in *Laing and Anti-Psychiatry* that these authors prefer the medical model, though some of the supposed disadvantages of the roles of analysand over that of patient are hardly to the point—for example they make play of the fact that it is difficult to get psychoanalytic treatment without paying, which is hardly the fault of psychoanalysts, any more than it is to the credit of the medical profession that—in some countries—their services are to be had for free.

From the point of view of interpreting Laing and other radical therapists, perhaps the most instructive aspect of this comparison of models is in connection with the 'conspiratorial model'—its contrast with the psychoanalytic and its similarities to the moral model. As Siegler and Osmond point out, the conspiracy-model is simply the inversion of the moral model. The moral model (in which they quite correctly include behaviourist theories of deviance) sees 'madness' as a perversity to be punished in order to bring the deviant into line with social conventions. It is useful to compare what they say of the moral and the psychoanalytical models under the heading: 'Behaviour: how it is to be interpreted'.

In the moral model, 'All behaviour is to be taken at face value; it requires evaluation rather than interpretation'. According to the psychoanalytical model on the other hand, 'All of the patient's behaviour is to be interpreted symbolically; it is the therapist's task to "de-code" it'. ('Models of Madness', in *The British Journal of Psychiatry*, 1966, pp. 1196–97)

The conspiracy model simply asserts the deviant's right to deviate (as a moral choice). Psychoanalysis is seen as having no right to pass comment on the moral judgements of the dissenter, just as the moral model denies its competence to comment on those of society. Essentially, this is in each case a Canute-like operation to protect the autonomy of morality as a science-free zone; it is designed to remove the critical potentialities of psychoanalysis in relation to moralities.

Siegler and Osmond take Szasz (author of *The Myth of Mental Illness*, *Ideology and Insanity* and other works in the same vein) as an example of a conspiracy theorist, and Laing cites him with approval in various places. There are certainly points of contact between Laing's views and those of Szasz—a personalist critique of scientific method in the human sciences and a scepticism about the concept of mental illness. But Szasz is mainly a polemical writer whose theoretical tools are chosen with a view to winning his case against medical and for moral judgements about 'mental illness'. His work lacks the theoretical interest of Laing's, and incidentally contains some very un-radical political ideas as well—e.g. his opposition to socialized medicine.[2]

I think it does Laing an injustice to lump him together with Szasz, even though he sometimes invites this treatment. It is not merely that Laing has other models than the conspiracy one. It is mistaken to regard him as subscribing to it at all, despite passages in which his *tone* lays him open to this charge, if only because he is always careful to point out that families do not as a rule consciously or deliberately victimize their members.

In the course of their defence of the medical model against conspiracy theories, Siegler *et al.* do make some valid points which might tell against Laing—e.g. that 'labelling' and reference to hypothetical entities play an honourable role in medical practice, so that it is by no means obvious that they should be regarded as malpractices in psychiatry, as Laing and others sometimes seem to suggest—though as we shall see, Laing may be arguing only against *certain* labels and hypotheses, which is a different matter.

One last point is worth mentioning about the article 'Laing's Models of Madness'. The specific strength of Laing's contribution to the understanding of psychosis is his work on family interaction; so, given that one of the models listed by Siegler and Osmond is the family interaction model, it is necessary to state the relation of his position to such a model.

Essentially, the relation of Laing's social phenomenology to the family interaction model is the same as that which traditional psychoanalysis bears to the medical model (see below). The family interaction model (as defined by Siegler *et al.*) locates mental illness in the family; for it, the family is diseased and requires treatment. Laing sees this as a category-mistake—treating a collective entity as if it were an organism (see the Introduction to *Sanity, Madness and the Family*). So Siegler, Osmond and Mann are quite correct in their contention (in 'Laing's models of Madness') that the place of family interaction in Laing's account is a different one:

He simply uses the information provided by the family interaction model to reinforce his argument that the schizophrenic patient has been driven mad by his family, a statement that is meaningless in any other model [than the psychoanalytic one]. (*Laing and Anti-Psychiatry*, p. 110)

However, their statement that 'Nowhere in this book' (i.e. *The Politics of Experience*) does he show 'the slightest concern for the experiences of other members of the family', should not blind us to the fact that he shows considerable concern for them elsewhere, without for a moment falling into a family interaction theory of madness, in the sense in question. Even in *The Politics of Experience*, Laing describes his project as 'social phenomenology' which indicates a theory of 'inter-experience'.

In the rest of this chapter I want to differentiate various points that Laing makes about sanity and madness, and to distinguish those implicit in any authentically psychoanalytical theory, those specific to social phenomenology, and those extreme sceptical positions which I think we must reject. There is probably no aspect of Laing's work which better illustrates the tensions and breaks in Laing's work.

Laing's criticisms of the concept of mental illness

Laing's sceptical statements about the sanity/madness distinction seem to be variations on eight, logically distinct positions, most of them mutually compatible, and some theoretically connected. They are (a) that illness is an unsatisfactory model for mental disorders; (b) that psychotic phenomena are intelligible; (c) that there are no objective criteria for applying the concept 'schizophrenia' (and more generally that it is a scientifically ill-founded concept); (d) that to understand madness one must study the family, not only the individual; (e) that people are often incorrectly classified as mad, and dissident members of a nexified family are specially prone to this fate; (f) that statistical normality is not preferable to madness; (g) that the concepts of sanity and madness are socially relative, and (h) that madness can be a natural curative process—perhaps the cure for sanity.

These positions do seem to fall into three groups: (a) and (b) are probably implicit in any psychoanalytic theory; (c), (d) and (e) belong to Laing's social phenomenology of the family; (f), (g) and (h) represent his later polemical position. I shall discuss them in turn.

The role played by the concepts 'illness', 'health', 'cure' etc. in psychoanalysis is not that which they play in orthodox medicine. They were the natural concepts for Freud to use, given that psychoanalysis did grow up as a branch of medicine in the first place, but their theoretical status must be seen as that of terms borrowed from another science and originally used in a meta-phorical sense, then given a new, independent sense within the new science. The phenomenon of the formation of scientific concepts in this way is quite common in all the sciences; at first the metaphorical borrowing serves as a model, enabling the new research to get its bearings, and making the new theory easier to understand. Later, the origin of the borrowed word is forgotten, as it comes to have a new sense, rigorously defined within the new science. Thus with 'energy' in its various scientific uses, 'wave', 'structure' and so on.

The danger in this (probably inevitable) practice is that it may give rise to mistaken arguments within the new science, based on the previous sense of the terminology—e.g. the continued postu-lation of ether on the assumption that a wave needed a medium. Arguments (usually from philosophical enemies of a new sci-ence) that it is unrigorous because it uses metaphors, or that it is confused because it uses words in a way in which they could

not be used in ordinary language, can be dismissed at the outset
as obscurantist.

However because psychoanalysis has remained (as a profession) close to the medical profession (in some countries, part
of it, and everywhere overlapping with it), and because psychiatrists (as distinct—in principle—from psychoanalysts) still
largely regard neurosis and psychosis as unambiguously forms
of illness, the confusion of the psychoanalytical sense of 'illness'
with the medical sense still needs to be criticized. It is for this
reason that many psychoanalysts resort to writing 'illness' in
quotes. It is not only Laing and his colleagues who do this: it is
done by disciples of Lacan (e.g. the Mannonis), who claim to be
returners to Freud, not revisers of him. Lidz, in the interview
published in *Laing and Anti-Psychiatry*, says, 'I personally, as
you may know, do not consider schizophrenia a disease or an
illness, but rather a type of reaction to a sick organization, a
personality disorder.' He also says, 'I think I would never say a
patient *has* schizophrenia. We say a patient *is* schizophrenic.'
This is close to Laing's earlier position; one might existentialize
the language even more, and say a patient be's schizophrenically.

The disadvantages of the use of the term 'illness' in psychiatric
contexts are repeatedly pointed out by Laing. Generally speaking, an illness is not something the causation of which lies in the
realm of mental processes, meanings, or human interaction, but
in purely organic processes. This is not to deny that there are
psychosomatic illnesses, or that socially determined factors can
result in physical diseases—e.g. industrial diseases. But the defining characteristics of diseases in general belong to the world of
the biological sciences rather than the social or human sciences.
The result of treating neurosis or psychosis as illness is that its
symptoms are then seen as explained simply by invoking the illness, and not as related to anything else in the person's life. Time
and again in Laing's case studies, he takes the patient's previous
psychiatrists to task for failure to notice or to investigate connections between the symptoms in the 'schizophrenic's' behaviour, and the family events he or she has experienced. In
doing this Laing is making a distinction which is implicit in all

psychoanalysis; in both Laing's thought and that of some more orthodox analysts, it is the converse of the next claim to be considered—that neurotic and psychotic phenomena are intelligible. But before going on to discuss this claim, it is worth noting that the use of the metaphors of illness and health in a wider sense than the physiological—I am tempted to say, in an existential sense—to denote the norm and pathology of human life, has had an honourable history long before Freud. Socrates' last wish was that a cock should be sacrificed to Aesculapius (the god of healing), implying that death is the cure of life; Jesus referred to himself as a physician; Kierkegaard wrote of despair as 'the sickness unto death'; and Spinoza and Nietzsche used the values sick/healthy as an alternative to moralistic values. None of these would be thought of as implying physiological reductionism, and in at least some of these cases, the implication is that human misery is a misfortune that befalls people, not the product of a voluntary choice of evil by anyone. If Laing's intention in criticizing medical terminology in psychiatry is to reject this implication, to see praxis instead of process, then I believe we should not follow him. But that is not the only meaning of the quest for intelligibility, and the abuse of medical metaphors to excuse turning a blind eye to unconscious or social meanings certainly justifies Laing's strictures.

. The intelligibility of a symptom lies in the fact that it expresses an idea, and, in Laing's studies, a set of ideas concerning the experience of the family. Ideas are not related to an individual's mental life in the same sort of way that a growth, an infection or an injury is related to the body. One can give a drug which lowers the general level of mental excitation, but one cannot give a drug which will kill the idea, and one cannot cut it out surgically. One operates on ideas by means of other ideas; this is essentially what differentiates all analytical schools including Laing's from other psychiatrists. Laing's version (along with some others) is marked by emphasis on transpersonal as well as intrapersonal processes as making symptoms intelligible, and by his success in the quest for intelligibility in relation with psychotic as well as neurotic symptoms.

The second group of Laing's contentions about 'madness' are not incompatible with the first, but they are based on his social phenomenology and not merely on spelling out the implications of shared psychoanalytical assumptions.

The first of this group—that there are no objective criteria for applying the concept of schizophrenia, which is scientifically redundant—though it does not necessarily depend on the use of a social-phenomenological method, makes its appearance in Laing's works along with this method. In *The Divided Self* he seems quite unworried about referring to schizophrenia, provided always that it is understood in mentalistic terms, not as a disease. But his search for intelligibility in schizophrenia is not seen as an easy task; he suggests that a lot of schizophrenic speech is 'purposefully' nonsensical—a ploy to confuse the psychiatrist (see p. 163). The only sign of his later scepticism about the concept (or rather, in this instance, of *any* 'labelling') is a rather mystified presentation of his case against the disease-model:

If we look at his actions as 'signs' of a 'disease', we are already imposing our categories of thought on to the patient. (p. 33)

I call this mystified because, of course, categories of thought are nobody's property, they are either applicable or inapplicable, independently of who applies them.

In *Self and Others* there is another such intimation, still in the context of the same mystification. There are, he argues, no valid criteria for attributing symptoms such as 'impoverished affect' and 'withdrawal'. These, he seems to be saying, are subjective judgements on the part of the doctors, and could not be otherwise. He goes on to argue for a Heideggerian concept of truth.

Whereas in natural science truth consists in a correspondence, an *adaequatio*, between what goes on *in intellectu* and what goes on *in re*, between the structure of a symbol system 'in the mind' and the structure of events 'in the world', another concept of truth is found in the Greek word ἀλήθεια In this concept, truth is literally that which is without secrecy, what discloses itself without a veil. (p. 129)

He seems to be implying in the context that there can be valid

F

and invalid ways of being subjective in the human sciences, but no valid way of being objective; for he blames misattributions of experience on what he regards as a faulty (natural scientific) concept of truth. I see no reason why the concept of truth he assigns to the natural sciences should not apply equally to the matter under consideration; if one ascribes experiences to the other which he does not have, then what goes on in one's mind does not correspond to what goes on in the world (i.e. in the other person's mind).

In general, however, Laing's position as stated in *Self and Others* seems to be that, while he claims that many people diagnosed as schizophrenic are different from the typical schizophrenic, he assumes the existence of such typical schizophrenics.

It is in the Introduction to *Sanity, Madness and the Family* that the scepticism about schizophrenia is first put forward as a considered position. Since this text, Laing's statements seem consistent enough on this matter. The position argued in this text is that, in view of the lack of agreed criteria for diagnozing schizophrenia, and of the fact that the 'disease' model is inadequate, there seems little point in postulating schizophrenia as a cause of particular peculiarities of experience and behaviour. It is better rather to look for specific causes of specific disturbances, than to explain the disturbances by 'schizophrenia' (which really adds nothing to their description, like the 'dormitive virtue' of opium) and then look around for causes of schizophrenia. Arguments such as that of Siegler and Osmond, that there is nothing wrong with hypothetical entities, as physical diseases are also hypothetical entities, miss this point. There is plenty wrong with hypothetical entities which contribute nothing to the explanation of the phenomena. If the symptoms of the patients (who had all been diagnozed schizophrenic) studied in *Sanity, Madness and the Family* can be explained in terms of the relations of those patients to their families, then one need only postulate the existence of those symptoms and those relations: to talk of schizophrenia is to multiply entities beyond necessity. As a vague, descriptive term, schizophrenia may still be useful, but should be regarded as pre-scientific; the only criterion Laing uses for applying it from *Sanity, Madness and the Family* onward, is its diagnosis by two doctors.

It should be noted that this scepticism is expressed about a specific concept—'schizophrenia'—not about psychosis in general, and that Laing still uses the word 'schizophrenia' in ways which imply that there is at least something in common between the various disturbances of experience and behaviour which psychiatrists tend to classify as schizophrenic. That two psychiatrists have given this diagnosis does apparently mean something: but it is not an explanation of the patient's experience or behaviour, and too often serves as an excuse for failing to look at the facts which might make that experience and behaviour intelligible— i.e. its relation to the past and present behaviour of other people towards the patient. But it is not being asserted by Laing at this stage that psychosis as such is unreal, or a mere 'label', let alone something enviable or admirable.

Associated with the notion that the concept of schizophrenia is scientifically redundant is the relocation of the area of psychiatric investigation, from the individual to the family. I have already said enough about this—the whole value of social phenomenology for psychotherapy is bound up with it. (I have already noted that it differs from the so-called family interaction model.) In the context of this understanding of the importance of the interaction between 'schizophrenics' and their families, one event, to the possibility of which Laing has alerted us, is that a family may find the diagnosis of schizophrenia in a dissident member a useful weapon in preserving their own defences against that member.

We now have a sketch of Laing's position in his social-phenomenological writings. This is compounded of (1) the assertion of the psychoanalytical position that mental 'illness' is intelligible in terms of meanings, and the insistence that this implies that it is not illness in the same sense as organic diseases (2) an extension of the search for meanings into the interpersonal sphere, (3) an awareness of the conflicts between the patient and his or her family, and the possibility that the diagnosis of schizophrenia is not merely an outcome of this, but also—perhaps mainly—a weapon in the hands of the family.

Certainly all this means that the division between sanity and madness is a matter of degree, and that the processes leading to mental breakdown are more widespread than might have been thought—they occur at least in the families of the patients, and are probably of the same kind as those which occur in all families. But none of this suggests either the relativization, or the inversion, or the denial of the distinction between sanity and madness.

In *The Politics of Experience* the final group of suggestions about madness make their appearance. That book is actually a collection of essays, the original versions of which were written at different times, and so it is not surprising that more than one position is represented in it. One unfortunate result of this is that it enables people to read Laing's earlier work through *The Politics of Experience*. Take, for example, the chapter 'The Schizophrenic Experience'. This is full of references to *Sanity, Madness and the Family*, and it may be that Laing already held the more extreme position of this essay when he wrote that book.[3] But he certainly makes explicit in the essay positions that are not defended in the book. For example he reasserts the original social-phenomenological position:

... to the best of my knowledge, *no* schizophrenic has been studied whose disturbed pattern of communication has not been shown to be a reflection of, and reaction to, the disturbed and disturbing pattern characterizing his or her family of origin. (pp. 94–95)

Something is wrong somewhere, but it can no longer be seen exclusively or even primarily 'in' the diagnosed patient (p. 96)

These are statements of the familiar position, but he draws the conclusion that

the experience and behaviour that gets labelled schizophrenic is *a special strategy that a person invents in order to live in an unlivable situation.* (p. 95)

This at least comes perilously close to saying what I have argued

Laing avoids saying in most of his writings—that because schizo-phrenic behaviour and experience is intelligible, it is also rational —a reasonable response to an unlivable situation, not just an understandable effect of it.

Although he is still careful to exonerate parents and psychia-trists from intent to harm (it is all unconscious) he does allow himself the liberty of using the word 'conspiracy' (in quotes) for the 'coalition' of family, doctors and others who treat the patient as schizophrenic. He approves a statement by Bateson that schizophrenia may be a natural curative process; and he points out that 'The perfectly adjusted, bomber pilot may be a greater threat to species survival than the hospitalized schizophrenic deluded that the Bomb is inside him' (p. 99). This of course is true, but it is one of those truths which seem profound at first, but turn out to be irrelevant. The solution to war is to change society, not to make bomber pilots maladjusted. And people are not (necessarily) classified as schizophrenics because they are dangerous to society—we distinguish crime from insanity.

He goes on to say that treating someone as a schizophrenic is a political fact. He implies that it is a form of violence perpetrated in order to maintain the existing order. The idea that psychiatry is intended to *help* the patient is presumably now regarded as, in most cases, a mystification; but this is very largely an unargued assumption. It is implicit in statements such as:

it is wrong to impute to someone a hypothetical disease of unknown aetiology and undiscovered pathology unless *he* can prove otherwise (p. 87)

No one would say the same about the diagnosis of a physical ill-ness. It is closer to what is said of accusation of a crime. This is not just the rejection of the medical model, it is (implicitly) the acceptance of a moral/criminological model. The criticisms Laing makes of existing psychiatric practices may be justified, and his concern with the civil rights aspect of mental health may be necessary, but his theorizations of this lead away from any psychoanalytical style of psychiatry towards something quite different. They also bring him close to the views of Szasz, whose book *The Myth of Mental Illness* he refers to in a footnote to the last quoted passage.

If 'the family' still comes in for criticism, it is not so much for driving people mad as for labelling them mad. The admirable tendency to take sides with the patient, when necessary, against his or her family, has been metamorphozed into the tendency to take sides with the patient's symptoms, i.e. with what was previously regarded as a misery inflicted by adverse patterns of family interaction. Madness, it seems, comes to have a fascination for Laing. The romantic idea of an affinity between madness and genius, supported by the eventual madness of certain men of genius such as Nietzsche and Van Gogh, makes its appearance here. I think at some points it is implied that we are all mad, only some forms of madness are useful to society and so not regarded as such; other forms would be potentially useful to a more liberated society.

But if Laing is really adopting a relativist position, I believe it undermines rather than supports his radicalism. For one of the features of a psychoanalytical account of neurosis and psychosis is that its definitions are independent of social forms, and are set up wholly in terms of the internal psychic economy of the individual, and thereby make it possible to criticize social institutions as merely socially approved forms of neurosis and psychosis, whereas on the relativist account such criticism is impossible, or is reduced to an empty value-judgement. For if sanity and madness are totally relative to the accepted values of society, one might still take up a position of rejecting the values of one's society, but one could not use the concepts 'sane', 'mad', 'neurotic' etc. to do so. A programme of social criticism based on applied psychoanalysis, such as those of Reich and Marcuse, rests precisely on the objectivity of psychoanalytic concepts, and their independence of socially relative values.

But if, at times, Laing seems to be relativizing the concepts of sanity and madness, at others he seems to be simply inverting the values of society, and preferring madness. It becomes difficult at points in *The Politics of Experience*, as it is throughout Cooper's *Death of the Family*, to tell whether Laing is still making criticisms of society for what it does to people, as evidenced by his clinical studies, or whether he is praising whatever sticks in the throat of society.

It must be admitted that there is a certain emotional appeal to this inversion of values. This can be illustrated by reference to an experiment on rats by a very different type of psychologist— namely Eysenck.

Having so trained them to run to the trough and devour the pellet, the experimenter then introduces a quite arbitrary social rule: to wit, that it is impolite to eat the pellet until three seconds have passed from the beginning of the signal. Any rat that eats before the three seconds are up is punished by a fairly mild electric shock to its feet.

... Each rat has a choice of three ways of behaving. It can either behave in a criminal or psychopathic manner by eating the food immediately it is put into the trough and thus brave the punishment which follows immediately; it can behave in a normal, socialized, integrated manner by waiting a few seconds and then eating the food when it is safe to do so; and it can, lastly, react in a neurotic manner by refusing to eat the food at all, even when it is perfectly safe to do so. (*Fact and Fiction in Psychology*, p. 266)

The instinctive anthropomorphic reaction of, I think, most people to this edifying little tale, is to admire the 'psychopathic' rats most, and feel some contempt for the 'normal, socialized, integrated' ones. We admire someone who is not the dupe of his social conditioning, even if his reaction against it brings no advantage to anyone.

But one rather important difference between rats and people is the human capacity to use language, think abstractly, and envisage situations which are not yet realized. The rat only has the choice of adjustment, electric shocks or hunger; but it is not the case that, for instance, a worker on an assembly line has to choose between adjustment, leaving his job, and say smashing up his machine 'by accident' from time to time to relieve his frustration. He can also envisage different possible situations in his factory, and can join a union and strike for shorter hours, for control of the flow of production by the workers on the line, and so on. There are ways of rebelling against repressive social structures which are fully rational, clearsighted and constructive. These depend on the capacity to live within these structures rather than attempting to drop out, while at the same time struggling within them, and learning to understand them and the conditions of their overthrow.

However there is one element of Laing's 'pro-madness' stance which has little to do with politics—whether micro or macro—and much to do with mysticism, though derived from sources such as Bateson. This is the idea of a natural curative process, which society treats as madness, thus preventing its natural outcome from occurring. 'Madness' is then a name for the curative process when stopped midway by adverse conditions (i.e. by psychiatric hospitals). The nature of this 'curative process' and the need for it, seem to be conceived as follows: we live in two worlds, an 'inner' and an 'outer'; 'sanity' is an impoverished form of experience, limited to the 'outer'; 'madness' is a corrective, a voyage into inner space; if one returns from the voyage, one will be able to pass between both worlds at will.

Now this *could* be simply a picturesque way of expressing the psychoanalytical idea already spoken of, that the neurotic (who is—statistically speaking—the normal individual) represses his instinctual wishes and the unconscious ideas derived from them in order to adapt to a frustrating reality; that the psychotic retreats into phantasy and remoulds the world in phantasy, ceasing to relate to it in reality; and that sanity consists in a transformation of the real world in accordance with ones wishes, which presupposes greater awareness of one's own phantasy-life than is usual. The temporal ordering of these states (from neurosis through psychosis to sanity) is new, but there are no theoretical reasons in psychoanalysis for thinking this to be impossible, and there is empirical evidence that it sometimes happens.

But Laing appears to be claiming more than this—namely that the entities encountered in 'inner space' are as objective and 'outer' as the 'real world'. Insofar as he intends this, he leaves the discourse of psychoanalysis and enters that of religion, and of a specific kind of religion: the cult of the inner life.

Now I have no intention here of discussing the question of the validity of religion or of any particular religion, though I shall say a little in the next chapter about Laing's 'gnosticism' insofar as it affects his idea of the self and of liberation. But Laing does seem to be attributing special insight into the spiritual world (to use a more accurate term than 'inner') to 'schizophrenics', and to see this as a contribution to the understanding of 'madness'. Yet he only claims this for some 'schizophrenics', and allows that some sane people have the same experiences—William Blake, for instance. But there remain important differences between Blake and the 'schizophrenic'; the latter generally lacks insight into 'this world', and is unable to lead a gratifying existence in it. Laing says of the 'madman' that he may be 'even through his profound wretchedness and disintegration, the hierophant of the sacred' (*The Politics of Experience*, pp. 109–10). For Blake on the other hand, 'Enjoyment & not Abstinence is the food of Intellect' (*Complete Writings*, p. 790). In which case surely, the task of the psychotherapist is to help the patient arrive at a point where he or she can know and enjoy life in this world, and leave possible transcendental experiences to take care of themselves.[4]

One of the serious disadvantages of this group of ideas is that it makes it once again unclear what the connection is between sane but neurotic experience and behaviour, and psychosis. It is precisely the continuity of these states that comes through most strongly in Laing's early writings and particularly *The Divided Self*. It is also a theme shared with orthodox psychoanalysis, and the extension of intelligibility to the psychoses has generally been based on the assumption of this continuity.

But most of the things said about 'madness' in *The Politics of Experience* and in texts by those associated with Laing's 'antipsychiatric' position are totally inapplicable to neurosis. A neurotic is not 'labelled' as such by 'the others'. He has problems within himself which prevent him living his own life in the way he wants to. He is not forced to see a psychoanalyst or psychiatrist; he is most likely discouraged by his friends, family, his doctor, his pride, and not least by the financial difficulties of getting psychoanalytic treatment. He does not (as a rule) have any excep-

tional experiences which he might take to reveal another order
of reality: rather his experience is likely to be marked by impoverishment, boredom and frustration.

In *The Divided Self* Laing saw precisely this vicious circle of
emptiness and isolation as pushing the severe neurotic 'perilously near to frank psychosis', which was an intelligible development of it. Are we now to believe that psychosis is a curative
process and simultaneously a voyage of discovery of profounder
orders of reality, which will lead to a higher sanity if only protected from the intrusions of psychiatrists?

If, as Laing tells us, a child born in modern Britain has a better
chance of getting into a mental hospital than into a university,
the chances of having one's happiness destroyed, at some time
in one's life, by neurotic symptoms, must be closer to those of
getting to primary school. This is the iceberg of which the small
minority who actually have treatment from a psychiatrist or
psychotherapist is the tip. So the promotion of analytic therapy
is surely a far more urgent task than the debunking of psychiatry.
Laing as a practising psychoanalyst can hardly be unaware of
this, but many of his readers, I fear, merely have their resistances
to analysis reinforced by the tone of his criticisms.

In all fairness, it should be noted that Laing's statements of the
so-called psychedelic model are hedged around with far more
reservations than one would guess from his interpreters, whether
friendly or hostile.

Anti-Psychiatry

If I have succeeded in disentangling various strands in Laing's
thinking about the sanity/madness distinction, it remains to discuss the effects of these theories for the criticism of existing mental health institutions, and for formulating proposals for
alternatives to them.

In the first place, there is the psychoanalytical criticism of the
reliance on physical treatments of mental 'illness' by most psychiatrists. A therapy which depends on words and on the abreac-

tion of emotions by the patient, does not easily co-exist with treatments such as heavy sedation, or ECT with its serious disturbance of short-term memory. Although psychoanalytic treatment does occur in some existing mental hospitals, it is in many ways in contradiction to their structure—i.e. to the authoritarian hierarchy which mars most hospitals, and psychiatric ones most of all. As Siegler and Osmond say in the section under the heading 'Treatment':

The nurses and attendants present a problem, because, unless they understand psychoanalytic principles, they may inadvertently undermine the therapy. (*British Journal of Psychiatry*, 1966, p. 1197)

This problem is also raised in David Cooper's *Psychiatry and Anti-Psychiatry* (a text which belongs with Laing's social-phenomenological works), which highlights the organisational problems of the infiltration of uncompromisingly psychoanalytical methods into a medical psychiatric framework.

Social phenomenology suggests its own additions to the psychoanalytic critique. Interviews with the patient's family become crucial, together with an awareness of the nature of the family mystifications in each case, to avoid the reinforcement of them by unsuspecting therapists. It also shows the need for a social environment which can provide support for the development of the individual's freedom and confidence, which the family has crushed. Hospital hierarchies, like every hierarchy, will spontaneously incline towards taking the side of the parents within a family.

So that even without taking into account the later and more extreme sceptical views about sanity and madness—his 'psychedelic model' and his gestures towards relativism and conspiracy-theories—it should not be surprising that Laing and others like him should find their aims obstructed by hospital hierarchies and should set up alternative communities.

The details of organization of such places can only be worked out by those with the requisite experience. I have no first-hand experience of them, but from the accounts of those who know them, there seems to be much to admire about them.[5] Only good can come of the elimination of petty hospital regulations, which seem to be based on a belief in the intrinsic value of authoritarianism, hierarchy and keeping people in ignorance. These principles are not an accidental feature of hospitals of course, but exist in some measure in all institutions in our society, from the armed forces to the education system. They serve the same function of repressive socialization in these institutions as they do in the patriarchal family itself.

At the same time, some accounts of these freer therapeutic communities (e.g. those printed in *Laing and Anti-Psychiatry*) strike me as slightly false in their claim that the staff-patient distinction had completely disappeared—like a white liberal schoolteacher pretending not to notice that some of the class are black. After all, not all the members of such communities are there for the same reason. The reality of the difference is certainly borne out by the more detailed account of life in such a community in *Mary Barnes* by Mary Barnes and Joseph Berke.

Even in a two-person psychoanalytic situation, where there is no question of 'psychosis', the relationship is not a symmetrical one. But this in no sense means that it is necessarily an authoritarian one, as is sometimes alleged—by Sartre for instance, for whom this allegation derives from his view of all human relations as relations between a subject (the desirable role) and an object (the undesirable one).[6] In a hierarchic society (which any society divided into classes must be), it is by no means easy to sort out asymmetrical from oppressive relationships within any micro-social unit; but this is one more matter to which more clarity must be brought before 'micro-politics' can be given a theoretically sound basis.

The increase in Laing's scepticism about psychosis is an aspect of a move from investigation to polemic. Polemic has a perfectly good place in scientific discourse if it is founded on knowledge; unfortunately, Laing's polemics tend to become mere re-iterations of value-judgements, and are less effective as criticism of psychiatric orthodoxies than are the careful presentations of clinical material in his earlier writings. As we shall see, this is also true in the wider area of social criticism and micro-politics.

Chapter 6

Roads to Freedom

In our society, at certain times, this interlaced set of systems may lend itself to revolutionary change, not at the extreme micro or macro ends; that is, not through the individual pirouette of solitary repentance on the one hand, or by a seizure of the machinery of the state on the other; but by sudden, structural, radical qualitative changes in the intermediate system levels; changes in a factory, a hospital, a school, a university, a set of schools, or a whole area of industry, medicine, education, etc.

This passage occurs in Laing's lecture 'The Obvious', read at the Dialectics of Liberation conference. He has just been elaborating his notion of intelligibility in terms of social context (see the quote on pp. 74–75 of the present work). There is nothing mysterious about the intelligibility of the 'micro' in terms of the 'macro' situations, as Laing speaks of it in this lecture. The individual is largely a product of his immediate social context from birth on.

Our own cities are our own animal factories; families, schools, churches are the slaughterhouses of our children; colleges and other places are the kitchens. As adults in marriages and business, we eat the product. (*The Politics of the Family*, p. 102)

Current social contexts obviously condition individual experience and behaviour as well, as the individual remains dependent on his social relationships. The nature of the micro-social group in turn is continually conditioned by the larger social context. The factory is a function of the firm, the firm of the economy, the economy of the world market; the case is similar with the other institutions Laing mentions. Laing also points out (correctly, as I believe) the 'paradox of the irrationality of the whole' (which has no larger context in terms of which it can be made intelligible, and on to which its irrationality can be displaced)—i.e. the entire world order is irrational. But this paradox does not require the solution that 'God has gone mad'; it requires us to look at the nature of the elements which are interrelated in these structures. For instance, an individual worker in a factory is dependent on the factory for his living, and his consciousness is partly the product of work in that factory. But he also has wants, needs, tastes, desires etc. which the factory, and the system of production of which it is part, thwart rather than satisfy. This generates not merely irrationality but also conflict within the system. Again, the state machinery is explicable not only in terms of its place in the context of world power politics, but also, and pre-eminently, in terms of the maintenance of order and property and the suppression of dissident groups within its home territory. So that the intelligibility of structures and their inner contradictions is a two-way matter. The economy itself for instance, which explains so much about social institutions and individual situations, is itself intelligible (in regard to the fact that there is an economy) only in terms of man's biologically given need to produce in order to live.

But what does stem from the structure of the economy—of particular economic systems—is that this need is turned against itself, that the worker's existence is overwhelmingly conditioned by the fact that, from the point of view of the economy as a whole, the worker is only entitled to live in order to produce. If the worker, who so far as his own desires are concerned, only works in order to live, finds himself allowed only that much life that is necessary in order for him to work, this 'irrationality' needs explanation in terms of the economic structure.

This is a methodological point. It is not within Laing's purpose as a psychologist or psychiatrist to analyse the economy—one can turn to Marx's *Capital* for such an analysis. Laing is concerned more with the institutions which mould the individual before he takes his place in the production line—the family, the school, etc., institutions which Louis Althusser has called the ideological apparatuses of the state.[1]

In explaining why these institutions are as they are, it will be necessary to look at the wider context of society—e.g. the need to produce individuals who are 'good' workers, bosses, housewives, policemen etc., i.e. nothing but workers, bosses, housewives, policemen. But Laing encounters these apparatuses in the first place not in connection with their function in capitalist society, but with their disastrous effects on the individuals who have been processed by them—all of us, that is. And just as the key which opened the door to knowledge of the system as a whole (for Marx) was the standpoint of the most oppressed class in the system—the workers: so Laing, like Freud, starts from the experience of the most manifest victims of the system of psychological repression. Marx produced a theory of the 'macro' levels of society, and based a political practice of liberation on that theory. Freud produced a theory of the individual psyche which was also social in that the foremost 'micro-social' unit, the family, is that which determines the vicissitudes of the individual's instincts. On this theory a therapeutic practice of individual liberation is based. Laing, as we have seen, has focused attention on the family and other micro-social units; he intends social phenomenology to be a theory on which a practice of liberation at the micro-social level can be based. This theory and practice would both link up with, and lead to the revision of, Marxism on the one hand and psychoanalysis on the other. It is worth examining the nature and pre-requisites of such a micro-social theory and micro-political practice.

Micro-politics as resistance to immediate authority

Micro-politics must not be seen as the importation of political values into the analysis of interpersonal relations and the dynamics of small groups. The starting point must always be the analysis of the pathology of the small groups themselves. We have seen Laing at work analysing the most important of such groups—the family. We have also seen the same concepts applied to psychoanalytical and hospital situations. These accounts stand or fall on their own merits without reference to any outside 'political' justifications.

At the same time, like any analysis—or at least any pathology —of a human situation, they do have implications about how things should be changed. In particular, we see in these micro-social processes a struggle of resistance to oppression by the authorities within them. This struggle does not need to be created by the psychotherapist as micro-political agitator; it is already present in the experience and behaviour of the micro-politically oppressed. It is present, however, largely in a mystified form, and, in micro- as in macro-politics, it is necessary to unite this spontaneous resistance with a theoretical analysis in order to produce a genuine practice of liberation.

But once such a theory is provided, even in outline, the connections between the micro-social level, and the global and personal levels, come into view. It is then necessary to ask: (a) how far micro-politics can go in isolation from other aspects of liberation; (b) how it can affect these other aspects; (c) what the pitfalls are for an isolated micro-politics, and how far Laing falls into them.

The social conditions which are most immediately effective in conditioning, restraining and frustrating the individuals in contemporary western society (or any other exploitative society) are at the 'micro-social' level. The worker experiences his exploitation by capital first of all in the overbearing manner of the foreman, the segregation of workers' and staff lavatories, etc. This is even more true in the case of oppressed groups other than the working class as such—housewives, students, patients in hospitals, children, soldiers and so on, whose oppression does not consist in economic exploitation, but to a large extent in the direct power of some other individuals to dominate them and restrict their possibilities.

But it may be asked: can the micro-social level of oppression and struggle for liberation be more than a link between individual liberation and macro-political struggle? Clearly the tyranny of the boss within the factory cannot be abolished within capitalism. Would not an attempt to achieve liberation at this level merely repeat the degeneration into moralism of individual liberation movements cut off from political perspectives? Already there are industrial psychologists collecting data on whether the workers in a particular factory are 'alienated' (read: fed up) and suggesting piped music and the like if they are.

In discussing Laing's claim about the possibility of revolutionary change at intermediate levels, we should remember two points: one concerning the role of ideology—the so-called subjective factor—in politics, and the nature of the institutions which sustain the ideology which holds repressive societies together; the other concerning a particular radical ideology which was flourishing at the time of the reading of Laing's paper.

The Dialectics of Liberation conference was held in July 1967. It was a manifestation of a style of left wing thought which came into fashion in the late 1960s, and has partly gone out of fashion since, as the left has returned to the struggles of the working class as the main field of operation. This style of leftism reflected the fact that it was not these struggles which gave rise to the resurgence of the left at that time, but rather student revolts, black power movements, women's and gay liberation movements, the 'counter-culture' based on rock music, mind-expanding drugs and relatively free sexual mores, etc. These movements were largely of people who were oppressed by the ideological institutions of capitalist society (the education system, the patriarchal family, racial discrimination, police interference in private life, etc.) rather than directly economically exploited. It was against these intermediate micro-social structures that the immediate revolt of the new left was directed. So it was natural enough to aim at forming a new kind of group rather than (or before) a new kind of individual or society, and to dream of success in the first place in revolutionizing these structures; they appeared to be the weakest link in the capitalist system. The importance of these institutions and the struggle within them cannot be denied—they are the places where we are made what we are. But the possibilities of transforming them without a complete social revolution needs to be looked at more closely.

In the first place it is necessary to distinguish the various institutions between the global and the individual levels. Those which are part of the economic system clearly cannot be altered within capitalism. A group of hippies can, under favourable circumstances, run a subsistence farm on land too poor to be desirable to capitalist farmers. But a group of steelworkers cannot, however affluent, club together and buy a steelworks. Outside the production process the possibilities are a little wider; one can found a free school, one can live in a commune. But—leaving aside the possibility of official interference—the financial difficulties are still grave enough to prevent such developments affecting more than a small minority. These difficulties are compounded by the fact that the individual participants of these enterprises have been formed in a repressive society. The liberated group is crushed between the millstones of the unliberated individual and the unliberated society.

This does not mean that the search for freer forms of organization in the school, the hospital, the domiciliary unit etc. are of no value; they are a symptom of a general weakening of repressive ideology, and to the extent that the new forms of organization correspond better to the desires of their participants than the old ones, they are a genuine improvement. But they are not —as they have often been seen—the first elements of the new society or a 'red base' from which the old one can be demolished.

On the other hand, movements for liberation at the intermediate levels may take the form, not of the establishment of alternative institutions 'outside' capitalist society (as monasteries in the middle ages claimed to be 'outside' the secular world, though they actually reflected, complemented and reinforced it), but of struggle against the authoritarian structure inside the micro-social institutions of capitalist society.

Thus the workers in a factory might, through struggle on the shop floor, make serious inroads on the authoritarian structure of the factory, and quite free themselves 'subjectively' of any deference towards those whom the capitalist system places above them—though it should be added that the tendency of the system is against this, and a constant defensive struggle must be maintained to protect these gains as long as the system lasts.

Similar achievements can be made by students in educational establishments, or in struggles for women's equality, children's rights etc. It is often this resistance struggle at the micro-social level, rather than the attempt to form alternative institutions within the existing social order, which both liberates individuals from their ideological mystifications, and contributes most to macro-political liberation. Those who were affected by the life-styles of the 'counter-culture' but who did not drop out of work or educational institutions were often referred to contemptuously as 'weekend hippies'; but it was weekend hippies (weekday workers) who were the potentially revolutionary part of the counter-culture—people who wanted the trendy clothes and stereo sets that capitalism can produce, but did not want to work (though they had to) all their life for a boss in order to get them. I think that there is no doubt that there is a greater freedom from 'internal' restraints against struggle for political liberation as a result of the growth of resistance to authority at the micro-social level.

So, sceptical as I am about the 'micro-red-base' theory intimated in Laing's lecture 'The Obvious', I think that the value of micro-politics can hardly be overestimated, not only for its own sake, but also for its relevance to political issues. To understand this relevance it is necessary to go into greater detail about the nature of ideology.

Micro-politics as ideological struggle

At this point a brief discussion of the Marxist notion of ideology is necessary, before considering the role of psychoanalysis and social phenomenology in this area.

The word 'ideology' originally signified the study of ideas, their origin, development and function. The term now refers, in Marxist usage, to systems of ideas themselves, rather than the study of them. But it retains the meaning, that ideas considered as ideology are considered with reference to their origin and function rather than their validity or truth-value. Ideology includes not only beliefs, theories and opinions, not just cognitive ideas, but the forms of emotion, evaluation, and what are commonly called 'attitudes'. It includes unconscious as well as conscious ideas.

For Marx, ideology is part of the superstructure of any society. Marxists have generally spoken of three levels of social organization—the economic, the political and the ideological, with the economic being basic or 'determinant in the last instance' of the political and ideological character of any society. This formula is oversimplified no doubt, but it goes some way towards locating ideology.

Ideology in any society tends to promote the cohesion of that society, and hence to perpetuate the form of society in question —e.g. the ideologies which prevail in capitalist societies serve to secure the acceptance of capitalist relations of production and the concomitant political institutions. This matter of the *function* of ideology is often confused with an independent, though related, issue—the way in which ideology is *produced*. The crudest way in which these two issues are confused is the notion that ideology is produced by acts of more or less deliberate deception of the people by the ruling class. On this view, there is no problem about how ideology comes to serve the interest of the ruling class (i.e. to perpetuate existing conditions)—it would be purpose-built to do so.

Few Marxists would admit to subscribing to such a conspiracy theory; yet many talk as if it were for practical purposes correct. For instance it is an obvious enough fact that 'the psychology of a class is not always identical with the material interests of that class' (Bukharin, *Historical Materialism*, pp. 287–88). The majority of workers in the West are not opposed to capitalism; the fascist movements of the 1920s and 1930s derived their strongest support from the class of small traders and minor officials, which had little to gain and much to lose by their power. There are many other instances.

Marxists have long taken cognizance of this fact; one of the themes of Lenin's *What is to be Done?* is that, without a scientific understanding of their plight, the workers themselves will spontaneously arrive at a 'bourgeois' ideology—i.e. one which serves to promote the continuance of bourgeois society. Yet one still reads Marxist accounts of such ideologies which speak of 'infiltration' of bourgeois ideas into the proletariat, which suggests the deception of a previously class-conscious proletariat by the guile of bourgeois propagandists. I think that the reason for this recurrent error in Marxist accounts of ideology, is that it is not in fact possible for Marxist theory by itself to deal adequately with this question. It is impossible because the objects of sciences other than that of social formations are involved in the production of ideology. In particular, the concepts of psychoanalysis are necessary in order to understand how the unconscious aspects of an individual's ideology are produced. Such fundamental areas of ideology as those concerning the family, sexuality, authority and obedience, and morality, cannot even begin to be understood without an account of the effects of the experience of the family on the unconscious of each individual—and that is a question for psychoanalysis, not for Marxism. Marxists who have not recognized this have tended to think that the dictum 'social existence determines consciousness' gives them a licence to explain conscious ideas directly in terms of economic relations. This has sometimes resulted in crude, mechanistic explanations of theoretical or cultural tendencies (Sartre mentions a 'simple-minded thinker who regarded Spinoza's philosophy as a direct reflection of the Dutch wheat trade')[2]—though it can also lead to an idealist overestimation of consciousness in relation to unconscious aspects of ideology.

Yet the notion that material production conditions the production of ideology (in a non-symmetrical way) by no means requires such crudity. In the first place because much of the effect of 'base' on 'superstructure' is indirect, working through institutions such as the school or the family, the 'ideological apparatuses'. But these are precisely the micro-social institutions of which Laing speaks. An 'ideological apparatus' produces ideology, not primarily because it is purpose-built to do so (though there are a few institutions—such as political parties—that are) but simply by the nature of the social relations into which it initiates people, and the way in which it causes people to apprehend those relations, through a veil of mystifications rooted in unconscious phantasies. For the most part, the primary function of an ideological apparatus is not an ideological one—e.g. the family, or for that matter the workplace, which, while it obviously exists for economic reasons, has a powerful effect in moulding the mentality of those who work in it. It is just these micro-social units in which we find ourselves, independently of our own choices or ideological tendencies, that are most effective as well as most universal in their effects. And their effectiveness rests not only in the ideas that they transmit by conscious communication, but also and predominantly in the effects of their structure on the unconscious. Given that for everyone the family is the micro-social unit in which the mind, both conscious and unconscious, is first formed, and which serves as model for all later patterns of relationship, it is the ideological effect of families on individuals which is the focal point of all analysis of ideology.

Thus, by starting 'from the other end', from a theory with primarily macro-political applications, we have arrived on the terrain mapped out by Laing and his colleagues—the psychoanalysis and social phenomenology of the small groups in which each individual lives out his or her everyday life, and through which the social structure is inevitably experienced (in a more or less mystified mode of experience).

This is not a question of trying to politicize personal relationships; the pathology of micro-social structures merits study and therapy for its own sake. But the micro-political practice of liberation indicated by this study is also an absolutely essential part of any larger movement for political and social liberation.

Once it is recognized that the ideology that has hitherto secured the cohesion of the capitalist system is not just something 'in the heads' of the masses, put there perhaps by the press, but a set of profound psychological modifications produced by and lived out in the micro-social structures in which everyone is moulded, it becomes clear that ideological struggle cannot be mere propaganda; it must be micro-politics. It is of the first importance then that we get clear what is at stake in that struggle, and what does and does not fall within its competence; also, that we base this struggle on *knowledge* of micro-social structures, not on ideological reflections of them, which are part of the problem. Now we must ask what indications Laing can give us of the lines on which this struggle can develop.

To evaluate Laing's contribution in this matter, we need to know his views on what it is about the existing micro-institutions that is so destructive. In the bulk of his work, two answers stand out as possibilities: (1) authoritarianism, and (2) misunderstandings. This applies in both the sorts of group with which Laing is 'professionally' concerned—the family and the psychiatric institution. I think it would not be unfair to describe the relation between these two problems in human relationships in the following way (using terms borrowed from Marxist theory): misunderstandings are the dominant problem, authoritarianism is determinant in the last instance.

In *Sanity, Madness and the Family* for instance, each family is a mass of mutual attributions etc. in which everyone's self-experience conflicts with everyone else's experience of them. No work of Laing's lacks this emphasis on the role of misunderstanding in human affairs, for which a notation is devised in *Interpersonal Perception,* and a theory developed in *Self and Others* and *Politics of the Family.* In *Knots* he gives terse little descriptions of the way misunderstandings reinforce one another, create 'spirals' and so on. Many of the situations he evokes are horribly recognizable; in others I feel he takes the spirals several twists beyond the level where they can be consciously experienced—e.g.:

. . . there is something the matter with him
because he thinks
   there must be something the matter with us
for trying to help him to see
that there must be something the matter with him
to think that there is something the matter with us
for trying to help him to see that
   we are helping him
to see that
   we are not persecuting him
   by helping him
   to see we are not persecuting him
   by helping him
   to see that
   he is refusing to see
   that there is something the matter with him
   for not seeing there is something the matter with him . . . (*Knots*,
p. 6)

(This 'Knot' is continued on the following page of *Knots*.) There is something almost obsessional about Laing's preoccupation with these multiple layers of disjunction between the inter-experience of individuals. But perhaps that is the effect of repeated experience of these disjunctions in the groups he has studied.

   In the Preface to *Knots*, Laing says: 'The patterns delineated here have not yet been classified by a Linnaeus of human bondage'. In many ways, Laing himself has done admirable Linnaean work of description and classification. But it is also necessary to pass beyond Linnaeus to Darwin—beyond the description and classification of phenomena, to an explanation of how they came to be as they are.

   The problem with the investigation of misunderstandings is that the light of truth does not dispel them—it is not just a

question of clearing them up by mutual sincerity and better communication. A superficial reading of Laing would indicate a
collective striptease of the soul as the way to unite 'knots'. But
the members of a family embroiled in spirals of misunderstandings have not necessarily kept their experience to themselves.
They may have talked endlessly and 'honestly' about their feelings about each other, only to become tied in more and more
complex knots; in the first place because what one honestly
thinks one feels for someone and what one actually feels (or the
feelings one acts on towards them) may be different. Also, to tell
the honest truth about one's feelings towards someone is not
necessarily either taken or meant as an exercise in communication and understanding; it may be experienced as an act of
aggression. If Jill tells Jack she feels frightened of him, this may
make him feel more frightened of her, hence more defensive and
more frightening. Communication of mutual experience between
people may, under favourable circumstances, be liberating, but
more often it is only the tying of another knot of suspicion and
disjunction

A truth that's told with bad intent
Beats all the lies you can invent (Blake)

No doubt one of the functions of a psychotherapist in such situations of disjunction is to serve as a neutral protagonist of truth,
who can help towards mutual understanding without taking
sides. But in order to understand where the dynamic of these
spiralling misunderstandings comes from, and why they are so
persistent, one needs to go beyond description to explanation.
Here we encounter the other aspect of the pathology of micro-
social structures in our society—authoritarianism.

The mystifying effect of authoritarianism can be seen behind
the failures in communication in Laing's descriptions. This can
be seen quite clearly for instance from the section on 'rules and
meta-rules' in *The Politics of the Family*; the child is commanded
under threat not to know what it does know, not to be what it is,
and not to know that it has been so commanded.

Authoritarianism within the small group (pre-eminently—

the family) always lies in the background as that which sets the
'spiralling' or 'knotted' effect in motion. In many cases, the
authoritarianism is still present, e.g. the family case histories in
which there is a one-way relationship of domination between the
patient and his/her parents. But even when a disjunction in the
inter-experience of two adults in an equal relationship is at
issue, the origins of the disjunction must be sought in their internalized parental authority. This is something which requires a
'politically' conscious application of psychoanalytical theory,
rather than (or in addition to) an account in terms of interpersonal perception.

Let us take as an example a situation set up in *Interpersonal
Perception* to illustrate a different point (concerning the relation
between experience and interpretation).

. . . a husband begins to cry. . . . For Jill, a man crying is inevitably to
be interpreted as a sign of weakness. For Jane, a man crying will be
interpreted as a sign of sensitivity. Each will react to a greater or lesser
extent according to a preconceived interpretive model which she may
or not be aware of. At its simplest level, Jill may have been taught by
her father that a man never cries, that only a sissy does. Jane may have
been taught by her father that a man can show emotion and that he is
a better man for having done so. Frequently such intermediary steps
(regulative schemata) that contribute to the determination of the experience are lost to awareness. Jill simply experiences her husband as
weak; Jane simply experiences hers as sensitive. Neither is clear why.
(pp. 10–11)

So far so good. But suppose it is pointed out to Jill that hers is
not the only or the best way of interpreting the situation, and
she assents to this. Will she forthwith cease to experience her
husband as weak? I think it is unlikely. We all cling to our own
ways of doing and of interpreting things, even when we acknow-
ledge consciously that there are other equally good ways. A
couple can have a bitter row over the correct way of peeling
potatoes or pronouncing the word 'either'. Each person invests
their own way of doing things with value, and takes the idea that
an alternative could be correct as a personal affront. Obviously
in a case as trivial as these there must be some displacement of

emotion from other matters, which remain unconscious. But what is involved in all such cases it, I think, a failure to emancipate oneself from an ego-ideal originally derived from an internalized parent, experienced as infallible and all-powerful. This accounts for the sheer obstinacy of misunderstandings. In addition to this, there is the fact that, to the extent that one has transferred feelings towards the parent of the opposite sex onto one's sexual partner, one invariably experiences one's partner as dominant and always at an advantage, oneself as the weaker and injured party in all antagonistic situations.[3] These matters must be taken into account if it is to be understood why it is that people so often appear to be intent on destroying each other, putting each other down, driving each other mad.

No doubt, if we are to avoid utopianism, we must admit that to some extent these are ineliminable features of the human condition, as every human being is dependent on adults for the early years of life. But inevitably, confronted with Laing's account of knots, disjunctions, misunderstandings in human relations, one asks how to prevent or cure them, and the relation of psychotherapy to the authoritarian form of family which at least exacerbates the difficulties attendant upon the fact that every person starts life as a child.

Psychoanalysis as a method of therapy can only remove or alleviate the effects of internalized parental authority. But those who have seen the political implications of psychoanalysis— such as Reich, Marcuse or Laing—have always posed the question, or encouraged their readers to pose the question, What could be done to create the conditions in which the problems, 'illnesses', entanglements, etc. which the psychoanalyst has to deal with would not arise?

To a limited extent this is a problem confronting the therapist himself, if he has a Laingian perspective on the effect of family and social contexts. He may be able to see what conditions in the life of the 'patient' cause (or 'render intelligible') the problem, and, if those conditions still obtain, take action to alter them. This approach is discussed by Laing in his essay 'Intervention in social situations' (reprinted in *The Politics of the Family*).

He gives the example of a nine-year-old boy who had been taken to a child guidance clinic by his mother. The child, as described by Laing, sounds normal enough and suffering from an authoritarian over-reaction by his mother to his 'naughtiness' (truancy from school etc.). Laing's conclusion was 'that there was as yet nothing seriously wrong with the boy, but there soon would be (poor prognosis), in that if everyone continued to treat him as they were doing, he would be "schizophrenic"' in six months' time'. His 'intervention' consisted of suggesting 'that no one should see the boy if he did not wish to see anyone, but that someone should have sessions with (the boy's mother) and her mother'. (*The Politics of the Family*, p. 31)

This is a good example of the practical value of inquiry into the social context of the individual who the psychiatrist is called in to help, in displacing the symptoms in need of analysis from one individual to another. Where the victim is a bit older, it might be possible to facilitate his or her leaving home. In these cases the radical psychotherapist acts as an 'outside agitator', armed with a theoretical knowledge and practical experience of oppression and mystification in the family, who helps the victims to fight a defensive struggle for their sanity and freedom. This, along with individual analysis are the possible soutions within the scope of the psychotherapist's work. There are two others: one is some sort of attempt to get individuals to 'change their heads'; the other is the replacement of the existing family structure by a different one, perhaps by communal living; parallel with this is the demand for the replacement of existing types of psychiatric institutions by new ones. Such proposals have been discussed in the last two chapters.

Inevitably, this account of what can actually be done to remedy the ills documented by Laing must seem an unsatisfying anti-climax after all the exposures of repressive ideology and the destructive socialization which installs it in us. But this is because we really are placed in a historical double bind in which there is little room for manoeuvre. On the one hand, as long as an essentially repressive civilization exists, psychoanalysis really can (as Freud thought) do no more than replace neurotic misery by ordinary human unhappiness, and micro-politics can at best create groups based on free solidarity among the oppressed, in resistance to their ongoing oppression. On the other hand, the forces that can create a free and classless society can only exist when the ideology that reconciles people to their oppression has been replaced by a clearsighted desire for liberation—that is, when the mass of people experience their oppression as intolerable. Political and ideological liberation seem to presuppose each other.

There is no easy way out of this dilemma; but it is important to avoid false exits from it. Just as an individual caught in an untenable position will be prone to find illusory ways out, the same temptation besets the politics and micro-politics of liberation. The utopian notion of liberation occurring first at the microsocial level is one such illusion. But there are more serious ones —ones which undermine the whole project of liberation—with which Laing toys at times, and which, in *The Politics of Experience*, sometimes take over completely.

False exits:

(*i*) *Moralism*

The political and moral changes that Laing refers to in the passage quoted at the head of this chapter are generally alternatives; would-be reformers and revolutionists have advocated either moral improvement or political change. The 'individual pirouette of solitary repentance' has been what most of the moral reformers and religious leaders of mankind have wished to promote. Of course they have organized, sometimes even taken over the reigns of civil government, but they have located the source of evil and the means of its correction in individual responsibility. The person who fails to live up to society's norms, rather than the antagonism of those norms to individual happiness, has been seen as the culprit. Thus the thinkers of late antiquity, from the cynics and stoics to St. Augustine, urged a retreat into oneself, a reliance on values which the misfortunes of earthly existence could not take away; for this reason independence of 'externals' was sought—including independence of things necessary to life, and including other people. No doubt this tendency in thought was a response to the impossibility, in the age after the Greek and Roman republics had fallen, of any kind of collective self-determination. It was a way of reconciliation to the impossibility of active transformation of the world, and making a virtue out of a necessity. But of course it did not stop anybody being dependent on the material world for survival, or on other people for happiness. Doctrines of individual liberation need not always be ways of resignation to frustration and unhappiness; they can also aim at removing 'inner' sources of frustration, and freeing the individual for fulfilment in the real world, including, if necessary, collective struggle to remove obstacles to fulfilment. Psychoanalysis when not corrupted into an instrument of adaptation would fall into this category. But the tendency is for any attempt at individual liberation to shut itself off from politics which it can not directly influence, and as soon as it does this, it is condemned to end as an attempt to secure happiness within existing conditions, however intolerable, and hence as a bypath from liberation and a justification of oppression and misery. Partisans of political liberation have therefore very often been suspicious of movements for individual liberation, and reasonably enough in most cases. As long as society is based on the exploitation and deprivation of the mass of people it will be necessary to fight within any movement for individual liberation to avoid this spontaneous tendency to become politically diversionary and personally enslaving. Reich and others have waged such a fight within psychoanalysis, and in many respects Laing has been their successor. But Laing has gone further in presenting theoretical reasons why the work of individual liberation must be linked, not so much with political movements as such (Laing presumably takes political leftism for granted, but says relatively little about it) but with micro-political movements.

But having a micro-political approach, not merely an individual one, does not in itself guarantee freedom from moralistic tendencies. It may merely change the direction in which the accusing finger is pointing. A realistic micro-politics will recognize the limits within which it operates until society as a whole is transformed. But such transformation seems remote, and it is tempting to look for an alternative. The alternative is a moralistic solution: attitudes of (some) parents are blamed for the plight of their children, and it is implied that what is required is 're-pentance' on the part of the parents. This is not something that Laing states, and against it must be set his warnings about witch-hunts against the mothers of schizophrenics, and his stressing of the importance of the social context of the family itself. The parents who put their children in double-bind situations have been put in such situations by their own parents, are put in them at work, etc. Laing even concedes that children can put their parents in such situations from birth on. But all this cannot eliminate the impression that Laing is also saying: people ought (morally) to treat each other differently from the way they do: if only they lived up to a certain standard, all this suffering would not occur.

There is an ideal implicit in Laing's criticism of existing conditions and this ideal is not merely a vision of life with certain present, clearly eliminable contradictions removed, but is an ideal of 'pure' emotions, to which existing emotions fail to approximate, and therefore stand condemned. Take for instance some of Laing's statements about love. He sees love as, at present, degraded and often destructive, but 'in essence' pure and altruistic. For example:

Love and violence, properly speaking, are polar opposites. Love lets the other be, but with affection and concern. Violence attempts to constrain the other's freedom, to force him to act in the way we desire, but with ultimate lack of concern . . . (*The Politics of Experience*, p. 50)

This is an acceptance at face value of the 'commonsense' and moralistic conception of the relation of love and violence, without any attempt to analyse the more complex relations they may have in the economy of the human psyche. Freud by contrast was not satisfied with this reassuring view of the matter:

In biological functions the two basic instincts [love and destruction] operate against each other or combine with each other. Thus, the act of eating is a destruction of the object with the final aim of incorporating it, and the sexual act is an act of aggression with the purpose of the most intimate union. This concurrent and mutually opposing action of the two basic instincts gives rise to the whole variegation of the phenomena of life. . . .

Modifications in the proportions of the fusion between the instincts have the most tangible results. A surplus of sexual aggressiveness will turn a lover into a sex-murderer, while a sharp diminution in the aggressive factor will make him bashful or impotent. (*Outline of Psychoanalysis*, p. 6)

(In fairness to Laing it should be noted that the expression 'lets the other be' in the above quote clearly has its existentialist sense of 'allows the other to have his own mode of being', not the colloquial English sense of 'leaves the other alone'.)

Again, Laing often appears to assume that if one expects something in return for what one does for someone, one does not do it out of true 'love'; that love would be content to be unreciprocated, and so on, though the passages where he does this could often be interpreted differently: Laing often describes a state of affairs with obvious distaste, but it is left to the readers to guess just what the distaste is for. For instance there is a passage in *Series and Nexus in the Family* (*New Left Review* No. 15, 1962) (the passage also occurs in *The Politics of Experience*, (pp. 75–76)) in which Laing appears to imply that love should be disinterested, and is violence when it expects reciprocity. (Peter Sedgwick has criticized this passage in his essay 'R. D. Laing: Self, Symptom and Society'.) This passage can however be interpreted as objecting only to the sort of moral blackmail which confers an unsolicited favour in order to extract an unintended favour in return:

'Sacrifice' under these circumstances consists in Peter impoverishing himself to do something for Paul. It is the tactic of *enforced debt*. One way of putting this is that each person *invests in the other*.

It is the contracting of the debt, not its payment, which is enforced here.

But Laing does seem to imply, here as elsewhere, that ideally every individual would be emotionally independent, and could confer love from a position of strength, as it were, not needing to be loved in return and hence able to afford to be altruistic. The ironic emphasis of the term 'invests' indicates this ideal, as does his talk elsewhere (*The Politics of Experience*, p. 62) about 'modern man' being 'addicted to other persons', as if this were a pathological condition.

My concern, my concern for your concern, your concern, and your concern for my concern, etc. is an infinite spiral, upon which rests my pride or shame in my father, sister, brother, my mother, my son, my daughter.

My security rests on his or her need for me. My need is for the *other's* need of me. His or her need is that I need him or her. My need is not simply 'need' to satisfy biological drives. It is my need to be needed by the other. My love is a thirst, not to satisfy my love, but a thirst to be loved. (*Series and Nexus in the Family*, New Left Review, No. 15 p. 13)

The latter paragraph is omitted from the passage in *The Politics of Experience* in which the adjacent paragraphs are printed. The context is a discussion of reciprocal terrorism in the family.

Is it implied here that one ought to need only satisfaction, not to be needed and loved? If so it stands in sharp contrast to the following passage from *Self and Others:*

Two basic intentions in sexuality are pleasurable relief from tension, and change in the other. . . . Any theory of sexuality which makes the 'aim' of the sexual 'instinct' the achievement of orgasmic potency alone, while the other, however selectively chosen, is a mere object, a means to this end, ignores the erotic desire to make a difference to the other. (pp. 84–85)

Both illustrate the persistent tension in Laing (as also in Sartre) between a sharp recognition of human interdependence on the one hand, and on the other, a resentment at the 'objectification' of the self by others, which is the corollary of such

G

interdependence. (This 'existentialist' conception of human relations can be seen as the origin of the slogan, once very popular in black power and women's liberationist circles, 'who defines whom?', with its mystifying implication that individuals or groups can define themselves and have the right to have their own self-conception recognized by others.) It is this tension which is reflected in the ambiguity about the preventive solution to the problems Laing describes: whether to transform the structures within which human interdependence is lived out, or to urge people to change their 'attitudes'.

(ii) Gnosticism and the inversion of personalism

Here we come back to Laing's personalism, this time to look at its political effects. Also it is time to mention another tendency running through Laing's works—his mysticism. In most of Laing's works, this tendency appears in asides only, but in *The Politics of Experience* he gives it free rein.

This is not in itself an objection. Most people have experiences which some would describe as mystical, whether induced by meditation, music, drugs or some other method. At a lecture once, where Laing mentioned this mysticism, he was asked how it affected his politics, the implication being that it would lead inevitably to quietism. He had been talking earlier about theories of perception, and he replied that his mysticism did not affect his politics, just as, if someone was dazzling him by shining a bright light in his eyes, he would go up and smash the light, whatever his theory of perception was. He was then asked if it helped in his psychoanalytic practice, and he replied that it only did insofar as it helped him understand other people with such experiences. He obviously felt that mystical or 'transcendental' experience was an end in itself, and was rejecting the utilitarian implications of the questions.

The idea of mysticism as a nice experience which is an end in itself is fair enough (if this is what he meant). But in *The Politics of Experience* the mysticism is of a special kind—a sort of gnostic idea of an inner self imprisoned in the socially conditioned self, and requiring deliverance. As this ties up with both his personalist ideology and his conception of liberation, it requires comment.

Much of the tone of *The Politics of Experience* is that of a Blakean protest against the impoverishment of experience and the imprisonment of the creative energies. Our imagination is systematically repressed from infancy on; the world we come to see is a product of the impoverished way we see it. Laing appears to agree with Blake that:

If the doors of perception were cleansed everything would appear to man as it is, infinite.

For man has closed himself up, till he sees all things thro' narrow chinks of his cavern.

and perhaps also that the cleansing of the doors of perception

will come to pass by an improvement of sensual enjoyment. (From 'The Marriage of Heaven and Hell' *Complete Writings*, p. 154)

Like Blake, Laing sees sexual repression in the family as the source of this impoverishment:

The Family's function is to repress Eros: to induce a false consciousness of security: to deny death by avoiding life: to cut off transcendence: to believe in God, not to experience the Void: to create, in short, one-dimensional man: to promote respect, conformity, obedience: to con children out of play: to induce a fear of failure: to promote a respect for work: to promote a respect for 'respectability'. (*The Politics of Experience*, p. 55)

The Family is, in the first place, the usual instrument for what is called socialization, that is, getting each new recruit to the human race to behave and experience in substantially the same way as those who have already got here. We are fallen Sons of Prophecy, who have learned to die in the Spirit and be reborn in the flesh.

This is known also as selling one's birthright for a mess of pottage. (*The Politics of Experience*, p. 57)

I have no fault to find with Laing's polemic against the impoverishment of human experience by the repressions imposed in family and school. What is interesting (and less acceptable)—specifically about the writings collected in *The Politics of Experi-*

ence—is the *metaphysic* of repression and liberation, with its suggestion of the Gnostic myths of the pre-existence of souls, their fall from a higher plain to be imprisoned in the flesh, and so on.[4] Is this just a poetic way of expressing the restriction of our possibilities through repression, or is it more?

It is revealing to compare it with the schizoid metaphysic described in *The Divided Self*.

... the 'true' self, being no longer anchored to the mortal body, becomes 'phantasticized', volatilized into a changeable phantom of the individual's own imagining. By the same token, isolated as is the self as a defence against the dangers from without which are felt as a threat to its identity, it loses what precarious identity it already has. (*The Divided Self*, p. 141)

This was part of the hell of schizophrenic experience as described in *The Divided Self*; has this embattled defence against the 'outer world' with the consequent disintegration of the self become the means of salvation in *The Politics of Experience*? On the one hand Laing has the idea of a self which ought not to be betrayed: love is seen as presenting a danger of betrayal. It begins to look like the schizoid 'true' self to which other people are always experienced as a threat.[5] On the other hand, Laing sometimes makes it sound as if the self itself is a prison which must be smashed, and this is particularly true in his more 'mystical' flights.

Is 'selfhood' the same as 'personality'? Both seem to be values for Laing in most of his work. In the earlier chapters of *The Politics of Experience* he seems chiefly concerned to defend 'personality' from rival theories which seem to him to depersonalize man (a person being defined as 'a centre of orientation of the objective universe' and 'the origin of actions'). This, as we have seen, has been a continuing preoccupation of Laing's. His practical concern seems to be the avoidance of 'betrayal of self' and the restitution of the betrayed self.

At this point it is worth comparing Laing's ideas with those of Marcuse in his political criticism of neo-Freudian revisionism in the appendix to *Eros and Civilization*.

Freud demonstrated that constraint, repression and renunciation are the stuff from which the 'free personality' is made

Freud recognized the work of repression in the highest values of Western civilization—which presuppose and perpetuate unfreedom and suffering. The Neo-Freudian schools promote the very same values as cure against unfreedom and suffering—as the triumph over repression. This intellectual feat is accomplished by expurgating the instinctual dynamic and reducing its part in the mental life. (*Eros and Civilization*, pp. 190 and 191)

The neo-Freudian revisionists as described by Marcuse have many ideas recognizable to readers of Laing.

The chief objections of the revisionists to Freud may be summed up as follows: Freud grossly underestimated the extent to which the individual and his neurosis are determined by conflicts with his environment. Freud's 'biological orientation' led him to concentrate on the phylogenetic and ontogenetic *past* of the individual: he considered the character as essentially fixed with the fifth or sixth year (if not earlier), and he interpreted the fate of the individual in terms of primary instincts and their vicissitudes, especially sexuality. In contrast, the revisionists shift the emphasis 'from the past to the present', from the biological to the cultural level, from the 'constitution' of the individual to his environment. 'One can understand the biological development better if one discards the concept of libido altogether' and instead interprets the different stages 'in terms of growth and of human relations'. Then the subject of psychoanalysis becomes the 'total personality' in its 'relatedness to the world'; and the 'constructive aspects of the individual', his 'productive and possible potentialities', receive the attention they deserve. (*Eros and Civilization*, pp. 196–97)

The 'free personality' according to Marcuse is precisely the result of repression, and to play down the instinctual dynamic in its name is to justify the repressions imposed by society. I have already discussed these aspects of post-Freudian developments in Chapter 2.

If Marcuse is correct, what follows about the fate of personality? If the personality formed by existing society is the product of repression and suffering, and serves to make possible adaptation to that society at the expense of instinctual gratification, that means that the idolization of personality at the expense of understanding its origins in the vicissitudes of the instincts in society is a repressive mystification. But it does not mean that personality as such should be seen as a disvalue. Its dependence should be recognized, but this theoretical depersonalization involved in Freudian interpretation does not lead to the breakdown of the personality by psychoanalysis, but only of certain of its defence-mechanisms—including perhaps its illusion of autonomy.

There is not, according to Freudian theory, a true self or personality alongside the false one imposed by repressive society: there is only the actual personality ('ego') and the instincts out of which it has been constructed. Liberation, then, consists not in the removal of the false self and the emergence of the true self, but in the transformation of the self from one which inhibits instinctual satisfaction to one which facilitates it.

All this is important because one aspect of Laing's mysticism seems to be a notion of the personality (or ego, or false self) as an incorrigible product of repressive society, which ought to be dissolved entirely. This appears at first in sharp contrast to his personalism: he has all along been saying: man is a self, not a bundle of processes. And now he says: selfhood is an illusion created by society's violence against the individual.

The ego is by definition an instrument of adaptation (*The Politics of Experience*, p. 57)

But somewhere—Laing seems to be assuming—there is another self, another centre of orientation and originator of actions, which, if only the 'egoic' self were eliminated, could be delivered.

There is a union here of a psychological critique of 'normal personality', not only with a political critique of the conditioning agencies which produced it, but also with a religious critique of the normal experience which fails to perceive spiritual beings and the like—a union unprecedented except in Blake. In the chapter of *The Politics of Experience* entitled 'Transcendental Experience' Laing appears to assume the reality of this spiritual world, and add to the indictment of repressive civilization that it incapacitates us for perceiving it. This is exactly Blake's position. It is not within the scope of this book to discuss the validity of this position, though it does seem to imply that previous, nonsecular civilizations were in some way less repressive.

It is the metapsychology implied that is interesting, as is also the 'way of liberation', it suggests. There is an almost exact replication of the themes of Gnosticism in *The Politics of Experience* (as also in David Cooper's *The Death of the Family*). This is not accidental. Cooper refers a number of times to 'Gnosis'. In *The Divided Self* Laing mentions Gnosticism in a footnote as expressing schizoid hatred of the body. In *The Politics of Experience* he adopts a very similar dualism of empirical (egoic) self and transcendental self. The political starting point of this Gnosticism is that western societies are capitalist ones based on exploitation, and their ideological apparatuses (agencies of socialization) are geared to producing suitable human material for exploitation; socialization by these agencies leads to a great restriction of human possibilities.

So far so good. But the position which Laing and Cooper base on this is mistaken. It seems to be as follows: (1) The empirical self is completely a product of capitalist ideological apparatuses; (2) it is therefore totally corrupt, as part of a totally corrupt society; (3) it must be destroyed to make way for the transcendental self.

As against this, it seems to me that the following are true: (1) The total being of each individual is produced by capitalist society and its agencies of socialization, though the raw material of this production process is a set of biologically given needs, dispositions, potentialities etc. (2) the transcendental self exists only as the ideal of the empirical self, and conforms more closely to the ideological requirements of capitalist society than any other aspect of the individual's being; (3) Capitalism does not *only* perpetuate exploitation; as a necessary condition of doing so it also produces (for the most part) the goods necessary for survival, and promotes the economic, scientific and cultural progress of mankind. We should never forget that it does exploit the workers, impoverish the under-developed world, waste resources, pollute the environment, frustrate basic human needs, and so on. But we should also not forget that it is not some monstrous calamity that has overtaken modern man, but the most progressive form of society that has hitherto been established. The fact that we acquire our socially determined characteristics within this society (how else could we acquire them?) should not make us think of them as contaminated—many of them are necessary conditions of life in any society. Take for instance the following passage from *The Politics of Experience:*

We are taught what to experience and what not to experience, as we are taught what movements to make and what sounds to emit. A child of two is already a moral mover and moral talker and moral experiencer. He already moves the 'right' way, makes the 'right' noises, and knows what he should feel and what he should not feel. His movements have become stereometric types, enabling the specialist anthropologist to identify, through his rhythm and style, his national, even his regional, characteristics. As he is taught to move in specific ways, out of the whole range of possible movements, so he is taught to experience, out of the whole range of possible experience. (p. 51)

The implication is clearly that what is described in this passage is a deplorable form of brainwashing; yet clearly in order to learn to talk, a child must learn some specific language and dialect within that language; he can later learn others only on this basis. It is absurd to find this fact, or any equivalent facts that there might be in relation to bodily movement and the like, in any way objectionable.

The capitalist mode of production with its ideological and political ramifications should be opposed because it frustrates the desires of the individuals within it, in quite specific ways determined by their economic class and position in relation to the ideological and political apparatuses. It should not be opposed *along with* these desires in favour of an ideal which anyway turns out to derive from the moral ideology of precisely that society. An inventory of the values held out as the basis of new and liberated personal relationships in works such as *The Death of the Family* or *The Politics of Experience*, shows them to be precisely the old repressive values of the bourgeois protestant tradition from Calvin through Kant and Fichte to the Festival of Light: individual independence, refusal to let oneself be 'used', the equation of active with good and passive with bad, the non-quantifiability of love, the outlawing of secrets in relationships, belief that 'sexual objectification' is degrading, etc.

Laing's differences from other related positions can be schematized without too much falsification in terms of the following metapsychological and therapeutic models:

(1) Freudian.

first there are the instincts;

their interaction with the outside world (mainly other people) leads to the formation of the ego, whose task is to mediate between the demands of the instincts and the real world;

psychic illness occurs when the ego fails to do this effectively in important respects;

cure consists of strengthening the ego by overcoming its obsolete defensive formations which it acquired in childhood, thus increasing the self-awareness of the ego (including awareness of the demands made on it by the instincts) and its effective functioning.

(2) Left Freudian.

as above, but adds that it is 'surplus-repression' required by societies based on class-exploitation which is largely the cause of the defence-mechanisms which prevent healthy ego-functioning.

(3) Personalist.

the ego is autonomous, though it is also a social product and only exists in relation to other people;

psychic illness occurs when ego loses autonomy;

cure = restoration of autonomy through self-awareness and supportive relationship with psychotherapist.

(4) Left Personalist.

as above, but adds that loss of autonomy is due to failure of society (notably, of parents) to recognize it.

I take it that 2 is roughly the position of Reich and Marcuse, and 3 that of most existential psychiatrists; most 'revisionist'

analysts tend towards 3 as well. 4 is clearly Laing's position in
The Divided Self; elsewhere he combines elements of 2 and 4;
but in the more 'mystical' passages of *The Politics of Experience* a new model seems to have emerged:
(5) Gnostic.

first there is the self;

it becomes imprisoned in the ego—which is an instrument
for living in *this* world—as a result of violence perpetrated by
this world;

this imprisonment constitutes 'psychic illness', but is also
the general state of 'normal' people;

cure is the breaking up of the ego (by drugs, religious experience or 'madness');

the self is then released and experiences 'other worlds' as
well (see the chapter 'Transcendental Experience' for this
model).

I once had to mark an exam paper in which one question
asked whether the correct conclusion to draw from Laing's *The
Politics of Experience* was to smash capitalism, to take LSD, or
to join a Buddhist monastery. One student answered: first to
take LSD (to rid one's mind of its conditioning); then to smash
capitalism (to prevent such conditioning in the future); then to
join a Buddhist monastery (to expand the new insights into the
'other world'). This programme seems to me exactly what is suggested by that book.

The problem, however, is what the self which is to be set free is.
If one is to remain within the bounds of science, nothing pre-existing the formation of the ego can have the characteristics of a self—
an organizing centre of experience and behaviour. The only self
is the ego. It can be antagonistic to the instincts or conducive
to their gratification and if the former it may progress to the
latter, perhaps with psychoanalytic help, but this is not the
emergence of another self which existed in an imprisoned state
all along; that would be at best a mythological expression of the
fact that certain *desires* emerge that were formerly repressed,
but these do not constitute a self. Maybe the 'non-egoic self' is a
way of referring to the instincts ('id' rather than 'ego' in Freudian

terms) but the breaking up of the ego would leave the instincts blind, unable to relate to the world.

Certain passages in Laing do suggest that the 'non-egoic self' would not be a self in the accepted sense:

This identity-anchored, space-and-time-bound experience has been studied philosophically by Kant, and later by the phenomenologists, e.g. Husserl, Merleau-Ponty. Its historical and ontological relativity should be fully realized by any contemporary student of the human scene. (*The Politics of Experience*, p. 113)

A 'self' which does not experience its own identity through space and time and its difference from other selves could not have any experience of the sort on which knowledge and action could be based—that is surely what Kant and the phenomenologists have shown. If anthropologists and neo-Marxists fall so far into their besetting fallacy of relativism that they think human society could exist without 'egoic' experience, they are simply confused.

At the same time, there is a sense in which Laing is right in saying that the ego is an illusion. 'Subjectivity'—our apparently self-validating self-experience as centres of the world and originators of action—is illusory insofar as it is not *knowledge* of ourselves. Human life is understood correctly when it is recognized that the 'subjects' of activity are not selves but a set of interacting psychic processes, many of them unconscious. Our egos are real alright, but they are only an aspect of these processes, and our inherent tendency—perhaps unavoidable at the level of everyday experience—to make our egos the centres and originators—in short the subjects—of human interaction, is an illusion.

But throughout most of his theoretical writings, Laing has been promoting and defending just this illusion against those who would make psychology a science of drives, desires, wishes, defence-mechanisms etc. rather than of 'persons'. He mentions on p. 113 of *The Politics of Experience* that 'egoic' experience gives 'a sense of ontological security'; his view in *The Divided Self* seemed to have been that a psychiatrist should promote ontological security by confirming egoic experience both in theory and in practice. Now, the dissolution of egoic experience seems to be his 'final solution'.

> If I could turn you on, if I could drive you out of your wretched mind,
> If I could tell you I would let you know. (*Bird of Paradise*, p. 156)

Perhaps what Laing found in Taoism and the mystical aspects of religion—though he could also have found it within psycho-analysis—was a recognition of the passivity and dependence of human beings in relation to nature both 'within' and 'without', and to other human beings; against this stands the idealist and moralist assertion that only what is conscious and active is human, and only what is human is good.

This insight which seems to have dawned on Laing belatedly as light from the East could have been derived from psycho-analysis and linked with a political, micro-political and thera-peutic programme free from the nightmare of anxiety and mutual destruction of egos which haunts much of Laing's work, like that of his existentialist predecessors. The aim might be, in Marcuse's terms:

> man intelligent enough and healthy enough to dispense with all heroes and heroic virtues, man without the impulse to live danger-ously, to meet the challenge; man with the good conscience to make life an end-in-itself, to live in joy without fear. 'Polymorphous sexual-ity' was the term which I used to indicate that the new direction of progress would depend completely on the opportunity to activate re-pressed or arrested *organic*, biological needs: to make the human body an instrument of pleasure rather than labor. (*Eros and Civiliza-tion*, p. 13)

But this does not mean that man could live without an ego, with-out conscious activity and struggle against the forces which prevent the realization of this vision of a 'pacified existence'. Unfortunately, Laing's involvement with anti-personalist mysti-cism led him out of these struggles for social liberation into a Theravada Buddhist monastery[6] (Theravada Buddhism is dis-tinguished by its rejection of the idea that there is a 'true' self to realize: there is only a false self to eliminate, and then Nir-vana).

By way of conclusion

> Do not adjust your minds—reality is out of focus
> (Graffito on lavatory wall at University College, London)

There are three theoretical operations going on in Laing's writings. The first is a scientific one—the extension of our knowledge of family and group interaction on the basis of psychoanalytic theory with some social-phenomenological accretions. The second is ideological, at the level of philosophical ideology; this is the revision of psychoanalytic theory to conform to a personalistic ethic and methodology derived from existentialism. The third is 'political' in the wider sense; the defence of the socially critical element in psychoanalysis, against every revision of therapeutic aims in the direction of 'adjustment'.

It should be clear that my own view is to value the first and third theoretical operations very highly, but to reject the second. I do not think this is merely an external judgement imposed on Laing's work from my own standpoint—I believe there are tensions within Laing's work itself between the second and third theoretical operations. For though superficially it seems plausible to use 'respect for persons' as a principle for opposing adjustment-therapies, the notion of personal responsibility has deeper roots in the practice of justifying society's demand for the conformity of the individual to its rules, and its claim to the right to condemn or punish those who do not conform. The 'personal' aspects of the human individual are precisely those aspects which are the product of adjustment to society's demands.

This tension explodes in *The Politics of Experience* into a denial *both* of the reality of the personal 'egoic' self, and that of the outside world.

Philosophically, Laing ends up in *The Politics of Experience* as an idealist of the purest type. The essence of idealism is the failure to distinguish theory (by which we know the world) from practice (by which we change it). Knowledge or perception are seen by the idealist as forms of action, which themselves change the world. There are two things which this idealist notion of the identity of theory and practice would make redundant—science, the effort to find out what the world is like independently of us; and practice, the attempt to change it. In place of these, an attempt to change one's head and *thereby* change everything, is indicated—a mystical practice which never gets outside the mind.

The graffito slogan above is unfortunately ambiguous, and the ambiguity is that of Laing's thought: does it mean 'do not adjust your *desires* to the situation—try to change your situation and fulfil them', or does it mean 'do not worry whether your beliefs are true or false of reality—believe what you wish, for reality is dependent on your way of seeing it'? The former is a formula for radicalism, the latter for idealism. But remembering Freud's formulations (see pp. 120–21 above) we can also say: the former is a formula for normality, the latter for psychosis. The 'normality' about which Laing is so scathing—the statistical normality of mystified and repressive families—is a neurotic position, and psychotherapists who advocate adjustment are prescribing neurosis as a cure for neurosis. Any protest against this is welcome, but it should avoid ending up by prescribing psychosis as a cure for neurosis.

In the end, one has to choose what one wants from Laing. If one reads the whole of his work through *The Politics of Experience* as many do, the earlier works become pointless in the last analysis. It is as if Marx had put his pen down after writing *Capital* and said 'So you see, the world is a vale of tears; best to forget it and contemplate our navels'.

On the other hand, one can concentrate on texts such as the case studies in *Sanity, Madness and the Family*, the second part of *Self and Others* and the papers collected in *The Politics of the Family*, and read Laing as a psychoanalyst with a keen eye for the effects of reality-problems in producing neurosis and especially psychosis, which might appear to be even further removed from them; and above all, one who described how one person's reality-problem is often an effect of the transpersonal defence-mechanisms of others. It is only such a reading that can help us understand and change the micro-social structures in which we find ourselves.

Notes to the Text

Chapter 1

1 Defined in the first sentence of *The Divided Self*, which reads: 'The term schizoid refers to an individual the totality of whose experience is split in two main ways: in the first place, there is a rent in his relation with his world and, in the second, there is a disruption of his relation with himself.' (p. 17)

2 The term 'depersonalization' appears in conventional psychiatric literature, meaning a feeling of the unreality of the self, but this is only one aspect of the meaning of this term for Laing.

3 The songs of *The Who* are particularly expressive of this mode of experience; indeed, the name of the group itself suggests ontological insecurity.

4 It is convenient when discussing existentialist ontology to conjugate the verb 'to be' in this non-standard manner. I mean to indicate thereby that the sentences concerned are to be read with a greater stress on the verb 'to be' than in normal English. The existentialists use this verb in an unusually active sense, and in Sartre it can even have the passive form 'is beed' (*est été*). Also it should take an adverbial rather than an adjectival complement in English, i.e. 'to be authentically'.

5 According to Blake: 'Men are admitted into Heaven not because they have curbed & govern'd their Passions or have No Passions, but because they have Cultivated their Understandings. The Treasures of Heaven are not Negations of Passion, but Realities of Intellect, from which all the Passions Emanate Uncurbed in their Eternal Glory.' (From 'A Vision of the Last Judgement', *Complete Writings*, p. 615)

6   cf. Peter Sedgwick: 'Laing has in fact been at deliberate pains, in his
    borrowings from the more opaque existentialist writers, to demystify
    their categories . . . "Being-in-the-world" means social interaction
    between persons, and Kierkegaard's "Sickness unto Death" is not the
    loneliness of the soul before God but the despair of the psychotic.
    Laing is, in short, naturalizing the mystical elements in one current of
    Continental existentialist thought.' (From 'R. D. Laing: self, symp-
    tom and society' in *Laing and Anti-Psychiatry*, ed. Boyers, p. 15)

7   For instance in *Self and Others* he says that, in the ontological in-
    security described in *The Divided Self*, '. . . man, as a person, encounters
    non-being, in a preliminary form, as partial loss of the synthetic unity
    of self . . .' among other things. (p. 51)
        I take it that by the term '*synthetic* unity' he means to indicate that
    this unity is the result of a process of unification, not an original unity.
    This point is made even more explicitly in *The Divided Self*, p. 77:
    '. . . the schizoid state we are describing, can be understood as an
    attempt to preserve a being that is precariously structured. We shall
    suggest later that the initial structuralization of being into its basic
    elements occurs in early infancy'.

8   In his book *The Leaves of Spring*, Esterson (Laing's collaborator on
    Sanity, Madness and the Family) recognizes that e.g. a family will
    produce an appearance of harmony, though actually riddled with
    conflicts. But he also speaks of some things being contradictions only
    because they conflict with our expectations, which again subjectivizes
    the notion of contradiction in an idealist fashion.

9   cf. Louis Althusser in his article 'Freud and Lacan', in *Lenin and
    Philosophy*: 'Since Copernicus, we have known that the earth is not
    the "centre" of the universe. Since Marx, we have known that the
    human subject, the economic, political or philosophical ego is not the
    "centre" of history—and even, in opposition to the philosophers of
    the Enlightenment and to Hegel, that history has no "centre" but
    possesses a structure which has no necessary "centre" except in
    ideological misrecognition. In turn, Freud has discovered for us that
    the real subject, the individual in his unique essence, has not the form
    of an ego, centred on the "ego", on "consciousness" or on "existence"
    —whether this is the existence of the for-itself, of the body-proper or
    of "behaviour"—that the human subject is de-centred, constituted by
    a structure that has no "centre" either, except in the imaginary mis-
    recognition of the "ego", i.e. in the ideological formations in which
    it "recognizes" itself.' (p. 201)

10 See for instance James Baldwin's comments on sexual myths about
    black people in his essay 'The Black Boy Looks at the White Boy' in
    his book *Nobody knows my Name*.

11 Esterson, op. cit. p. 220: 'For some time now psychiatrists have been
    urging that "schizophrenics" be treated as persons. This seems an
    implicit attempt to break out of the natural scientific way of seeing
    them which involves studying them as if they were things or organ-
    isms.' Yet doctors in non-psychiatric specialties which clearly, from

a scientific point of view, treat the patient as an organism not as a person, can also cause offence by a cold and indifferent manner, or, alternatively, make things pleasanter for the patient by their warmth and concern. This has nothing to do with the way the patient is constituted as an object of medical science.

12 Esterson, op. cit. p. 248: '. . . the method of therapeutic regression, intended to help free the person from carry-overs bedevilling his relations, requires him to accept what is in effect an experience of radical personal defeat. He must let himself fail in his experience of himself as rational, integrated and autonomous in the presence of the analyst, discovering, reliving, and working through the relevant childhood phantasy relations, finding in weakness strength, in defeat a moment of healing. Said William Blake, "A fool, if he persists in his foolishness, may become wise".' Is this not a 'good depersonalization', which may be necessary in order to achieve self-awareness and the capacity for gratification?

13 In his article 'Sanity, Madness and the Problem of Knowledge' in *Radical Philosophy*, No. 1, 1972. I shall say more about this notion below (in Chapter 3).

Chapter 2

1 cf. what Lévi-Strauss says in relation to Durkheim's method: 'In all forms of human thought and activity, one cannot ask questions regarding nature or origin before having identified and analysed phenomena and discovered to what extent their interrelations suffice to explain them. It is impossible to discuss an object, to reconstruct the process of its coming into being without knowing first *what it is*; in other words, without having exhausted the inventory of its internal determinants.' (*The Scope of Anthropology*, p. 11)

2 At the end of the chapter on 'The Abbotts' in *Sanity, Madness and the Family*, Maya's symptoms are said to be 'the outcome of her inter-experience and interaction with her parents'. What does 'outcome' mean here if it is not a causal notion?

3 In *Politics and History*, and elsewhere.

4 Hegel. Quoted by Engels in *Anti-Duhring*, part I, chapter XI. Engels comments: 'Freedom does not consist in the dream of independence from natural laws, but in the knowledge of these laws, and in the possibility this gives of systematically making them work towards definite ends. This holds good in relation both to the laws of external nature and to those which govern the bodily and mental existence of men themselves.' (pp. 136–37)

5 It is instructive to compare Freud's account of the actual neuroses in several of the papers in his *Collected Papers*, vol. I, with the entry on actual neurosis in Rycroft's *Critical Dictionary of Psychoanalysis*. In Freud it is sexual frustration or inadequate forms of gratification which are considered pathogenic; Rycroft speaks of 'sexual excess'

and 'unrelieved sexual stimulation' as causing these neuroses. In place of the economic principle, with its implication that frustration is pathogenic, we have a formula compatible with a moralistic conception of 'unwise' sexual behaviour.

6   See his paper, 'The Loss of Reality in Neurosis and Psychosis' in his *Collected Papers*, vol. II, which is best read in conjunction with his paper 'The Two Principles of Mental Functioning' in the *Collected Papers*, vol. IV.

7   On this practical contradiction in the work of an analyst, and its theoretical effects, see Sean Sayers' paper 'Mental Illness as a Moral Concept' in *Radical Philosophy*, No. 5, Summer 1973.

8   This should not be taken as meaning that a union of social phenomenology and psychoanalysis would leave social phenomenology purely descriptive and introduce causal notions only in the psychoanalysis of the individuals. The explanatory role of social phenomenology is dangerous only when isolated from psychoanalytical explanation, and therefore permitted to ignore the intra-personal aspect.

Chapter 3

1   As Freud says: 'With the introduction of the reality-principle one mode of thought-activity was split off; it was kept free from reality-testing and remained subordinated to the pleasure-principle alone. This is the act of *phantasy-making* . . .' He adds in a footnote: 'Just as a nation whose wealth rests on the exploitation of its land yet reserves certain territory to be preserved in its original state and protected from cultural alterations, e.g. Yellowstone Park.' (*Collected Papers*, vol. IV, pp. 16–17)

2   *Critique of Pure Reason*, A58–59. Kant likens the pursuit of a general criterion of truth to 'one man milking a he-goat, and the other holding a sieve underneath'.

3   In a reply to Pateman's article, in *Radical Philosophy*, No. 2, 1972, Martin Skelton-Robinson interprets him as meaning that parents are *legitimate* epistemological authorities, but nothing in Pateman's article suggests this, and nothing in it implies a relativistic conception of truth (though Pateman is in fact a relativist—see his article 'Language, Truth and Politics', in *Radical Philosophy*, No. 8, 1974).

4   Of course the 'schizophrenics' studied in Laing's works are not children but generally young adults. But the disorientation of their experience through the transpersonal defences at work in their families of origin had started when they were children. The possibility of making schizophrenia intelligible in terms of later relationships is quite a different matter.

5   See Freud's paper on 'Family Romances' in his *Collected Papers*, vol. V. It is interesting that the opening paragraph of this paper is very close to Laingian themes: 'The freeing of the individual, as he grows

up, from the authority of his parents is one of the most necessary though one of the most painful results brought about by the course of his development. It is quite essential that that liberation should occur and it may be presumed that it has been to some extent achieved by everyone who has reached a normal state. Indeed the whole progress of society rests upon the opposition between successive generations. On the other hand, there is a class of neurotics whose condition is recognisably determined by their having failed in this task.'

6 Agnes Lawson's mother's attitude is described in the following terms: 'Mrs. Lawson had no objection to Agnes going to dances or going out with boys—she should go out, but Agnes had never been one for doing so. However, she wouldn't like Agnes to be like some of the types today. As for the boys, she didn't mind what boy she went out with provided he intended to marry her and was not flighty. She never objected to Agnes kissing boys. It was natural, provided it wasn't done openly, but that was Agnes' business. She would not interfere, unless he wasn't Agnes' type.' (*Sanity, Madness and the Family*, p. 242)

Chapter 4

1 Something similar is argued by Reimut Reiche in *Sexuality and the Class Struggle* (New Left Books). For a critical review of this book, see David Fernbach, 'Sexual Oppression and Political Practice' in *New Left Review*, No. 64, November–December 1970.

2 This is one of Juliet Mitchell's criticisms of Laing. Her extremely interesting and important book *Psychoanalysis and Feminism* was published while I was in the process of writing the present book; the two chapters in it on Laing are certainly the best commentary and criticism of his work that I have seen. But while she gives him credit as an 'ideologist' for his descriptions and his polemical position, I feel that she does not do justice to his scientific contribution—notably to the theory of trans-personal defences. This is because she sees him as rejecting explanation in terms of infantile experience and unconscious phantasy in favour of contextual explanation, whereas I think that, in his best work (e.g. *Sanity, Madness and the Family* and *The Politics of the Family*) he is assuming the validity of the former sort of explanation, but extending the field of inquiry to interpersonal relations. With Juliet Mitchell's criticisms of Laing's existentialist heritage and personalist methodology I am in complete agreement, as should already be clear.

3 cf. Marx: 'I paint the capitalist and the landlord in no sense *couleur de rose*. But here individuals are dealt with only in so far as they are the personifications of economic categories, embodiments of particular class-relations and class-interests. My standpoint, from which the evolution of the economic formation of society is viewed as a process of natural history, can less than any other make the individual re-

sponsible for relations whose creature he socially remains, however much he may subjectively raise himself above them.' (*Capital*, vol. I, p. 10)

An analysis of micro-social structures such as the family should observe a similar principle.

Chapter 5

1 For instance, in *The Psychotic*, which is a popular account of psychosis by Andrew Crowcroft, a psychiatrist with a psychoanalytical (Kleinian) orientation, great stress is laid on getting people to see psychosis as an illness that happens to people, like any other; yet the same book also stresses that psychosis is understandable in terms of the same concepts which we use to understand normal experience.

2 See Sean Sayers' review of Szasz's *Ideology and Insanity*, in *The Human Context*, Summer 1975.

3 The essay dates from 1964, the same year in which *Sanity, Madness and the Family* was published.

4 cf. Juliet Mitchell: 'Religious mystics may have the capacity to temporarily abandon their ego-boundaries; the chronic schizophrenic has none properly developed to give up. The ecstasy of the mystic, the choice of the drug-taker, is the predicament of the psychotic.' (*Psychoanalysis and Feminism*, p. 267)

5 There is a moving account of (among other things) one person's experience of such a community in *Mary Barnes—two accounts of a journey through madness* by Mary Barnes and Joseph Berke.

6 See, if you must, the section on psychoanalysis in *Between Existentialism and Marxism*, a collection of recent writings by Sartre. This consists of a bootleg transcription of a conversation between an analyst and his patient, in a potentially violent situation, together with a preface by Sartre and replies by Pontalis and Pingaud, which to my mind effectively destroy Sartre's case. I must admit that I cannot see Sartre's publication of this dialogue as other than an irresponsible act of sabotage against psychoanalysis, unworthy of a thinker of Sartre's calibre.

Chapter 6

1 In his paper 'Ideology and the State' in *Lenin and Philosophy*, New Left Books.

2 *Literary and Philosophical Essays* (p. 198).

3 It is interesting in this connection to note the relative rarity of such disputes between heterosexual members of the same sex living together.

4 For a full account of Gnosticism, see *The Gnostic Religion* by Hans Jonas. There is a shorter account (referred to by Laing in *The Divided*

Self) in Rudolf Bultmann's *Primitive Christianity in its Contemporary Setting*. Both books are written from a perspective influenced by Heidegger's existentialism.

5 To these 'existentialistic' parts of *The Politics of Experience*, all the criticisms I level against such tendencies as they appear in *The Divided Self* are applicable, without the considerable reservations I make about applying them to that book.

6 This occurred in 1971 (see the postscript to Peter Sedgwick's paper in *Laing and Anti-Psychiatry*). Laing has not published any new books since this date, although he is now again practising as a psychoanalyst. (Since the time of writing, another book by Laing has appeared, *The Facts of Life* (Pantheon, 1976).) I should perhaps point out that I do not share Sedgwick's view that this action of Laing's was in some way a political betrayal. No doubt there is plenty wrong with Ceylon, but there is plenty wrong with Britain too. Laing's motives are no one's concern but his own, but his published writings are everyone's concern, and there is a tendency to nihilistic mysticism in the later ones, which I believe is a false path.

Bibliography

Editions are cited in the following order: American hardcover; American paperback; British hardback; British paperback.

Works by Laing

The Divided Self, New York, Pantheon Books, 1969; Baltimore, Penguin, 1971; London, Tavistock, 1960; Harmondsworth, Penguin, 1970

The Self and Others, New York, Pantheon Books, 1970; Baltimore, Penguin, 1972; London, Tavistock, 1961; a revised edition entitled *Self and Others* was issued in 1971 by Tavistock, London, and Penguin, Harmondsworth; all references are to the Penguin edition

'Series and Nexus in the Family', *New Left Review*, no. 15, 1962

Sanity, Madness and the Family (with Aaron Esterson), New York, Basic Books, 1971; Baltimore, Penguin, 1972; London, Tavistock, 1964; Harmondsworth, Penguin, 1970

Reason and Violence (with David Cooper), New York, Pantheon Books, 1971; New York, Vintage Books, 1971; Tavistock, London, 1964, revised edition 1971

Interpersonal Perception (with Phillipson and Lee), New York, Springer Publishing Co., 1966; New York, Harper & Row, 1972; London, Tavistock, 1966

The Politics of Experience, New York, Pantheon Books, 1967; New York, Ballantine Books, 1968; Harmondsworth, Penguin, 1970 (paperback)

'The Obvious' in David Cooper (ed.), *The Dialectics of Liberation*, New York, Collier Books, 1969 (paperback); Harmondsworth, Penguin, 1968 (paperback)

The Politics of the Family, New York, Pantheon Books, 1971; New York, Vintage Books, 1972; London, Tavistock, 1971; Harmondsworth, Penguin, 1971

Knots, New York, Pantheon Books, 1970; New York, Vintage Books, 1972; London, Tavistock, 1970; Harmondsworth, Penguin, 1972

The Facts of Life, New York, Pantheon Books, 1976

Other works referred to in the text

Althusser, Louis, *For Marx*, New York, Pantheon Books, 1970; New York, Vintage Books, 1970; London, Allen Lane, 1970
   Politics and History, London, New Left Books, 1972
   Lenin and Philosophy, New York, Monthly Review Press, 1972 (hardcover and paperback); London, New Left Books, 1971

Baldwin, James, *Nobody Knows My Name*, New York, Dial Press, 1961; New York, Dell Publishing Co., 1962; London, Michael Joseph, 1964; London, Corgi, 1969

Barnes, Mary, and Berke, Joseph, *Mary Barnes*, New York, Harcourt, Brace, Jovanovich, 1972; New York, Ballantine Books, 1973; London, MacGibbon & Kee, 1971; Harmondsworth, Penguin, 1973

Bateson, Gregory, *Steps to an Ecology of Mind*, Corte Madera, California, Chandler & Sharp, 1972; New York, Ballantine Books, 1972; London, Intertext, 1972; London, Paladin, 1973

Beauvoir, Simone de, *The Second Sex*, New York, Knopf, 1953; New York, Vintage Books, 1974; London, Cape, 1968; Harmondsworth, Penguin, 1972

Blake, William, *Complete Writings*, New York and London, Oxford University Press, 1966 (hardcover and paperback)

Boyers, Robert, and Orrill, Robert (eds.), *Laing and Anti-Psychiatry*, New York, Octagon Books, 1971; New York, Harper & Row, 1971; Harmondsworth, Penguin, 1972

Brentano, Franz, *Psychology from an Empirical Standpoint*, Atlantic Highlands, New Jersey, Humanities Press, 1973; London, Routledge & Kegan Paul, 1973

Bukharin, Nicolai, *Historical Materialism*, Ann Arbor and London, University of Michigan Press, 1970

Bultmann, Rudolf, *Primitive Christianity in its Contemporary Setting*, New York, New American Library, Meridian Books, 1956 (paperback); London, Collins, 1960

Cooper, David, *Psychiatry and Anti-Psychiatry*, New York, Barnes & Noble, 1967; New York, Ballantine Books, 1971; London, Paladin, 1970 (paperback)
   The Death of the Family, New York, Pantheon Books, 1970; New York, Vintage Books, 1971; London, Allen Lane, 1971; Harmondsworth, Penguin, 1972
   (ed.), *To Free a Generation: The Dialectics of Liberation*, New York, Collier Books, 1969 (paperback); Harmondsworth, Penguin, 1968 (paperback)

The Grammar of Living, New York, Pantheon Books, 1974; London, Allen Lane, 1974

Davidson, Donald, 'Actions, Reasons and Causes' in White, Alan R. (ed.), *The Philosophy of Action*, New York, Oxford University Press, 1968 (paperback); London, Oxford University Press, 1968

Engels, Friedrich (see also under Marx), *Anti-Dühring*, New York, International Publishers Co., 1966 (hardcover and paperback); London, Lawrence & Wishart, 1955

Esterson, Aaron, *The Leaves of Spring*, New York, Barnes & Noble, 1970; Baltimore, Penguin, 1972; London, Tavistock, 1970; Harmondsworth, Penguin, 1972

Evans, R. I., *R. D. Laing, The Man and His Ideas*, New York, Dutton, 1976 (paperback)

Eysenck, H. J., *Fact and Fiction in Psychology*, Santa Fe, New Mexico, William Gannon, 1972; Baltimore, Penguin, 1965; Harmondsworth, Penguin, 1970 (paperback)

Fernbach, David, 'Sexual Oppression and Political Practice', *New Left Review*, no. 64, 1970

Flügel, J. C., *The Psychoanalytic Study of the Family*, Atlantic Highlands, New Jersey, Humanities Press, 1960; London, Hogarth Press, 1960

Foucault, Michel, *Madness and Civilization*, New York, Pantheon Books, 1965; New York, Vintage Books, 1973; London, Tavistock, 1971

Foulkes, S. H., and Anthony, E. J., *Group Psychotherapy*, 2nd edition, Santa Fe, New Mexico, William Gannon; Baltimore, Penguin, 1965; Harmondsworth, Penguin, 1965 (paperback)

Frankl, Viktor, *Psychotherapy and Existentialism*, New York, Simon & Schuster, Touchstone-Clarion, 1968 (paperback); London, Souvenir Press, 1970; Harmondsworth, Penguin, 1973

Friedenberg, Edgar, *R. D. Laing*, New York, Viking, 1974 (hardcover and paperback); London, Woburn Press, 1974; London, Fontana, 1973

Freud, Sigmund, *The Interpretation of Dreams*, New York, Basic Books, 1954; New York, Avon Books, 1967; London, Allen & Unwin, 1955

Jokes and Their Relation to the Unconscious, New York, Norton, 1961 (paperback); London, Routledge & Kegan Paul, 1966

The Psychopathology of Everyday Life, New York, Norton, 1971 (paperback); London, Benn, 1966; Harmondsworth, Penguin, 1975

Introductory Lectures on Psychoanalysis, New York, Norton, 1966 (paperback); London, Hogarth Press, 1974; Harmondsworth, Penguin, 1973

The Ego and the Id, New York, Norton, 1962; London, Hogarth Press, 1962

Group Psychology and the Analysis of the Ego, New York, Norton, 1975 (paperback); London, Hogarth Press, 1959

An Outline of Psychoanalysis, New York, Norton, 1970 (paperback); London, Hogarth Press, 1969

Collected Papers, New York, Basic Books, 1959; the Standard Edition, London, Hogarth Press, 1950, is published in the United States by Macmillan, New York

Freud, Sigmund, and Breuer, Joseph, *Studies in Hysteria*, New York, Avon Books, 1966 (paperback); London, Hogarth Press, 1955; Harmondsworth, Penguin, 1973

Goffman, Erving, *Asylums*, Chicago, Aldine, 1961; New York, Doubleday, Anchor Books, 1963; Harmondsworth, Penguin, 1970

    The Presentation of the Self in Everyday Life, New York, Overlook Press, 1974; New York, Doubleday, Anchor Books, 1959; London, Allen Lane, 1969; Harmondsworth, Penguin, 1971

Heidegger, Martin, *Being and Time*, New York, Harper & Row, 1962; Oxford, Basil Blackwell, 1967

Husserl, Edmund, *Logical Investigations*, Atlantic Highlands, New Jersey, Humanities Press, 1970; London, Routledge & Kegan Paul, 1970

Jonas, Hans, *The Gnostic Religion*, 2nd revised edition, Gloucester, Massachusetts, Peter Smith, 1964; Boston, Beacon Press, 1963

Kant, Immanuel, *Critique of Pure Reason*, New York, St Martin's Press, 1929; New York, Dutton; London, Macmillan, 1929

Kierkegaard, Sören, *The Last Years: Journals 1853–1855f* New York, Harper & Row, 1965; London, Collins, 1965

    The Sickness unto Death, Princeton, New Jersey, Princeton University Press, 1941; London, Oxford University Press, 1941

    The Concept of Dread, Princeton, New Jersey, Princeton University Press, 1944; London, Oxford University Press, 1944

    Attack on 'Christendom', Princeton, New Jersey, Princeton University Press, 1968

Lacan, Jacques, 'The Mirror Phase', *New Left Review*, no. 5, 1968

    'The Function of Language in Psychoanalysis', see below under Wilden

Laplanche, J., and Pontalis, J. B., *The Language of Psychoanalysis*, New York, Norton, 1974; London, Hogarth Press, 1973

Lenin, V. I., *What Is To Be Done?*, New York, International Publishers Co., 1969; London, Oxford University Press, 1963; London, Panther, 1970

Lévi-Strauss, Claude, *The Scope of Anthropology*, New York, Grossman, 1968; London, Cape, 1967

Lidz, Theodore, *The Family and Human Adaptation*, New York, International Universities Press, 1963; London, Hogarth Press; see also Boyers and Orrill, op. cit.

Lomas, Peter (ed.), *The Predicament of the Family*, New York, International Universities Press, 1967; London, Hogarth Press, 1967

MacIntyre, Alasdair, *The Unconscious*, Atlantic Highlands, New Jersey, Humanities Press, 1962; London, Routledge & Kegan Paul, 1958

Mannoni, Maud, *The Child, His 'Illness', and the Others*, New York, Pantheon Books, 1970; London, Tavistock, 1970; Harmondsworth, Penguin, 1973

Mannoni, Octave, *Freud*, New York, Pantheon Books, 1970; New York, Vintage, 1974; published in London as *Freud: the Theory of the Unconscious*, New Left Books, 1972

Marcuse, Herbert, *Eros and Civilization*, Boston, Beacon Press, 1955, and 1974 (paperback); London, Allen Lane, 1969; London, Sphere, 1972

Studies in Critical Philosophy, London, New Left Books, 1972

Negations, London, Allen Lane, 1968; Harmondsworth, Penguin, 1972

Marx, Karl, *Early Writings*, New York, Vintage Books, 1975 (paperback); Harmondsworth, Penguin, 1975 (paperback)

Grundrisse, New York, Random House, 1974; New York, Vintage Books, 1974; London, Allen Lane, 1973; Harmondsworth, Penguin, 1973

Capital, New York, International Publishers Co., 1967, 3 vols., and 1974, 1 vol. (paperback); London, Lawrence & Wishart, 1973

Marx, Karl, and Engels, Friedrich, *The German Ideology*, New York, International Publishers Co., 1970; London, Lawrence & Wishart

Selected Works, New York, International Publishers Co., 1968; London, Lawrence & Wishart, 1969

Merleau-Ponty, Maurice, *The Phenomenology of Perception*, Atlantic Highlands, New Jersey, Humanities Press, 1962; London, Routledge & Kegan Paul, 1962

Mitchell, Juliet, *Women's Estate*, New York, Pantheon, 1972; New York, Vintage Books, 1973; Harmondsworth, Penguin, 1971

Psychoanalysis and Feminism, Pantheon Books, New York, 1974; New York, Vintage Books, 1975; London, Allen Lane, 1974

Nietzsche, Friedrich, *On the Genealogy of Morals*, New York, Vintage Books, 1973

Pateman, Trevor, 'Sanity, Madness and the Problem of Knowledge', *Radical Philosophy*, no. 1

'Language, Truth and Politics', *Radical Philosophy*, no. 8

Poulantzas, Nicos, *Political Power and Social Classes*, New York, Humanities Press, 1975; London, New Left Books, 1973

Reich, Wilhelm, *Character Analysis*, New York, Farrar, Strauss & Giroux, 1972; New York, Simon & Schuster, Touchstone-Clarion, 1974; London, Vision, 1969

The Sexual Revolution, New York, Farrar, Strauss & Giroux, 1974 (hardcover and paperback); London, Vision, 1969

The Mass Psychology of Fascism, New York, Farrar, Strauss, 1970; New York, Simon & Schuster, Touchstone-Clarion, 1974; London, Souvenir, 1972; Harmondsworth, Penguin, 1976

Reiche, Reimut, *Sexuality and Class Struggle*, New York, Praeger, 1971; London, New Left Books, 1970

Ricoeur, Paul, *Freud and Philosophy: an essay on interpretation*, New Haven, Connecticut, Yale University Press, 1970

Russell, Bertrand, and Whitehead, A. N., *Principia Mathematica*, London, Cambridge University Press, 1962

Rycroft, Charles, *A Critical Dictionary of Psychoanalysis*, New York, Basic Books, 1969; Totowa, New Jersey, Littlefield, Adams & Co., 1973; London, Nelson, 1968

(ed.), *Psychoanalysis Observed*, New York, Coward, McCann & Geoghegan, 1967; Baltimore, Penguin, 1969; London, Constable, 1966; Harmondsworth, Penguin, 1968

Sartre, Jean-Paul, *Being and Nothingness*, Secaucus, New Jersey, Citadel Press, 1965 (paperback); London, Methuen, 1969
Saint Genet, New York, George Braziller, 1964; New York, New American Library, 1964; London, W. H. Allen, 1964
Between Existentialism and Marxism, New York, Pantheon Books, 1974; London, New Left Books
No Exit, New York, Knopf, 1947; *No Exit and Three Other Plays*, New York, Vintage Books, 1955
Search for a Method, New York, Knopf, 1963; published in Great Britain as *The Problem of Method*, London, Methuen, 1963
Critique de la Raison Dialectique, translation forthcoming from New Left Books
Sayers, Sean, 'Mental Illness as a Moral Concept', *Radical Philosophy*, no. 5
Review of Szasz, T., *Ideology and Insanity* (qv.) in *The Human Context*, 1975
Siegler, Miriam, and Osmond, Humphrey, 'Models of Madness', *British Journal of Psychiatry*, vol. 112, no. 493, 1966
Steinbeck, John, *East of Eden*, New York, Viking, 1952; New York, Bantam, 1974; London, Heinemann, 1968; London, Pan, 1970
Szasz, Thomas, *Ideology and Insanity*, New York, Doubleday, Anchor Books, 1970 (paperback); Harmondsworth, Penguin, 1974 (paperback)
The Myth of Mental Illness, revised edition, New York, Harper & Row, 1974 (hardcover and paperback); London, Paladin, 1972 (paperback)
Tillich, Paul, *The Courage To Be*, New Haven, Connecticut, Yale University Press, 1952 (hardcover and paperback); London, Nisbet, 1952; London, Fontana, 1962
Wiggins, David, 'Freedom, Knowledge, Belief and Causality', Royal Institute of Philosophy lectures 1968–69, New York, St Martin's Press, London, Macmillan
Wilden, Anthony, *The Language of the Self*, Johns Hopkins University Press
Wollheim, Richard, *Freud*, London, Fontana, 1971 (paperback)

Chapter-by-chapter appendices on further reading

Chapter 1

Freud's method can be seen at work in his *Introductory Lectures on Psychoanalysis*, or in the case studies in volume III of his *Collected Papers*. His ideas are elaborated theoretically in the metapsychological papers in volume IV of the *Collected Papers*.

Probably the best accounts of Freud's theory are in Professor Wollheim's *Freud* and Octave Mannoni's *Freud: the Theory of the Unconscious*. A valuable aid to the study of Freudian theory is *The Language of Psycho-*

analysis by Laplanche and Pontalis—a dictionary of psychoanalytic concepts.

A good example of phenomenology at work is *The Phenomenology of Perception* by Merleau-Ponty. On existentialism, see Sören Kierkegaard's *The Sickness unto Death*, and Jean-Paul Sartre's *The Transcendence of the Ego*, and *Being and Nothingness* (the chapters on bad faith, and existential psychoanalysis).

For the Marxist version of the dialectic, see Marx's Introduction to *Grundrisse*, and Althusser's essays 'Contradiction and Overdetermination' and 'The Materialist Dialectic' in *For Marx*.

Chapter 2

The Leaves of Spring, by Laing's colleague Aaron Esterson, is essential reading on the topics discussed in this chapter. For anti-causalist interpretations of psychoanalysis see Rycroft (ed.) *Psychoanalysis Observed*, and *The Unconscious* by Alasdair MacIntyre. The causalist version should be clear from Freud's own writing, and from Wollheim's *Freud*. The relation of causes and meanings in psychoanalysis is also discussed from a phenomenological standpoint as 'energetics and hermeneutics' in *Freud and Philosophy: an essay on interpretation* by Paul Ricoeur.

On the relative roles of infantile and current experiences in producing mental disturbances, see the papers on the classification and aetiology of neuroses in volume I of Freud's *Collected Papers*, and also *Character Analysis* by Wilhelm Reich.

The Sartre texts most relevant to Laing's social phenomenology are the later ones, i.e. *The Problem of Method*, *Saint Genet*, *Between Existentialism and Marxism*, and the *Critique de la Raison Dialectique*.

Chapter 3

For developments parallel to Laing's in the field of interpersonal experience and behaviour, see Bateson's *Steps to an Ecology of Mind*, and the work of Erving Goffman, to which his book *The Presentation of the Self in Everyday Life* is a good introduction. See also *Group Psychotherapy* by Foulkes and Anthony.

For the philosophical background, see part 3 of Sartre's *Being and Nothingness*, and his play *No Exit*.

Chapter 4

There are three volumes in the International Psycho-Analytical Library concerned with the family: *The Psychoanalytical Study of the Family* (1921) by Flügel; Lidz's *The Family and Human Adaptation* (which is discussed above), and *The Predicament of the Family*, a collection of essays edited by Peter Lomas, including Laing's essay 'Family and Individual Structure'.

The use of psychoanalytical ideas (albeit unorthodox ones) to criticize the nuclear patriarchal family can be seen in the whole of Wilhelm Reich's work.

The feminist writings most relevant in the present context are *The Second Sex* by Simone de Beauvoir, which is existentialist in its philosophical assumptions, and Juliet Mitchell's books *Woman's Estate* and *Psychoanalysis and Feminism*. Mitchell is one of the very few feminist writers to accept the scientific validity of Freudian theory.

Chapter 5

The essays collected in *Laing and Anti-Psychiatry* represent a variety of views on this subject. For the extreme sceptical and anti-psychiatric case, see Szasz's works, e.g. *The Myth of Mental Illness* and *Ideology and Insanity*. Sean Sayers' review of the latter in *The Human Context*, Summer 1975f is an excellent criticism of Szasz's viewpoint; see also Sayers' paper 'Mental Illness as a Moral Concept' in *Radical Philosophy*, no. 5.

On the origin, function and ideology of mental hospitals in Western society, see Foucault's *Madness and Civilisation* and Goffman's *Asylums*.

Chapter 6

On the theory of ideology in Marx and Engels, see *The German Ideology* (part I) and the 'Letters on Historical Materialism' in their *Selected Works*. For the notion of 'ideological apparatuses' see Althusser's essay 'Ideology and the State' in his *Lenin and Philosophy* and the sections on ideology in *Political Power and Social Classes* by Poulantzas. On the use that can be made of psychoanalytic concepts in analysing ideologies and ideological apparatuses, see Freud's *Group Psychology and the Analysis of the Ego*, and Reich's *The Mass Psychology of Fascism*.

Marcuse, in addition to his political criticism of neo-Freudian revisionism in *Eros and Civilisation*, has written an essay 'Love Mystified' criticizing Norman O. Brown's attempt to build a mystical metaphysics on psychoanalysis. This essay is printed, together with Brown's reply, in *Negations*.

Ideas similar to those expressed in *The Politics of Experience* can be found in David Cooper's *The Death of the Family* and *The Grammar of Living*; they are open to the same objections.

Index